WHEN CHILDREN BECOME PARENTS

Welfare state responses to teenage pregnancy

Edited by Anne Daguerre and Corinne Nativel

First published in Great Britain in November 2006 by

The Policy Press
University of Bristol
Fourth Floor
Beacon House
Queen's Road
Bristol BS8 1QU
UK

Tel +44 (0)117 331 4054
Fax +44 (0)117 331 4093
e-mail tpp-info@bristol.ac.uk
www.policypress.org.uk

© Anne Daguerre and Corinne Nativel 2006

British Library Cataloguing in Publication Data
A catalogue record for this book is available from the British Library.

Library of Congress Cataloging-in-Publication Data
A catalog record for this book has been requested.

ISBN-10 1 86134 678 6 paperback
ISBN-13 978 1 86134 678 0 paperback
ISBN-10 978 1 86134 679 4 hardcover
ISBN-13 978 1 86134 679 7 hardcover

Cover design by Qube Design Associates, Bristol.
Front cover: kindly supplied by www.third-avenue.co.uk
Printed and bound in Great Britain by MPG Books Ltd, Bodmin.

Contents

When children become parents

List of figures and tables

Figures

Tables

Acknowledgements

The editors, Anne Daguerre and Corinne Nativel, would like to express their thanks to the French Family Allowance Fund (*Caisse Nationale des Allocations Familiales*), for entrusting them with the preparation of a report entitled 'Early motherhood in developed countries: problems, instruments and policy issues' (*Les maternités précoces dans les pays développés: problèmes, dispositifs, enjeux politiques*). The report was influential in the genesis of this book.

We would like to express our gratitude to Middlesex University and the Science and Technology Department at the French Embassy for their financial and logistical support in the organisation of a conference in July 2005, which gathered all the contributors of this volume.

Lastly, we would like to thank UNICEF (United Nations Children's Fund) and Susheela Singh from the Alan Guttmacher Institute for permission to use material calculated from published work (see Statistical appendix) as well as Mathilde Darley, Gilles Favarel-Garrigues and Daniel Sabbagh for their helpful comments on various chapters.

Notes on contributors

Johanne Charbonneau is the Director of the Urbanisation, Culture and Society research centre (Institut National de la Recherche Scientifique at the Université du Québec in Montreal). She has been a professor in this research centre since 1993. Her research interests include social networks, family ties, social support, life trajectories and neighbourhoods. Her most recent book is *Adolescentes et mères: Histoires de maternités précoces et soutien du réseau social (Teenagers and Mothers: Stories of Early Motherhood and Social Network Support)* (Presses de l'Université de Laval, 2003).

Anne Daguerre is a senior research fellow at Middlesex University. Her publications include *La protection de l'enfance en France et en Angleterre 1980-1989 (Child protection policies in France and England 1980-1989)* (l'Harmattan, 1999); 'Policy Networks in England and France: The Case of Child Care Policy 1980-1989' (*Journal of European Public Policy*, 2000); 'Importing Workfare: Policy Transfer in Labour Market Policies under New Labour' (*Social Policy and Administration*, 2004); and 'Neglecting Europe: Explaining the Predominance of American Ideas in New Labour's Employment Policies since 1997' (*Journal of European Social Policy*, 2004).

Elena Ivanova is a senior researcher at the Centre of Demography and Human Ecology at the Russian Academy of Sciences and an Associate Professor in the Department for Applied Sociology at the Russian State University for the Humanities, both located in Moscow. Her research interests include demography, social policy, sociology, family, young generations and intergenerational relations. She has published in several journals such as the *Russian Demographic Journal*, *Sotsiologicheskie Issledovaniya* and *Population et Société*.

Lisbeth B. Knudsen is a reader in the Department of Sociology, Social Work and Organisation at Aalborg University in Denmark. Her research focuses on the demography and sociology of reproductive behaviour in Nordic countries. She has published on fertility trends, induced abortion, family structure and the role of the welfare state in Nordic countries in *Scandinavian Population Studies*, *Demographic Research*, *Acta Obstetrica et Gynecologica Scandinavia*, *Population Studies*, *Contraception* and *Dansk Sociologi (Danish Sociology)*.

Kristin Luker is a professor in the Department of Sociology and Boalt Hall School of Law at the University of California, Berkeley. She is author of *Dubious Conceptions:The Politics of the Teenage Pregnancy Crisis* (Harvard University Press, 1995) and *When Sex Goes to School* (W.W. Norton, 2006). She has published in *American Prospect*, *Contemporary Sociology* and *Family Planning Perspectives* among others. She is a member of the Advisory Board of the Program on Reproductive Health and Rights, Open Society Institute.

Christine Carter McLaughlin is the director of strategic planning and devlopment at the UC Berkeley Center for the Development of Peace and Well-being. She is also a researcher and doctoral candidate in sociology at the University of California, Berkeley. Her work centres on the effects of family and the social structure on childhood well-being. Her next book, *Who Gets to be Happy in America?*, examines factors that cause the stratification of happiness in children.

Georg Menz is a lecturer in political economy at Goldsmiths College, University of London. His research interests include political economy, the labour market and social policy and the politics of immigration. His publications include *Varieties of Capitalism and Europeanization: National Response Strategies to the Single European Market* (Oxford University Press, 2005), *The Future of European Migration Policy* (Lynne Rienner, 2006) and *Internalizing Globalization: The Rise of Neoliberalism and the Decline of National Varieties of Capitalism* (co-edited with Susanne Soederberg and Philip Cerny) (Palgrave, 2005).

Corinne Nativel is a research fellow in the Department of Geographical and Earth Sciences at the University of Glasgow and a Teaching Fellow at the Universities of Paris III-Sorbonne Nouvelle and Paris X-Nanterre. Her research is concerned with the geography of welfare restructuring, labour market policy and the global justice movement. Recent publications include *Economic Transition, Unemployment and Active Labour Market Policy: Lessons and Perspectives from the East German Bundesländer* (Continuum Publishing, 2004) and *Putting Workfare in Place: Local Labour Markets and the New Deal* (with Peter Sunley and Ron Martin) (Blackwell Publishing, 2006).

Elisabetta Pernigotti is a doctoral candidate at the University of Paris VII-Denis Diderot and the Faculty of Political Sciences at the

University of Torino. She was previously a Marie Curie Fellow at the National Research Institute on Contemporary Societies (IRESCO) in Paris and at the Comparative Social Law Institute (COMPTRASEC) at the University of Bordeaux. Her research interests include women's rights, the gendered dimension of social exclusion and comparative social policy.

Stéphane Portet is a lecturer and a research fellow at the École des Hautes Etudes en Sciences Sociales (EHESS-Paris) and coordinator of the French–Polish Social Sciences Research and Training Centre organised by the EHESS at the University of Warsaw. He is a member of the Simone-SAGESSE Research Team, University of Toulouse le Mirail. His main research interests are labour markets, social policy, gender issues in communist and post-communist Poland and European enlargement. His publications include book chapters, and articles in various Francophone journals such as *Lien Social et Politique* (2001); *Travail Genre et Société* (2004); *Nouvelles Questions Féministes* (2004); and the *Chronique Internationales de l'IRES* (2004).

Elisabetta Ruspini is associate professor in the Department of Sociology and Social Research at the University of Milano-Bicocca. Her main research interests are lone parenthood, gender and the welfare state, constructions of masculinity and femininity, and longitudinal research. She is the author of *Introduction to Longitudinal Research* (Routledge, 2002) and (with Angela Dale) of *The Gender Dimension of Social Change: The Contribution of Dynamic Research to the Study of Women's Life Courses* (The Policy Press, 2002).

Ann-Karin Valle is an associate professor at Akershus University College and a doctoral candidate in public health at the University of Oslo. Her PhD thesis is entitled 'Teenage sexual and reproductive health among urban youth: concepts of the self and sociological variations in sexual behaviour'. She is the author of 'Social class, gender and psychosocial predictors for early sexual debut among 16 year olds in Oslo' (published in the *European Journal of Public Health* in April 2005). She has worked as an advisor on women's health in the Norwegian Directorate of Health and co-authored several evaluation reports published by Options Consultancy Services Ltd (London) on behalf of the International Planned Parenthood Federation (IPPF).

ONE

Introduction: the construction of teenage pregnancy as a social problem

Anne Daguerre with Corinne Nativel

The title of this volume, *When children become parents*, is deliberately provocative. Indeed, in the US, this slogan has been used to render teenage pregnancy a key social concern (Pearce, 1993; Maynard, 1997). The phrase implicitly denies teenagers the capacity to make autonomous choices since young people are not considered as adults (Pearce, 1993, p 46). The main reason why this phenomenon has become a public issue is because successive governments, regardless of their political orientations, have portrayed it as a social problem since the early 1980s. As delayed childbearing is becoming the norm in Western societies, teenage pregnancy is being portrayed as a socially deviant phenomenon called 'early motherhood'. Young people who have children while they are still financially dependent can thus be referred to as 'children having children', an expression that reflects a moral judgement made on their behaviour. They are stigmatised because they are seen as socially deviant. Indeed, in industrialised countries the average age at first birth has increased while births to teenagers have more than halved since the early 1970s (see Table A1 in Statistical Appendix at p 244). Moreover, the births to younger teenagers (aged 15-17) are a very small proportion of all teenage births. As early motherhood is declining and as births to older teenagers (aged 17-19) represent the vast majority of teenage births, the concern with teenage pregnancy in industrialised nations might seem paradoxical. This concern reflects a change in social attitudes. According to the United Nations Children's Fund (UNICEF), 'the reason for this change is that teenage parenthood has come to be regarded as a significant disadvantage in a world which increasingly demands an extended education, and in which delayed childbearing, smaller families, two-income households, and careers for women are increasingly becoming the norm' (UNICEF,

2001a, pp 5-6). According to the report, teenage births represent between 6 and 14 per 1,000 in Continental Western European countries, between 18 and 31 per 1,000 in the UK and some other English-speaking countries and as high as 52 per 1,000 in the US (see Statistical Appendix, Figure A1 at p 241 for more recent data).

Policies are based on ideas, value judgements and causal assumptions, which are not clearly spelled out. Hall (1993) defines the notion of policy paradigm as 'a framework of ideas and standards that specifies not only the goals of policy and the kind of instruments that can be used to attain them, but also the very nature of the problems they are meant to be addressing' (Hall, 1993, p 279). So, policy paradigms relate to core beliefs and ideas about the nature of the problem and in turn shape public policies. It is thus essential to identify the main competing policy ideas and discourses concerning teenage pregnancy.

Contemporary policy discourses on teenage pregnancy are historically and culturally constructed. It is the social context in which teenage motherhood takes place that makes the phenomenon problematic. In Western societies, the concern with teenage pregnancy can be traced back to the late 1960s; it is strongly linked to demographic transitions, that is, the shift from traditional family patterns to individualist family patterns. In the traditional system that still prevails in much of the developing world, teenage childbearing is by and large perceived as the reproductive outcome of early marriage and family formation. According to the UNICEF report *Early Marriage* (2001b, p 6), 'the familialist system is characterised by extended families, communal households, authoritarian exercise of power by men, young age at marriage, spouses chosen by elders, absorption of the newly-wed into an existing household, no non-household role for women'. This is the dominant pattern in some developing countries, where teenage motherhood is extremely common. UNICEF states that 'among women aged 15-24, 48% were married before the age of 18 in South Asia (9.7 million girls), 42% in Africa, and 29% in Latin America and the Caribbean (UNICEF, 2005a, p 4) and '78% of Nigerian women, 72% of Chadian women and 55% of Bangladeshi women aged 20-24 were in union by age 18' (UNICEF, 2005a, p 4). By contrast, in Western Europe and North America broad social and economic changes have led to a rise in age at first birth, falling fertility rates, the dissociation between sex and marriage, and the lengthening period of contraceptive use. In the Western world, the dominant family pattern is 'individualist', characterised by nuclear families, relative independence of the young couple in relation to their parents, and late age at marriage and childbearing. Teenage pregnancy is in rapid decline (see Figure A3 in the Statistical Appendix) and is correlated with single motherhood.

There are four major arguments invoked in policy discourses to justify the need for state intervention with regard to teenage pregnancy. According to the first argument, teenagers are too young to bring up children. There is both an 'essentialist' and a sociological argument to this assumption. On the essentialist side, it is argued that young women, by the very nature of their physiology, are too immature to carry a child. The physiological definition of youth refers to a brief life span – between the ages of 12 and 18 – during which puberty takes place. Emotional and psychological developments also occur during this period. It is in this particular period of life that the child comes to terms with a new adult identity. Rapid physiological and psychological changes imply that adolescence is an inappropriate time span to bear a child. This naturalist view has inspired a range of research, especially in public health and demography. Pregnancy in adolescence is associated with an increased risk of poor outcomes for children, including a premature birth, low birth weight, and death during the first year of life (Fraser et al, 1995). According to UNICEF (2001b, p 11), 'pregnancy-related deaths are the leading cause of mortality for 15-19 year old girls world wide. Mothers in this age group face a 20 to 200% greater chance of dying in pregnancy than women aged 20 to 24. Those under age 15 are five times as likely to die as women in their twenties'. However, the jury is still out as to whether 'the adverse outcomes experienced by some mothers and children of teenage pregnancies are causally related to the age of the mother, or whether there are other factors that lead to adverse outcomes for both mother and baby' (Lawlor and Shaw, 2002, p 552). The evidence is inconclusive, and adverse health outcomes might well be more related to poverty and lack of antenatal and obstetric care than age. Physical immaturity is a key risk mostly for girls under the age of 15, but this is much less true of girls aged 17-19. As young women tend to report their pregnancies relatively late, they do not receive appropriate antenatal care and are more at risk than their older counterparts. They are also more likely to be poor, which in turn affects their ability to have a nutritious diet and healthy lifestyle. But pregnancy at age 17-19 seems to carry fewer health risks than delayed childbearing. Moreover, a pregnancy at age 35+ also poses significant risks to the health of both mother and child. In the words of Lawson and Rhode (1993, p 5): 'Older teenagers are physically much better suited for childbearing than older women'. For the vast majority of teenage births, it is not the age of the mother that poses significant health risks but the social, economic and psychological circumstances within which the pregnancy takes place.

The concern about the physiological age of young mothers is embedded in a broader social script, which assigns specific functions and/or roles to particular age spans. In this 'socio-cultural' reading, young people are seen as too immature and unfit for the task of bringing up children in an optimum fashion. In fact, the root of the problem is not so much the biological age but the socially acceptable time to bear and bring up children. Both the expressions 'early motherhood' and 'late pregnancy' carry a strong value judgement about the 'right' age for embracing motherhood (less so of fatherhood).

In the second argument in public discourse it is suggested that adolescents lack maturity to make informed decisions concerning their sexuality. Public discourses tend to adopt two contradictory stances. The first stance relates adolescence to childhood and focuses on the need to protect children from sexual abuse by adults. Therefore sexual experimentation and/or exposure to sexual knowledge are associated with a premature loss of innocence, which can only damage children. Indeed, sex is portrayed as an adult activity, which is imposed by predatory characters on innocent children in exploitative contexts. The child or young person is never a consenting adult and cannot have access to consensual sex (Thomson, 2004, pp 90-1). If sex occurs between two young persons, the protagonists are seen as victims unable to exercise their free will. For instance, young women may feel pressurised to have sex for fear of losing their boyfriend. Similarly, young men can be subject to peer pressures: they may have sexual intercourse despite not being fully prepared for dealing with the complex and contradictory emotions associated with sex. Since the late 1990s, the US has experienced a trend towards sexual abstinence, with faith-based organisations such as 'True Love Waits' and 'Silver Ring Thing'[1] urging young people to keep their virginity until marriage. The second assumption according to which adolescence is a period characterised by risk taking is more pragmatic and value free. In this perspective, sexual experimentation is an unavoidable rite of passage, which entails particular risks such as unwanted pregnancies and sexually transmitted diseases. Teenagers need to be made aware of these risks in order to be able to prevent them. This pragmatic stance underlies the implementation of relatively value-free and 'hygienist'[2] policies in relation to teenage sexual health.

The third argument in policy discourse with regard to teenage parenthood relates to poverty. According to UNICEF (2001a), mothers who give birth as teenagers are markedly worse off than women who give birth in their twenties. On average, teenage mothers are twice as likely to be living in poverty as women who give birth later in life. The association between disadvantage later in life and poverty both for mothers and children is one of the main reasons for current governmental concern in Organisation for Economic Co-operation and Development (OECD) countries. Policies that aim to reduce teenage conception rates are based on the assumption that a reduction in teenage birth rates will reduce poverty and play a key role in the fight against social exclusion. This is the assumption that is at the heart of New Labour policies in the UK. However, the extent to which teenage pregnancy is the cause or the consequence of poverty remains unclear. In fact, according to a study by the Institute for Fiscal Studies (IFS) (Goodman et al, 2004), the negative effect of teenage motherhood may be relatively small compared to the role of other socioeconomic factors. In the words of the IFS study report: 'The pathway to disadvantage started much earlier in the young woman's life and cannot be entirely attributed to early motherhood. If this is the case, policies which are aimed at preventing teenage conceptions or births will be less effective in ameliorating the negative outcomes of concern than the raw data would otherwise suggest' (Goodman et al, p 2). Although early motherhood appears to be primarily a consequence of material disadvantage and a lack of educational achievement; it is nevertheless equally clear that teenage pregnancy exacerbates pre-existing social disadvantage.

The fourth type of argument in public discourse in relation to teenage pregnancy relates to the parent's financial dependency. Young people's lives are characterised by a state of semi-autonomy. While adulthood is equated with financial independence and citizenship status, youth is 'an extended period in which a gradual transition is effected between childhood and citizenship, mediated by the family and the state' (Jones, 1995, p 1). Full financial independence is almost impossible to achieve at the age of 18. Transition into adulthood involves several stages. Young people typically leave school, have their first sexual encounter, leave the parental home, find paid employment and then form a household with their own partners and children. Most authors (for example, Jones, 1995; Furlong and Cartmel, 1999) acknowledge that transitions into adulthood are becoming increasingly lengthy and complicated due to a lack of demand for young and unskilled labour. The path to financial independence is paved with various obstacles and impasses. In this context, young people postpone family formation and childbearing until their mid- to late twenties, or even later. Raising children is one of the last stages of adulthood status in Western societies, before retirement. Life trajectories can differ from this accepted norm, but there is usually a heavy price to pay if they do. Teenagers who keep their babies often suffer from social isolation and are victims of strong moral stigma (Whitehead, 2001).

The immediate consequence of having a child at a very young age is increased financial dependency on the welfare state and/or the family. Teenage parents will usually need stronger financial and emotional support to bring up their children than older families. This is especially problematic in societies where the state refrains from financially supporting the family. In liberal welfare states such as the US and the UK, children are traditionally seen as the parents' responsibility. State assistance is a last-resort resource and is granted only in cases of acute need. Teenage pregnancy is stigmatised because of its association with welfare dependency. Early motherhood raises questions about the amount and the type of support that should be made available to children and families in contemporary societies. If the family is seen as an essentially private/individual matter, teenage parents are likely to experience acute isolation and stigmatisation.

Central argument and hypotheses

In Western societies, the vast majority of policy actors (policymakers, non-governmental organisations, faith-based organisations and conservative family lobbies) identify teenage pregnancy as a social problem that can be solved by state intervention. The scope of the phenomenon is clearly greater in some countries than others. Anglophone countries continue to be over-represented in statistics on teenage pregnancy. By contrast, France, Denmark, Italy and Sweden have reduced their teenage birth rates by three quarters or more since the early 1970s (UNICEF, 2001a). The Netherlands and Norway have achieved a reduction of two thirds or more. But the fall in teenage births is much less pronounced in Anglophone countries such as the UK, the US and New-Zealand. Norway and the UK had similar teenage birth rates in 1970 but since then Norway has seen teenage birth rates fall by 72% – almost double the 38% drop seen in the UK (UNICEF, 2001a, p 10). How can the variations in teenage pregnancy rates be explained? What is the role of political actors and cultural forces in the treatment of this issue?

This book has three principal objectives:

(1) to contribute to the comparative literature on welfare states by analysing the links between welfare state provision and teenage reproductive behaviour across a range of countries with differing welfare regimes;
(2) to examine the public policy responses to teenage parenthood among the national models of welfare states;
(3) to present and discuss the construction of teenage pregnancy as a social problem in case studies drawn from various industrialised countries.

The comparative method used in the book draws on a small number of cases; data are collected from these cases according to a a common set of research questions. We use primarily the most similar approach, according to which cases are selected that share certain similarities (Przeworski and Teune, 1970; Lijphart, 1975). We have limited our cases to advanced industrialised societies with stable democratic systems: the UK (focusing on England), the US, New Zealand, France, the Canadian province of Québec, Italy, Denmark and Norway. Two transition countries, Russia and Poland, emblematically illustrate the difficulties of transition from communism to economic liberalism and democracy. Both Russia and Poland have been characterised by rising income inequality and child poverty since the early 1980s. The health of Russian youth has been especially affected by rising social inequalities (UNICEF, 2004), despite some small progress very recently: 'In Russia the infant mortality rate in 2004 was 11.5 deaths of babies under one year per 1,000 live births; in 2002 it amounted to 13.3 deaths (*UN in Russia*, 2005, p 14). Both countries have witnessed a steep decline in teenage pregnancy rates as a result of the decline in early marriages.

We assume that, to a large extent, variations in teenage pregnancy between countries are affected by the nature of welfare provision and the regulation of teenage sexuality. The welfare regime typology is useful for understanding public responses to the challenge of adolescent parenthood. Indeed, conservative and Scandinavian welfare states tend to have a significantly lower teenage pregnancy rate than liberal welfare states.

- Our first hypothesis is that there is a strong negative correlation between the amount of financial support available to the family and the occurrence of teenage pregnancy.

In other words, the type of welfare regime has an impact on the level of family support and social solidarity, which in turn makes a significant difference to the occurrence of teenage parenthood. Since teenage mothers are most likely to have experienced poverty, the extent to which the welfare state can mitigate the failure of the market and/or the family has a crucial role to play in the politics of adolescent pregnancy and parenthood. Inegalitarian societies tend to foster low expectations for their disadvantaged youth who might be tempted to consider early motherhood as one way to achieve personal fulfilment and obtain a social status. In liberal welfare states, teenage pregnancy is analysed through the prism of welfare dependency. This is especially true in the US and New Zealand, and to a lesser extent in the UK. In Russia, the implementation of liberal policies has destroyed previous safety nets, thus reinforcing social exclusion. Teenagers tend to be left on their own, which is less true in Scandinavia and France. In Italy, teenagers are traditionally part of an extended family network (single parents stay home with their parents and remain in the same household).

- Our second hypothesis is that the ability to help prepare teenagers to cope with sexuality is crucial to young people's well-being.

Adolescents are now living in eroticised societies where traditional, established social conventions such as the loss of virginity as a taboo and the postponing of sex before marriage are being broken (UNICEF, 2001a). Moreover, the mass media, including teenage magazines, increasingly portray regular, 'safe sex' as a necessary condition for individual fulfilment and happiness. Those who do not comply with these new sexual norms feel left out. It should then come as no surprise that sexual activity among teenagers has increased. In the US, the percentage of all adolescents aged 15-18 who have sex by the age of 18 has doubled since the 1950s. In the UK, in the 1960s the average age at first sexual intercourse was 20 for males and 21 for females; today it is 17 for both sexes. More recent data suggest that the number of girls having under-age sex (under the age of 16) has doubled since 1990, and that almost 40% of 15-year-old girls have had full sexual intercourse (UNICEF, 2001a, p 13) (see also Figure A2 in the Statistical Appendix at p 242). The easy availability of affordable contraception, liberal abortion laws, comprehensive sex education and, perhaps more crucially, cultural openness to sex, help to reduce the occurrence of teenage pregnancy and sexually transmitted diseases.

- Our third hypothesis is that the cultural value system within which public authorities operate is a key variable for explaining differences in state intervention towards teenage pregnancy.

In the words of UNICEF, 'those countries with the highest teenage birth rates tend to be those that have marched furthest along the road from traditional values whilst doing little to prepare adolescents to socio-sexual changes' (UNICEF, 2001a, p 19). Teenage sexuality is conceived as a problem because adolescents, characterised by their financial and emotional dependence, assert themselves sexually while being unable to financially care for their child. The slogan 'children having children' encapsulates the moral judgement of adult authorities towards the irresponsible child. The gender dimension is especially important as young women can be stigmatised for engaging in 'promiscuous behaviour'. In sex education programmes, young women tend to be portrayed as the objects of sexual desire whereas men are portrayed as sexual predators who actively choose to have sex. Girls continue to value romance and love in sexual relationships whereas boys are more 'love-free' and can assert their masculinity in casual intercourse. Even when young women are portrayed as active agents who can experience sexual desire as well as men, they are encouraged to avoid sexual activity rather than seek it. Young women are usually more aware of the dangers and the pitfalls of sex than young men, and experience greater ambivalence in relation to sexual activity (Carpenter, 1998).

It is no coincidence that Anglophone countries such as the US, the UK and New Zealand have persistently high teenage pregnancy rates. The US administration has encouraged the implementation of abstinence-based sex education programmes since the mid-1990s. According to sex abstinence education advocates, teenage sex is harmful and immoral. New-born Christian movements propose to re-establish traditional orientations to sexuality such as the belief that sex should be reserved for marriage, and the stigmatisation of non-procreative behaviour such as masturbation, oral sex, homosexuality and often contraception. If sex is taboo and stigmatised, discussions about contraceptive use are simply forbidden or impossible. The fact that US teenagers fail to make effective use of contraceptive methods is linked to the lack of education and discussion about sexual matters, which leaves young people ignorant and vulnerable when dealing with sexual encounters and relationships. To a lesser extent, a persisting atmosphere of shame and secrecy also explains UK teenagers' failure to use contraception effectively. For instance, Wellings et al (2001, p 1847) find that 'the prevalence of non-use of contraception is higher among men and women who do not discuss sexual matters with parents'.

By contrast, the more a society recognises the right of teenagers to have sex, the less adolescent sexuality is being portrayed as a social problem. Moreover, societies that have pioneered gender equality policies are less likely to apply double standards to young males' and females' sexual activity. 'Under-age sex' is seen in a much more pragmatic way in Scandinavian countries such as Sweden, Denmark and Norway, which developed the use of contraceptive campaigns and family planning centres for teenagers as early as the 1970s. The Nordic welfare regime has pioneered a pragmatic response towards adolescent sexuality (UNICEF, 2001a). The Netherlands has promoted comprehensive and efficient sex education policies (Lewis and Knijn, 2003). Other Continental welfare states such as France and Germany have also adopted similarly pragmatic views and tend to allow teenagers to control their sexuality with the discreet support of public authorities and adults. Lastly, strong social and family control in Southern European countries is linked to lower teenage pregnancy rates in these countries than in other OECD countries.

Two bodies of literature are drawn upon and engaged in this volume. The first is the comparative welfare state literature developed by Esping-Andersen (1990; see also Esping-Andersen et al, 2002). The redistribution of wealth substantially reduces the scope of childhood poverty. As teenage pregnancy has been found to be both the cause and the consequence of early disadvantage, the nature of welfare provision can significantly reduce the occurrence of teenage pregnancy. The welfare state literature is used to examine the role of welfare state provision in preventing child poverty and social disadvantage. According to Esping-Andersen's acclaimed classification of welfare states based on the distinction between conservative, liberal and Scandinavian regimes (1990), generous welfare provision, especially extensive family policies, reduces the occurrence of child poverty, which in turn reduces the occurrence of teenage pregnancy. According to UNICEF (2000, 2005b), higher government spending on family and social benefits is correlated with low child poverty rates. There is a very strong association between low income in childhood and outcomes later in life. Indeed, 'children from poor families are much more likely to have low educational achievement, to become teenage parents and to have less success in the labour market' (UNICEF, 2000, p 12). In liberal welfare states where social rights are linked to demonstrable needs and where social spending on families is kept to a minimum, child poverty rates (21.9% in the US, 16.3% in New Zealand and 15.4% in the UK) are typically high. The US and the UK also have high teenage live birth rates (respectively 50 per 1,000 in the US and 42 per 1,000 in the UK). By contrast, Scandinavian welfare states such as Norway and Denmark, which provide generous, universal benefits to their citizens, have low levels of child poverty (4% in Norway and 5% in Denmark) and low teenage pregnancy rates (14 per 1,000 in Norway and 10 per 1,000 in Denmark).

The Continental Welfare Model in Esping-Andersen's typology 'espouses compulsory state social insurance with fairly strong entitlements' (Esping-Andersen, 1990, p 22). Income maintenance is based on occupational status. This model is dominant in France, Germany, Italy, Austria, the Netherlands and Belgium. The French welfare state is characterised by generous support for families and children and by relatively low rates of child poverty (7.5%) and teenage pregnancy (10 per 1,000). Eastern European welfare states such as Poland, Hungary, Slovenia and the Czech Republic are developing a conservative corporatist kind of policy but are increasingly borrowing some features of the liberal model with a shift towards means-tested intervention (Deacon, 2000; Förster and Toth, 2001; Manning, 2004). Although family policies used to be an important feature of post-communist states such as Poland and Russia, this is no longer the case. In Poland, welfare retrenchment, in particular the reduction of family benefits, has led to a 4.3% increase in child poverty since the mid-1990s. Child poverty is now 12.7% (UNICEF, 2005b). Poland has a relatively high teenage birth rate (21.1 per 1,000). Russia has the one of the highest child poverty rates in industrialised countries (23.5%). However, in both countries the rise in child poverty and youth unemployment has had no significant effect on teenage pregnancy rates, which have been declining since the mid-1990s.

Italy is representative of the Southern variant of the Continental Welfare Model analysed by Ferrera (1996). The Southern welfare state is characterised by the dualistic nature of social protection. Social insurance schemes are targeted at the core sectors of the labour force located within the institutional labour market (Ferrera, 1996, p 19). Social assistance schemes are targeted at older people. Thus, outsiders are virtually excluded from social insurance and assistance schemes. As state support for families and children is extremely weak, single parents and young people are left in an extremely vulnerable position. Child poverty is endemic, especially in the South, and has increased by 2.5% since the 1990s. Although Italy has now the highest child poverty rate in Europe (16.6%), teenage pregnancy rates remain low (6 per 1,000). Strong parental control and the importance of traditional attitudes towards sex due to the influence of the Catholic Church help explain the low occurrence of teenage pregnancy.

Feminist theories of the welfare state represent the second body of literature addressed in this volume. Indeed, it would be wrong to assume that income transfers alone eliminate teenage pregnancy and improve children's well-being. Traditional welfare regime categories as developed by Esping-Andersen in 1990 paid little attention to women's status in social policies. Yet family-friendly policies and gender equality measures aimed at favouring women's paid employment are found to substantially improve child well-being (Kamerman et al, 2003). Here feminist theories of the welfare state are particularly useful. A common feminist critique of the mainstream welfare state literature is that it neglects the gender dimension in the establishment of modern welfare regimes. Yet, historically women and children's rights are interlocked. The extent to which the welfare state sees women as mothers or workers and enables them to form an autonomous household has received considerable attention since the early 1990s (Lewis, 1992; Orloff, 1993; Sainsbury, 1994, 1999; Daly and Rake, 2003). Conventional wisdom assumes that child care facilities, parental leave provisions and generous family benefits reflect the nature of the gender contract, that is, the extent to which welfare settlements developed along the lines of female paid work or women's care in the private sphere. Lewis and Ostner (1995) rate modern welfare states according to the degree of women's independence from a male breadwinner model on a scale of weak, moderate or strong breadwinner models. In a strong breadwinner model, women and children are dependent on the husband's income while the mother looks after the children. The Netherlands, Germany, the UK and Switzerland are typical strong breadwinner regimes whereas France and Sweden are weak male breadwinner regimes where both parents are expected to be wage earners (Lewis and Ostner, 1995; Naumann, 2001).

In France and Scandinavia the gender contract is relatively equalitarian in the sense that women's participation in the labour market is seen both as a right and an economic necessity. This has important implications for the formation of female identity. When young women can obtain a sense of self-worth in the public and professional spheres, they are less likely to view intimacy with the opposite sex and motherhood as their only sources of status and gratification. A review of the data on teenage conception in Europe found that educated women are less likely to be sexually active at a very young age than women with low educational achievements and aspirations, and are more likely to postpone family formation or to have an abortion if they become pregnant: 'The higher the level of educational achievement the higher the age at first sexual activity and the lower the likelihood of teenage birth. Abortion, on the other hand, is a more common outcome of conception among higher educational achievers' (Kane and Wellings, 1999, p 23). Similarly, educated young men have less traditional attitudes to gender roles and are more likely to use a condom. In sum, a gender-equality-oriented consensus is more conducive to egalitarian attitudes in relation to sex and family formation. Young women who have reasonable hopes that their social aspirations will be supported by the wider value system are more likely to delay family formation and less likely to choose early motherhood to gain a form of social status. In Scandinavian welfare states, the gender contract is egalitarian. Women are actively encouraged to participate in the labour force and can rely on a comprehensive system of child care. This is also the case in France, which is characterised by a high female participation rate in the labour market. The dominant assumption is that women are both workers and mothers and that these roles are not mutually exclusive. Moreover, countries with family-friendly policies rate women's and children's well-being extremely highly. These policies convey the message that young people are valuable human beings. This positive attitude towards young people and families is part of a cultural consensus in France and Scandinavian countries. By contrast, in Russia and Poland commitment towards young people's well-being remains virtually non-existent.

The book enhances and contributes to this literature by including another dimension: the way in which teenagers, especially young women, are allowed to have control over their sexuality; a right long denied to adult women, which was at the heart of the second-wave feminist movement in the 1970s. Women's sexual rights as measured by access to contraception and abortion vary greatly in our sample.

Generally, welfare retrenchment and the erosion of women's rights go hand in hand, as the contrasting cases of Poland and the US clearly demonstrate.

Outline of the book

This book proceeds to analyse the way in which teenage pregnancy is deemed a social problem in contrasting welfare states. It is divided into three sections. Part One analyses policy responses to teenage pregnancy in three liberal welfare states. In Chapter Two, Christine Carter McLaughlin and Kristin Luker discuss the emergence of teenage pregnancy as a social problem in the US, paradoxically at a time when teenage pregnancy is declining. The ideology of welfare dependency has prevented the development of comprehensive policy responses to teenage pregnancy. The US administration is pursuing a Conservative neoliberal agenda. In Chapter Three, Georg Menz analyses the evolution of public policies towards teenage pregnancy in New Zealand. While the Conservative government implemented punitive measures towards young single mothers in the 1980s, the Labour government has implemented various programmes that aim to prevent teenage pregnancy but also positively support teenage parents. In Chapter Four, Anne Daguerre notes that although the New Labour government in the UK has taken visible steps to reduce teenage pregnancy as part of a wider commitment to the fight against social exclusion and the improvement of young people's sexual health since the late 1990s, sex education remains highly controversial owing to recurrent outbursts of moral panic over the 'teenage pregnancy crisis'.

Part Two focuses on Continental and Scandinavian welfare states and attempts to identify the factors underlying the prevalence of low teenage pregnancy rates in Québec, France, Italy, Denmark and Norway. In Chapter Five, Johanne Charbonneau describes how a real commitment to children's and women's well-being has resulted in lower teenage birth rates in Québec compared to the Anglophone parts of Canada. In Chapter Six, Corinne Nativel explains that universalist family policies, coupled with a special emphasis on maternal and infant care, account for low teenage pregnancy rates in France. This represents an apparent paradox since teenage pregnancy rates remain very low despite the fact that there is no specific programme for very young parents. In Italy, the low occurrence of teenage pregnancy is primarily explained by cultural factors, according to Elisabetta Pernigotti and Elisabetta Ruspini (Chapter Seven). Despite high child poverty rates, teenage motherhood continues to be an 'invisible phenomenon'. Family care and control and the resilience of traditional values in relation to family formation and sexual relationships explain low teenage pregnancy rates. Analysing teenage pregnancy trends in Denmark and Norway, Lisbeth B. Knudsen and Ann-Karin Valle (Chapter Eight) show that comprehensive sex education coupled with a commitment to children's and women's well-being account for low teenage birth rates. Part Three analyses policy responses to teenage pregnancy in two transition states, Russia and Poland. Elena Ivanova (Chapter Nine) and Stéphane Portet (Chapter Ten) describe how teenage pregnancy, which was relatively common during the communist period, declined in the 1990s. Early marriage was also widespread due, in particular, to public housing provision that enabled young couples to get married and start a family earlier than their Western counterparts. Starting in the early 1990s, patterns of family formation have changed. Like their adult counterparts, adolescents tend to delay marriage and family formation. In both countries, economic liberalism has been accompanied by a religious backlash that has eroded women's reproductive rights. In particular, access to abortion, which used to be a major family planning method in both countries, has been severely restricted, thus prompting a rise in backstreet abortions.

The comparative study detailed in this volume shows that teenage pregnancy rates and policy responses to the phenomenon vary tremendously depending on a variety of complex factors such as the existence of gender-equality and family-friendly policies, the integration of young people in family networks, the influence of religion and the pre-eminence of liberal or conservative attitudes in relation to sex. More importantly, as argued in the Conclusion to the book (Chapter Eleven), it is the way in which these factors interact that accounts for the singularity of national responses to teenage pregnancy within similar welfare regime categories.

Notes
[1] See the following websites: www.lifeway.com/tlw/ (True Love Waits) and www.silverringthing.com/index.html (Silver Ring Thing) (accessed December 2005).

[2] Hygienist policies were born in the 19th century with the aim to fight against avoidable diseases caused by bacteria. The development of basic hygienist rules (such as systematic hand washing in order to avoid infection by bacteria) saved many human lives. But

hygienism also embodies less positive connotations as it is often associated with positivism, that is, an almost religious faith in science and medicine.

References

Carpenter, L. (1998) 'From Girls into Women: Scripts for Sexuality and Romance in Seventeen Magazine 1974-1994', *Journal of Sex Research*, vol 35, no 2, pp 158-67.

Daly, M. and Rake, K. (2003) *Gender and the Welfare State: Care Work and Welfare in Europe and the USA*, Oxford: Polity Press.

Deacon, B. (2000) 'Eastern European Welfare States: The Impact of the Politics of Globalization', *Journal of European Social Policy*, vol 10, no 2, pp 146-61.

Esping-Andersen, G. (1990) *The Three Worlds of Welfare Capitalism*, Oxford: Polity Press.

Esping-Andersen, G., with Gallie, D., Hemerijck, A. and Myles, J. (2002) *Why We Need a New Welfare State*, Oxford: Oxford University Press.

Ferrera, M. (1996) 'The Southern Model of Welfare', *Journal of European Social Policy*, vol 6, no 11, pp 17-37.

Förster, M. and Toth, I. (2001) 'Child Poverty and Family Transfers in the Czech Republic, Hungary and Poland', *Journal of European Social Policy*, vol 11, no 4, pp 324-41.

Fraser, A.M., Brockert, J.E. and Ward, R.H. (1995) 'Association of Young Maternal Age with Adverse Reproductive Outcomes', *The New England Journal of Medicine*, vol 332, no 17, pp 1113-18.

Furlong, A. and Cartmel, F. (1999) *Young People and Social Change*, Buckingham: Open University Press.

Goodman, A., Kaplan, G. and Walker, I. (2004) *Understanding the Effects of Early Motherhood in Britain: The Effects on Mothers*, London: Institute for Fiscal Studies.

Hall, P.A. (1993) 'Policy Paradigms, Social Learning and the State: The Case of Economic Policy-making in Britain', *Comparative Politics*, vol 25, no 3, pp 275-96.

Jones, G. (1995) *Leaving Home*, Buckingham: Open University Press.

Kamerman, S., Kamerman, S.B., Neuman, M., Waldfogel, J. and Brooks-Gunn, J. (2003) *Social Policies, Family Types and Child Outcomes in Selected OECD Countries*, OECD Social Employment and Migration Working Papers, Paris: OECD.

Kane, R. and Wellings, K. (1999) *Reducing the Rate of Teenage Conceptions – An International Review of the Evidence: Data from Europe*, London: Health Education Authority.

Lawlor, D.A. and Shaw, M. (2002) 'Too Much Too Young? Teenage Pregnancy is not a Public Health Problem', *International Journal of Epidemiology*, vol 31, no 3, pp 552-53.

Lawson, A. and Rhode, D. (1993) *The Politics of Teenage Pregnancy*, Yale, CT: Yale University Press.

Lewis, J. (1992) 'Gender and the Development of Welfare Regimes', *Journal of European Social Policy*, vol 2, no 3, pp 159-73.

Lewis, J. and Knijn, T. (2003) 'Sex Education Materials in the Netherlands and in England and Wales: A Comparison of Content, Use and Teaching Practice', *Oxford Review of Education*, vol 29, no 1, pp 113-50.

Lewis, J. and Ostner, I. (1995) 'Gender and the Evolution of European Social Policies', in S. Liebfried and P. Pierson (eds) *European Social Policies*, Washington, DC: Brookings, pp 159-93.

Lijphart, A. (1975) 'The Comparable Cases Strategy in Comparative Research', *Comparative Political Studies*, vol 8, no 2, pp 481-96.

Macintyre, S. and Cunningham–Burley, S. (1993) 'Teenage Pregnancy as a Social Problem: A Perspective from the United-Kingdom', in A. Lawson and D. Rhode (eds) *The Politics of Pregnancy*, Yale, CT: Yale University Press, pp 59-73.

Manning, N. (2004) 'Diversity and Change in Pre-accession Central and Eastern Europe since 1989', *Journal of European Social Policy*, vol 14, no 3, pp 211-32.

Maynard, R. (1997) *Kids Having Kids: Economic Costs and Social Consequences of Teenage Pregnancy*, Washington, DC: Urban Institute Press.

Naumann, I.K. (2001) 'The Politics of Child Care: Swedish Women's Mobilization for Public Child Care in the 1960s and 1970s', Paper presented at the ECSR Summer School: Family, Gender and Social Stratification, Stockholm, 2001.

Orloff, A. (1993) 'Gender and the Social Rights of Citizenship: The Comparative Analysis of Gender Relations and Welfare States', *American Sociological Review*, vol 58, no 3, pp 303-28.

Pearce, D.M. (1993) 'Children having Children: Teenage Pregnancy and Public Policy from the Woman's Perspective', in A. Lawson and D. Rhode (eds) *The Politics of Pregnancy*, Yale, CT: Yale University Press, pp 46-73.

Przeworski, A. and Teune, H. (1970) *The Logic of Comparative Social Inquiry*, New York, NY: John Wiley.

Sainsbury, D. (ed) (1994) *Gendering Welfare States*, London: Sage Publications.

Sainsbury, D. (ed) (1999) *Gender and Welfare State Regimes*, Oxford: Oxford University Press.

Thomson, R. (2004) 'Sexuality and Young People: Policies, Practices and Identities', in J. Carabine (ed) *Sexualities*, Milton Keynes: Open University Press, pp 86-119.

UNICEF (United Nations Children's Fund) (2000) *Child Poverty in Rich Nations*, Florence: Innocenti Research Centre.

UNICEF (2001a) *A League Table of Teenage Births in Rich Nations*, Innocenti Report Card No. 3, Florence: Innocenti Research Centre.

UNICEF (2001b) *Early Marriage, Child Spouses*, Florence: Innocenti Research Centre.

UNICEF (2004) *Economic Growth and Child Poverty in the CEE/CIS and the Baltic States*, Florence: Innocenti Research Centre.

UNICEF (2005a) *Early Marriage, a Harmful Traditional Practice*, Florence: Innocenti Research Centre.

UNICEF (2005b) *Child Poverty in Rich Countries*, Florence: Innocenti Research Centre.

UN in Russia (2005) No. 2 (39), Moscow: United Nations Office in the Russian Federation.

Wellings, K., Nanchahal, K., Macdowall, W., McManus, S., Erens, B., Mercer, C.H., Johnson, A.M., Copas, A.J., Korovessis, C., Fenton, K.A. and Field, J. (2001) 'Sexual Behaviour in Britain: Early Heterosexual Experience', *The Lancet*, vol 358, no 9296, pp 1843-50.

Whitehead, E. (2001) 'Teenage Pregnancy: On the Road to Social Death', *International Journal of Nursing Studies*, vol 38, no 4, pp 437-46.

Part One
Liberal welfare states

TWO

Young single mothers and 'welfare reform' in the US

Christine Carter McLaughlin and Kristin Luker

Introduction

Teenage pregnancy in the US is a topic rife with moral inferences and political implications. Three important questions surround the increasing tendency for adolescent childbearing to be cited as evidence of social and moral decline in the US. First, why did policymakers in the US declare an 'epidemic' of teenage pregnancies at precisely the time that birth rates to adolescents were actually beginning to decline? Second, why did lawmakers revoke financial support for poor mothers – including the young mothers who most need help – as a response to the said 'epidemic'? Finally, if teenage pregnancy is perhaps *not* an epidemic, is it even a problem in the US? Answering these questions permits us to explore changing gender roles and public policy in relation to adolescent motherhood.

Statistical trends

Adolescent birth rates in the US reached their peak in the post-war Baby Boom, reaching a level of 96 births per 1,000 women under age 20 in 1957 (Ventura et al, 2001, p 10). Importantly, most of those births were to married parents. Teenage birth rates in the US have ranged from 63 per 1,000 in 1920, to 82 in 1950, to 89 in 1960 (Heuser, 1976, p 16). They went back down to 68 in 1970, and ironically were at 56 per 1,000 in 1975 when the 'epidemic' was declared – and they continued to fall from there to 53 in 1980. They rose to 63 in 1990, but went back down again to 49 per 1,000 in 2000 (Heuser, 1976; Ventura et al, 2001). Pregnancy rates are also declining, from 99 per 1,000 women under 20 in 1973 to 86 in 2000 (see Figure 2.1). The teenage pregnancy rate is down 29% since its most recent peak in 1990. Estimated abortion rates are also falling;

the abortion rate has dropped 83% since it peaked in 1985.[1] Birth rates are down 30% since their 1991 high.[2]

Why are adolescent pregnancy and birth rates falling in the US? Although the US has spent hundreds of millions of dollars in federal and state funds on educational programmes promoting abstinence, data from the National Survey of Family Growth show that the percentage of teenage girls who report having had sexual intercourse has declined only one percentage point, from 52.6% to 51.5% (Alan Guttmacher Institute, 2004). The US decline in teenage pregnancy has been driven in large part by fewer pregnancies among *sexually experienced* teens (Darroch and Singh, 1999; UNICEF, 2001). This is significant for a few reasons. Nearly half of US high school students report having had sexual intercourse, and a third say they are currently sexually active (CDC, 2004). Because there has been no corresponding fall in the frequency of intercourse among sexually experienced teenagers, the decline in teenage pregnancy is most likely to be due to improved contraceptive use (Saul, 1999).

Indeed, one in ten sexually active teens now uses one of the long-acting injectable or implanted contraceptives, which were not

Figure 2.1: Birth, pregnancy and abortion rates for US women under the age of 20

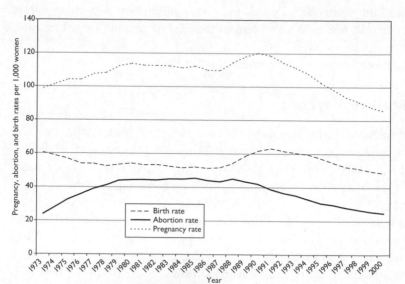

Sources: The National Center for Health Statistics of the US Department of Health and Human Services (number of births); the Alan Guttmacher Institute (number of abortions); US Bureau of the Census (population estimates). For exact sources, see www.guttmacher.org/pubs.teen_stats.html

widely available until after the peak in teenage pregnancies. This shift in contraceptive use, mostly from the pill to these long-acting forms, appears to be having a dramatic impact on overall adolescent pregnancy rates. Furthermore, long-acting forms of contraception are likely to be playing a large role in reducing the *second* pregnancies of teenage mothers, whose pregnancy rates have dropped even more dramatically (Saul, 1999). A relatively high proportion of teenage mothers (25%) use long-acting contraceptives (Saul, 1999). An analysis from the Alan Guttmacher Institute concludes that 'about 80% of the decline in overall teenage pregnancy rates since the late 1980s reflects this improved contraceptive use among sexually active teenagers. At the same time, it also confirms a decline – or, at least, a leveling off – in the proportion of teenagers who have ever had sexual intercourse' (Saul, 1999, p 7).

Despite considerable concern at the political level about the teenage pregnancy rate, pregnancy, abortion and birth rates among adolescents are all in decline. The US is not experiencing an epidemic of teenage parenthood. The rhetoric of 'children having children' is a cover for moral concern about sexually active unwed women and single mothers – not teenage mothers. However, just because teenage pregnancy is not the problem it is portrayed to be does not mean that it is not a real problem for teenagers who become pregnant. Importantly, current 'welfare-to-work' policy is likely to be fundamentally ineffective in bringing about positive change – say, in reducing poverty among young mothers or even in reducing the rates of sexually active unwed women or the rates of single motherhood – because it is not connected to the motivational roots of the *actual* problem. Without a better understanding of the women for whom government support is designed, and the social and economic context of their lives, there can be no useful understanding of adolescent motherhood and no basis for preventing it.

Sociological explanations of teenage pregnancy

Young women who are poor and otherwise disadvantaged are far more likely to have children as teenagers than are their better-off peers. Forty per cent of poor women in the US have children before they are 20 years old, while only 7% of those in high economic status groups do (Singh et al, 2001).[3] Eighteen per cent of poor mothers give birth by the age of 18, while only 3% of their wealthier counterparts do. Thirty-four per cent of those with less than a high school education give birth before they are 18, compared to 3% of those with some college education. And while 7% of young women with some college education give birth before the age of 20 in the US, a stunning 66% of those with less than a high school education do so (Singh et al, 2001).

Knowing that adolescent mothers in the US are comparatively disadvantaged helps us understand, at least in part, why the birth rate among teenagers is higher in the US than it is in all other Organisation for Economic Co-operation and Development (OECD) countries. Relative to other developed countries, the number of young people growing up in disadvantaged conditions is widespread in the US (Jones et al, 1985). For example, 17% of the US population's income is below 50% of the median, compared to 8% and 9% in France and Sweden, respectively (Singh et al, 2001).

Poverty and disadvantage bring increased social and environmental risk factors such as failing schools, dangerous neighbourhoods and violent families (Kirby et al, 2001; Waller, 2001). Judith Musick, who studied disadvantaged youth and adolescent mothers extensively, documents how the lives of adolescent girls raised in poverty are different in every dimension relative to those raised in middle-class families and neighbourhoods. Disadvantaged 'girls frequently have grown up in damaged and damaging family situations where the basic developmental foundation has been poorly laid or is lacking altogether.... Their external supports and their opportunities to find alternative models of coping are fewer and far less adequate' (Musick, 1993, pp 58-9). Taught that education will not help them out of poverty by the experiences of the people around them, the life options for disadvantaged youth are limited in number and offer little hope of life outside of poverty (Kaplan, 1997). American public schools in low-income neighbourhoods are notoriously troubled places, offering teenagers little hope or inspiration for a better life (Kozol, 1991).

Adolescent mothers in the US are not just likely to be suffering from a poverty of occupational and educational opportunities, however. They are also more likely than their better-off peers to be experiencing what Elaine Bell Kaplan (1997) calls a 'poverty of relationships'. Like Kaplan, Musick has found that disadvantaged teenagers have often experienced 'frequent separations from primary attachment figures in early life, which leave residues of vulnerability to threats of abandonment' (Musick, 1993, pp 41-2). In her ethnography of poor adolescent teenagers, Kaplan found that there was often little 'consistent, useful guidance from significant adults and few positive alternate role models' (Kaplan, 1997, p 179). Although teenage girls are at a point in their development where they need affirmation by and connection to others, 'many feel unloved by their mothers, ignored by their schools, and rejected by their fathers and boyfriends' (Kaplan, 1997, p xii). This absence of familial and other forms of social support in the lives of teenage mothers helps us to understand why they get pregnant and want to keep their children. Sexual activity creates at least the illusion of connection to a male figure. Fathering a baby has the potential to draw that male father into a girl's life. Pregnancy also draws attention to girls who are otherwise often isolated. One teenage mother wrote in her journal, 'I like it when people notice I'm having a baby. It gives me a good feeling inside and makes me feel important' (Musick, 1993, p 109). Pregnancy and childbearing represents, for some girls, the most obvious way for them to try to create the loving and attentive family they crave.

Poverty also brings with it a dramatically increased risk of sexual abuse, which sadly becomes *the* significant form of sexual socialisation for many young women – and which also explains why some girls are more likely to become pregnant as adolescents. A study conducted by the Ounce of Prevention Fund found that 61% of its US sample of 445 black, white and Hispanic pregnant and parenting teens had been sexually abused. Sixty-five per cent of these victims reported abuse by more than one perpetrator, and three quarters of them had been abused more than once. Other research reports similar findings (Boyer and Fine, 1992; Roosa et al, 1997; Blinn-Pike et al, 2002). The Ounce of Prevention Fund study found that one quarter of the victims of sexual abuse became pregnant by the perpetrator, and that sexual abuse increased the likelihood of pregnancy between the ages of 14 and 16 (Boyer and Fine, 1992). In addition to causing pregnancy, trauma caused by sexual abuse usually has lasting and profound psychological effects. Girls who have been raped or molested often mistake sex for love and caregiving, and are confused about what is and is not healthy sexually behaviour. 'Repeated violation of personal boundaries is a kind of brainwashing,' writes Musick, who is a psychologist. 'It saps the will, destroys self-efficacy, and leads to a perception of self as a victim' (1993, pp 95-6). Girls who know themselves as victims are less likely to feel the sort of control over their own bodies that would lead them to use contraception, even in consensual sexual encounters.

The prevalence of sexual abuse in US communities, and in particular among young single mothers, makes abstinence and marriage promotion programmes seem ludicrous. When girls are socialised for promiscuous and compulsive sexual behaviour by abusive men – who are most often kin or near-kin, such as the boyfriends of their mothers – it seems unlikely that an educational programme promoting abstinence until marriage would bear any relation to the sexual reality of these girls (Gershenson et al, 1989; see also Geronimus, 1992, 1997).

The pervasive poverty – of economic and emotional resources and of relationships – and sexual abuse in the lives of young unwed mothers reframes popular perception of single motherhood from an active choice motivated by welfare assistance to one that represents a highly constrained choice among limited options. As Linda Gordon (1976) notes, many of these women find themselves 'falling into motherhood'. The future is particularly bleak for many teenage mothers. Sexual abuse and lack of developmentally appropriate nurturance can stunt cognitive and academic development, setting even smart and talented teenagers up for failure in school (Boyer and Fine, 1992). Parents often offer little in the way of hopeful role modelling. Parental employment in impoverished neighbourhoods usually has little prospects. One girl in Kaplan's study explained that most of the women she knew in her mother's generation were on welfare, cleaned houses, or worked in the fast food industry for the minimum wage – not something to look forward to (1997, pp 32-3). Moreover, mothers who themselves gave birth as teenagers model behaviour their daughters are likely to replicate: seeking gratification through early motherhood (Michaels, 1988).

In addition to understanding the life circumstances and motivational forces of teenage mothers in the US, it is also critical to understand why such girls are seen as so undeserving of governmental support and are viewed by so many with contempt rather than empathy. It is important to bear in mind that while adolescent parenthood is many things, it is not occurring at epidemic proportions, and as we have seen, it is not the problem commonly portrayed by political and moral rhetoric. So why is concern over an increase in single motherhood framed as an epidemic of teenage pregnancy – what purpose does this serve policymakers and pundits?

Early parenthood can be viewed as some girls' attempts to gain meaningful familial relationships – or some meaning at all in their otherwise bleak lives. But this individual striving can also be seen in a wider cultural context, one in which all Americans are expected to achieve some level of both financial and emotional independence from their families and from the state. 'DeVonya Smalls was trying to achieve the American Dream,' writes Kaplan about a teenage mother whose motivations seemed typical of the other mothers she studied.

'In her version of the Dream, having a baby was an act of individualism and achievement' (Kaplan, 1997, p xix). Smalls' decision to have a baby is a paradoxical search for independence, on the one hand, and familial relationships, on the other.

It is in this cultural context, within an economically and educationally bleak landscape, that girls like DeVonya Smalls look for their path to the American Dream. The traditionally masculine route – work hard in school, get a job and work your way up – is closed to her on many levels. School is not the opportunity it is supposed to be. Her job opportunities are meagre; even if she worked her way up from a minimum-wage job at McDonald's she would be unlikely to pull herself, much less her family, out of poverty. The traditional feminine route – marry and raise children – is also likely to be closed to girls like DeVonya Smalls. Although, given her poverty of relationships, women like Smalls might want marriage, there are not enough suitable men around to make that a likely possibility. In one analysis, Christopher Jenks estimates that, by traditional American standards, the number of men available to marry is probably no more than two thirds the number of women who want children – and this includes those who would not make good husbands (Jenks, 1995).

DeVonya Smalls' decision to have a baby is also rooted in American notions of independence. To understand this point it is helpful to understand the historical context behind American notions of independence and the American Dream. In their genealogy of American dependency, Nancy Fraser and Linda Gordon trace the American notion of dependency from one with neutral connotations used to describe classes of people to its current-day negative meaning, used more often to describe individuals' psychological and economic states. In hierarchical pre-industrial British and American societies, dependency is described as a normative social condition rather than an individual trait. The pre-industrial meaning of dependence was thus closer to our current meanings of interdependence and dependable – 'implying trusting, relying on, counting on another' (Fraser and Gordon, 1994, p 37). The word 'dependence' was then linked to how people made their livelihoods, but the term was not yet so explicitly gendered. Industrialisation brought a massive shift in the meaning of dependence (and equally its opposite, independence) and in so doing, shifted the way women's labour is valued. With the rise of wage labour and the rights of the male worker came the stigmatisation of those who did not earn a wage. 'As wage labour became increasingly normative – and increasingly definitive of independence – it was precisely those excluded from wage labour who appeared to personify dependency' (p 40). With this emergence of an idealised notion of men's independence, women became framed as un-working dependants.

Not only did women's labour become all but invisible, but women's perceived economic dependence on men carried a negative stigma similar to that borne by others also excluded from wage labour – namely, those who received government assistance, colonial natives, and slaves. This notion of intrinsic dependency justified colonisation, slavery, and the exclusion of women from paid work, while at the same time it made wage-earning men heroically independent. This valorisation of men's wage work celebrated men's independence as a personality trait. In contrast, dependency came to be seen as a personal flaw.

These historical meanings of dependency remain with us today. Dependence is an ideological and political term, which references poor people 'dependent' on government assistance and housewives 'dependent' on their husbands. Now considered more a moral and psychological trait than a purely economic condition, dependence has become a synonym for addiction and is considered pathology. Furthermore, the term dependence remains explicitly gendered. Our ideologies of manhood still imbue working men with the independence and therefore respect originally linked to family wage work, while our ideologies of motherhood are still linked to the invisibility of women's contributions to the family economy and their resulting embodiment of dependency. Popular beliefs about poor mothers further embody this pathology of weakness dictated by dependence. We envision poor mothers as black inner-city teenagers and as white rural 'trailer trash' – saddled with both dependent children and dependence on welfare. Poor black mothers shoulder a triple burden, as they are also often imagined to be dependent on drugs. Such women are seen as too ignorant to understand the concept of birth control, too morally inferior to attract and keep a decent working husband, and totally undeserving of their children. The difficulty and disadvantage of their lives is rarely acknowledged as anything other than their own fault.

Girls like DeVonya Smalls, who want the independence and achievement that the American Dream represents, see motherhood as their most vivid and viable route. Although mothers are often imbued with the dependence of their children, paradoxically American mothers are *also* viewed omnipotent figures in family life, with the power to make or break the lives of their children (Chodorow and Contratto, 1989). This makes motherhood seem like a feasible arena for personal power, independence and life-meaning to a young woman whose life lacks all of these things. A baby promises both love and the independence revered in American culture, simultaneously seeming to solve a girl's felt problems of exclusion from the American Dream (caused by economic poverty) and her poverty of relationships.

In light of the motivational forces drawing disadvantaged young women to early sexual activity and parenthood, the choice to have a baby *seems* rational given their limited options. But because teenage mothers are wrestling with their own childhood developmental tasks, the combination of their depleted social networks, the poverty of the institutions and neighbourhoods they face, and the psychological tasks they face within the context of their own development, young mothers often do not make exemplary mothers. While they may work very hard raising their children, if they go on welfare they are still deemed unemployed slackers. The work they do to ensure their children's survival usually does not earn them the social independence, and therefore the moral superiority, granted to those with good educations and paying jobs. Anchored to their dependencies, adolescent mothers are seen as moral failures.

Teenage pregnancy as a political problem

Teenage pregnancy in the US has become first and foremost a political problem rather than a demographic one. For almost half a century, the US has arguably been a 'laggard' welfare state. Alone among mature economies, it lacks universal health care, extended unemployment benefits, paid leave for childbearing, and it grants only minimal support for its most impoverished citizens (Flora and Alba, 1981; Skocpol, 1984; Quadagno, 2005). Pensions and health care are predominantly provided by private employers rather than publicly by the state (Quadagno, 1988). Moreover, in a dramatic move in 1996 designed to end 'welfare as we know it', even this minimal safety net was severely cut back. For the first time since 1935, a new legal regime was created by the 1996 Personal Responsibility and Work Opportunity Reconciliation Act (PRWORA). At present, poor people in the US have no legal rights to social provision from the state beyond the meagre time limits provided under the rubric of 'welfare reform'.[4] Should a person use up the short-term benefits under Temporary Assistance to Needy Families (TANF), as welfare is now called, any additional support is at the discretion of individual states, rather than an entitlement based on need.

The limited welfare state that does exist in the US began in the depths of the Great Depression, when the 1935 Social Security Act created for the first time almost-universal social provision by providing a national old-age pension *for people who were regularly employed in the mainstream economy.* It was almost-universal in that agricultural workers and domestic workers, the two most common occupations for African American men and women, respectively, were not covered by Old Age Insurance (Quadagno, 1994). At the same time, the state-level mothers' pensions that had previously provided for needy mothers were incorporated into the 1935 Social Security Act in the form of Aid to Dependent Children (later called Aid to Families with Dependent Children, or AFDC). Relevantly, while old-age pensions were administered at the federal level, were not means-tested and were presumed to be universal, AFDC was largely administered at the state level, was means-tested and continued the tradition of supporting only those mothers deemed to be both needy and 'deserving'.

As a result, AFDC from the outset was a stigmatised form of social provision while old-age pensions were not. AFDC was the only part of the 1935 Social Security Act popularly called 'welfare' in common parlance; old-age pensions were and are called 'social security', although both forms derive from the 1935 Social Security Act. Despite the fact that both AFDC and old-age pensions are forms of income transfer, most Americans believe that old-age pensions are personally earned savings accounts being held in trust for them by the federal government, an idea fostered by the fact that most individuals employed in the mainstream economy see a monthly deduction from their paychecks for 'social security'.

The seeds of the 'teenage pregnancy crisis' were planted in the 1960s, when, in the face of rising affluence, the US began to confront the paradoxes involved in its patchwork and limited forms of social provision. In a 16 March 1964 address to Congress, President Lyndon Johnson proposed the 1964 Economic Opportunity Act, an ambitious set of programmes designed to reduce inequality in the US. One key part of the Economic Opportunity Act dealt with the federal provision of birth control supplies to poor people. Birth control had been nominally illegal in the US since 1873, and the net effect was to stratify access to birth control such that it was often difficult for poor people to obtain. This led, in turn, to a wide disparity between well-to-do and poor women in numbers of 'unwanted' births (Campbell, 1968; Levitan, 1969). In addition, because the US lacked (and still lacks) a national health care system, providing birth control was a popular form of social provision among bureaucrats, on the logic that reducing fertility would reduce births among the poor (Gordon, 1976; Littlewood, 1977).

The 1964 federal provision of birth control was an unqualified success: within a few years after the new policy was enacted, poor and affluent wives, African American and white alike, reported remarkably similar abilities to plan their families in the ways that they wanted. An important caveat is that two key groups of women took advantage of the new policy, while another one did not. First were the intended recipients of the policy, namely married women at the end of their childbearing years. Most 'unwanted' births measured in national surveys prior to this point were from women who had found themselves pregnant once again after having already achieved the size of family that they wanted. A second group of women were at the opposite end of the family-building spectrum. As sexual mores changed during the 'sexual revolution' of the late 1960s, young women who were not yet married became increasingly likely to have sex. These women were gradually, albeit gingerly, incorporated into the group of women imagined as 'targets' of federally subsidised family planning under the rubric of 'teenagers'; by 1972 many teenagers were obtaining their contraceptives from these governmentally subsidised categorical programmes.

For affluent and middle-class teenagers, these programmes did just exactly what they were supposed to do, allowing them to manage the timing of their fertility. But for a third and final group of women, these programmes did not successfully prevent pregnancy, in large part because the women involved were not strongly motivated to do so. Family planners, flushed with the success of their programmes with older and already married women in reducing unwanted fertility, and impressed with the willingness of affluent and middle-class teenagers to use contraception in order to postpone pregnancy, concluded that births to young, poor and often minority women, particularly when out of wedlock (as increasing proportions of them were), must of necessity be 'unwanted'. Accordingly, they and other campaigners began to advocate increased attention to these young women, who were 'failing' to take advantage of low-cost contraception in order to postpone their births until they were older and married.

It was in this context that liberals began to talk about a 'crisis' in teenage pregnancy, and to call for expanded services aimed more precisely at young people. Particularly influential was a 1976 publication, *Eleven Million Teenagers*, by the Alan Guttmacher Institute (then the research wing of Planned Parenthood) depicting an 'epidemic' of teenage births (Alan Guttmacher Institute, 1976). Although the figure of 11 million described the numbers of sexually active teenagers, the focus was on the high – mostly unmarried – teenage birth rate as well as the high abortion rate.[5]

In the years since the mid-1970s, young women have emerged on the front lines of new forms of sexual and reproductive behaviour. Although most visible among African Americans and among the young and the poor, single motherhood in the US has become more common in all age groups and in all classes. The growing importance of single motherhood, however, is problematic both to the general public and for the welfare state. Because it is coupled with a decline in marriage, the welfare state is now in a contradictory position. Single motherhood puts severe stress both on the categorical form of social provision and on the rhetoric of deserving motherhood on which it was based. 'Welfare', first in the form of mothers' pensions and then in the form of AFDC, had traditionally presumed that women and their children were impoverished by no fault of their own: the canonical single mother was the worthy, respectable (and usually white) widow. The increase in young women who were becoming single mothers not through the death or desertion of a spouse but by the failure to marry vastly expanded the numbers of people who needed support, and did so in a way that many Americans viewed as immoral.

Americans often take for granted that an increase in choice increases individual autonomy. In this case, the vast expansion of federal provision of birth control for the young and the poor seems to have set the stage for the paradoxical willingness to see young unmarried mothers as exercising the *wrong* choice, namely the choice to have a child out of wedlock. These women came to seem perverse, or, worse yet, rational actors out to take advantage of an unwitting welfare scheme that encouraged such socially stigmatised behaviour.

Starting in the 1980s, American conservatives began to attack the sexual and gender changes of the 1960s that threatened constructions of masculinity and male independence. They focused on the problem of teenage pregnancy, challenging the definition put on the table by liberals. Rather than seeing pregnant teenagers as young women who were not being adequately supported by the larger society, or as a product of the decline in stable working-class jobs that had historically aided family formation, conservatives defined the existence of teenage pregnancy as the product of a cultural breakdown. For example, one conservative commentator, William

Bennett, uses the out-of-wedlock birth rates as one of his 'leading cultural indicators' of social disarray. Conservatives saw teenage pregnancy as the inability of parents to control their children (read: daughters) and blamed the welfare system for creating the 'moral hazard' of unwed motherhood (Bennett, 1994).

By the end of the 1980s, teenage pregnancy – first put on the public agenda by liberals hoping to increase services to disadvantaged young people – provided a ready symbol that united both fiscal and social conservatives in the US. Fiscal conservatives were alarmed by levels of welfare provision (although these levels were both low by international standards and, because they were not indexed to inflation, were actually *decreasing* in real dollar terms); they were eager to free up dollars from welfare to use in other government expenditures. Because 'welfare' (AFDC) was a legal entitlement under the 1935 Social Security Act, individual states were obligated prior to 1996 to provide benefits to all individuals who met the statutory requirements, as those requirements were defined by the individual states. Thus, AFDC payments were an inflexible part of both state and federal budgets, and could not be reallocated in times of fiscal crisis.

Social conservatives were alarmed by women who controlled their own fertility (abortion has been one of the single most politically mobilising issues in the US since the early 1970s) and by patterns of family formation different from the traditional nuclear family. Although liberals continued to argue that part of the problem was a lack of well-paying jobs with benefits, conservatives were eminently successful in arguing that teenage pregnancy – by now a trope for a mixed bag of social issues including unmarried sexuality, an abortion rate shockingly high by international standards, and unwed motherhood – was a *moral* problem that, at a minimum, demanded the reform of the welfare system to eliminate its imagined inducements to deviant practices.

Current policy initiatives and evaluations

Because of the vagaries of the US federal system, states varied in the level of benefits they provided to needy mothers prior to the 1996 PRWORA. In addition, the real value of welfare benefits declined over time as inflation increased. Thus, two kinds of natural experiments – over time and across states – have led scholars to conclude that welfare has very modest effects, if any, on fertility rates. For white teenagers in particular, states with higher rates of benefits may have lower 'legitimation' rates, that is, rates of marriage among already pregnant couples (Rank, 1989; Lundberg and Plotnick, 1990; Plotnick, 1999; Ellwood and Jencks, 2004). But the 'moral panic' over teenage pregnancy and out-of-wedlock births had already set the stage for a union of fiscal and social conservatives to put an end to almost 60 years of social provision. Although there is considerable evidence that President Bill Clinton imagined replacing welfare with more generous efforts to help needy individuals enter the paid workforce, the Bill that eventuated from his campaign promise to 'end welfare as we know it' mixes together moral and social anxiety about sexuality, changing gender relations, and new family forms.

In the US system, Congress often inserts a section in new legislation called 'Findings', which plays an important legal role as a directive to courts confronting subsequent ambiguities in the legislation under consideration. US courts often turn to these Findings sections in an attempt to understand the 'intent of Congress' when they are called upon to resolve contested issues in federal legislation (Frickey, 1996, p 695). Most interestingly, when read carefully, the Findings section of the 1996 welfare reform Bill makes clear that the new legislation is only indirectly about government financial assistance or work, two items readers could be forgiven for thinking are most central to questions of poverty and its alleviation. Rather, the Findings section is about sex, teenagers, and single motherhood. The key point here is that the Findings section shifted the debate at a national level from a debate about poverty and jobs to one about marriage and unwed sexuality. Feminist scholars have pointed out that debates about welfare have always been about regulating the sexuality and the motherhood of poor women. Our point is that the purpose of such regulation has gone from implicit to explicit in this Bill. So when the House and Senate met to reconcile differences between the two chambers' versions, the point when the Findings section was written, the reconciliation committee inserted Section 510, which provided US$50 million a year for abstinence education. Because the welfare Bill was itself amending the 1935 Social Security Act of 1935, two consequences flowed from this addition. First, because Title V of the Social Security Act provides for states to match three dollars for every four dollars that the federal government spends, the total funding in this Bill is projected to amount to US$88 million a year for abstinence. Second, because the section on abstinence was attached to a series of 'entitlements', abstinence education became an entitlement too, meaning in this context that it could be neither voted on nor debated for five years until the Bill came up for reauthorisation (Sonfield and Gold, 2001).

The first two items in the Findings section of the welfare reform Bill note that 'marriage is the foundation of a successful society', and 'marriage is an essential institution of a successful society which promotes the interests of children' (Public Law 104-193, The Personal Responsibility and Work Opportunity Reconciliation Act of 1996, section 101). The Findings section then moves from marriage to a consideration of how it is related to the need for welfare reform: 89% of children receiving AFDC are in homes where no father is present; this in turn is due to an increased propensity for unmarried women to get pregnant; that the rates for younger women are increasing more quickly than the rates for older women; and that non-marital births are associated with negative outcomes for women, for children and for society. Almost imperceptibly, the categories of pregnancy, unwed births and teenage births became collapsed into one another, and the resulting amalgam of teenage unwed births becomes identified as the *source* of poverty rather than as a *result* of it.

On a simple statistical level, the arguments made in the Findings section are undeniably true. Single-parent families, which are most often single-mother families, are poorer than two-parent families; this holds true even in nations with generous social provision (Casper et al, 1994). While not always teenagers, single mothers are, of course, young: rates of unmarried births are increasing faster among young women than older women, mostly because younger women have more of their reproductive years ahead of them and are still building their (possibly unmarried) families.

Moreover, the 'problem of children having children' is seen by Congress as a willful refusal among some women to marry rather than the simple but unfortunate fact that many poor young women cannot find men who will commit to them through marriage, or cannot find men who are able, most often through no fault of their own, to earn enough money to pull them out of poverty (Wilson, 1987; Tucker and Mitchell-Kernan, 1995; Levy, 1998). Welfare is seen as the problem, not the solution, in that it is assumed to motivate or at least enable unmarried childbearing. The Findings section of the Bill, and the sections that follow, make clear that the national panic driving welfare reform is about a rise in *single* parenting rather than *teenage* parenting. Time limits on welfare are designed to make alternatives to marriage less reliable and more daunting, and a national commitment to abstinence is designed to make marriage more alluring.

To make absolutely clear that the money was earmarked for *abstinence*, the money came with clear guidelines for its use. For instance, sex education eligible for funding had to have the 'exclusive purpose' of deterring all sex outside of marriage by 'teaching the social, psychological, and health gains to be realized by abstaining from sexual activity' and 'abstinence from sexual activity outside marriage is the expected standard for all school age children'. The guidelines also specified that abstinence education must teach that 'abstinence from sexual activity is the only certain way to avoid out-of-wedlock pregnancy, sexually transmitted diseases, and other associated health problems'. Furthermore, this money was earmarked only for sex education that 'teaches that bearing children out-of-wedlock is likely to have harmful consequences for the child, the child's parents, and society' and that teaches the 'importance of attaining self-sufficiency before engaging in sexual activity'.[6] This abstinence education provision defines a new notion of what public policy is expected to do: promote marriage as a way of reducing the welfare burden in the US.

Nearly all US states are using these abstinence-only funds; in 1999, more than one in ten Section 510 dollars funded programmes in faith-based organisations (Sonfield and Gold, 2001). Like sex education in the US, abstinence-only programmes vary dramatically by state, school district and the organisation that implements them. Perhaps because of this variation, it is unclear whether abstinence-only education is effective. Although conservative think tanks such as the Heritage Foundation (Rector, 2002) tout the success of abstinence-only education in quasi-academic papers, scholarly evaluations – which insist on higher standards of evidence, rigorous research design and proper statistical analyses – find little to no evidence that abstinence-only programmes change sexual behaviour (Kirby, 2002; Rector, 2002). But again, the results of these studies depend on many factors, especially the actual content of the educational programme and the age of the teenagers enrolled in it.

When Congress approved the Section 510 Abstinence Education Programme, it also authorised an evaluation of abstinence-only programmes funded by this policy. The resulting multi-year evaluation estimates the effects of a select group of the strongest abstinence-only programmes. Findings from this study unfortunately do not yet include behavioural outcomes such as actual sexual activity, risks of contracting sexually transmitted diseases, and risks of pregnancy in teenagers;

however, the study does measure impact on *intermediate* outcomes that 'may be related to teen sexual activity, such as the views of youth on abstinence and teen sex and their expectations to abstain' (Maynard et al, 2005, p xix).

The abstinence–only programmes evaluated by the policy research firm Mathematica did affect some of the intermediate outcomes examined. Teenagers receiving abstinence-only education 'reported views that, on average, are more supportive of abstinence and less supportive of teen sex than did their control group counterparts' (Maynard et al, 2005, p xxxii). The programmes also 'increased perceptions of potential adverse consequences of teen and non-marital sex' (Maynard et al, 2005, p xx). Evidence that the programmes increased teenagers' expectations that they would abstain from sex is extremely weak.

Programmes that promote abstinence by encouraging adolescents to make pledges to remain virgins until marriage have drawn a lot of attention precisely because they may actually increase the risk of sexually transmitted diseases and decrease contraceptive use at first intercourse. Peter Bearman and Hannah Bruckner (2001) found that, for some teenagers, pledging to stay abstinent until married did delay the onset of sexual intercourse for an average of 18 months. However, they also found that the adolescents who took the pledge were one third less likely than their non-pledging peers to use contraception when they did become sexually active – which they often did well before they were married. Teenagers who made the pledge had the same rate of sexually transmitted diseases as their non-pledging peers, but were actually *less* likely to use condoms or seek medical testing and treatment for sexually transmitted diseases, thereby increasing the possibility that they would transmit diseases (Bruckner and Bearman, 2005).

The most effective sexual education programmes for teenagers in the US are not 'abstinence-only' programmes but rather are comprehensive ones that include information about both contraception and abstinence (Kirby, 1997). These programmes provide truthful information about the risks of unprotected sex as well as methods teens can use to avoid unprotected intercourse (Kirby, 1997). Comprehensive programmes have been found to delay the onset of sexual intercourse, reduce the number of sexual partners a teenager has, and increase their contraception use (Kirby, 1997, 2001).

Conclusion

By changing the rhetoric around teenage pregnancy from one where young women are portrayed as manipulative actors taking advantage of generous government hand-outs to an examination of the *actual* problem of teenage pregnancy, we hope to increase the understanding that in the US teenage pregnancy is a marker for just how bleak life has become for some people. These young mothers suffer from more than economic poverty: they also suffer from a poverty of hope, a poverty of viable roads to success; and a poverty of social connectedness.

Young poor mothers are not caught in a 'culture of poverty' as conservative commentators in the US would have us believe: they are caught in a *cycle* of poverty. This distinction between a *culture* of poverty and a *cycle* of poverty is critical. Believing that the poor live in a culture that perpetuates unemployment, promiscuous sex, unfinished education and early childbearing moves the blame for such symptoms of poverty from unequal *economic structures* and failing government institutions, such as schools and job markets, to *the people themselves*. While families can get caught in downward spirals of poverty and dysfunction, it is usually not because of their values. In her ethnography of teenage mothers, Kaplan (1997) demonstrates that many adolescent mothers value the same things that the 'moral majority' does: family, love, marriage, independence and personal achievement. Having a baby is their way of exercising those values. Where they differ from the daughters of the 'moral majority', however, is in the economic structures they are embedded in, and therefore the resources they have access to in order to fulfil their values.

It is critical for us to understand the ways in which gender roles and deep gender insecurity, as well as our notions of independence and dependency, are playing a part in keeping adolescent mothers in poverty. As women have steadily entered the paid labour force over the last 50 or so years, they have threatened American notions of heroic male independence and, with it, masculinity. Women are no longer necessarily economically dependent on men, and so men are no longer independent in the traditional sense. An increasing rate of single motherhood – which indicates that women are even *less* dependent on men – is causing moral alarm in those who fear, and feel, this crisis in masculinity.

Instead of treating the less fortunate with such contempt, we Americans might reconsider what we value. If it is education and the American Dream we value, if we want DeVonya Smalls to work rather than receive welfare, we would do well to make sure that she gets the same education as her middle-class peers, and that a job which has the potential to lift her out of poverty is available to her. If we value marriage and stable relationships, we would do well to help the men in DeVonya's community participate in both childrearing and in the paid labour force. Americans may value independence and self-striving, but we also have a rich history of helping others in need. Not until American lawmakers and the people they govern extend their empathy to girls like DeVonya will we begin to truly understand, and therefore to end, the cycle of poverty that she is caught in.

Notes

[1] European readers should be cautioned that abortion rates in the US are estimates, not vital statistics.

[2] Data comes from the National Center for Health Statistics of the US Department of Health and Human Series (number of births); the Alan Guttmacher Institute (number of abortions); and the US Bureau of the Census (population estimates). For exact sources, see www.guttmacher.org/pubs/teen_stats.html

[3] Women with family incomes less than 149% of the poverty threshold rate are categorised as poor; those in high economic status groups have a family income of 300% or more of the poverty threshold rate.

[4] Under PRWORA (Public Law 104-193), needy individuals no longer have a legal entitlement to support, but states receive 'block-granted' funds, which they may then allocate as they wish. In any event, needy people are also limited to a lifetime total of 60 months of assistance, and can be sanctioned (have benefits reduced) for not attempting to find work or engage in state-provided training.

[5] Both American adults and teenagers have very high rates of abortion by international standards; since abortions are more common among unmarried women, and young women are disproportionately unmarried, abortions appeared to be concentrated among the young.

⁶ Public Law 104–193, The Personal Responsibility and Work Opportunity Reconciliation Act of 1996, Section 510(b).

References

Alan Guttmacher Institute (1976) *Eleven Million Teenagers*, New York, NY: Alan Guttmacher Institute.

Alan Guttmacher Institute (2004) *US Teenage Pregnancy Statistics with Comparative Statistics for Women Aged 20-24*, New York, NY: Alan Guttmacher Institute, available at www.guttmacher.org/pubs/teen_stats.html

Bearman, P. and Bruckner, H. (2001) 'Promising the Future: Virginity Pledges and the Transition to First Intercourse', *American Journal of Sociology*, vol 106, no 4, pp 859-912.

Bennett, W.J. (1994) *The Index of Leading Cultural Indicators: Facts and Figures on the State of American Society*, New York, NY: Simon and Schuster.

Blinn-Pike, L., Berger, T., Dixon, D., Kuschel, D. and Kaplan, M. (2002) 'Is there a Causal Link between Maltreatment and Adolescent Pregnancy? A Literature Review', *Perspectives on Sexual and Reproductive Health*, vol 34, no 2, pp 68-75.

Boyer, D. and Fine, D. (1992) 'Sexual Abuse as a Factor in Adolescent Pregnancy and Child Maltreatment', *Family Planning Perspectives*, vol 24, no 4, pp 4-19.

Bruckner, H. and Bearman, P. (2005) 'After the Promise: The STD Consequences of Adolescent Virginity Pledges', *Journal of Adolescent Health*, vol 36, no 4, pp 271-78.

Campbell, A.A. (1968) 'The Role of Family Planning in the Reduction of Poverty', *Journal of Marriage and the Family*, vol 30, no 2, pp 236-45.

Casper, L.M., McLanahan, S.S., Garfinkel, I., Sigle-Rushton, W., McLanahan, S., Hanson, T.L. and Miller, C.K. (1994) 'The Gender-Poverty Gap: What We Can Learn from Other Countries', *American Sociological Review*, vol 59, no 4, pp 594-605.

CDC (National Center for Chronic Disease Prevention and Health Promotion) (2004) *Despite Improvements, Many High School Students Still Engaging in Risky Health Behaviors*, Atlanta, GA: CDC, available at: www.cdc.gov/HealthyYouth/pdf/YRBSpress-release.pdf

Chodorow, N. and Contratto, S. (1989) 'The Fantasy of the Perfect Mother', in N. Chodorow (ed) *Feminism and Psychoanalytic Theory*, New Haven, CT: Yale University Press, pp 79-97.

Darroch, J.E. and Singh, S. (1999) *Why is Teenage Pregnancy Declining? The Roles of Abstinence, Sexual Activity, and Contraceptive Use, Occasional Report No. 1*, New York, NY: Alan Guttmacher Institute.

Ellwood, D.T. and Jencks, C. (2004) 'The Uneven Spread of Single-Parent Families: What Do We Know? Where Do We Look for Answers?', in K.M. Neckerman (ed) *Social Inequality*, New York, NY: Russell Sage Foundation, pp 3–78.

Flora, P. and Alba, J. (1981) *The Development of Welfare States in Europe and America*, New Brunswick, NJ: Transaction Books.

Fraser, N. and Gordon, L. (1994) 'A Genealogy of Dependency: Tracing a Keyword of the US Welfare State', in B. Laslett, J. Brenner and Y. Arat (eds) *Rethinking the Political: Gender, Resistance, and the State*, Chicago, IL: University of Chicago Press, pp 33–59.

Frickey, P. (1996) 'The Fool on the Hill: Congressional Findings, Constitutional Adjudication, and *US v Lopez*', 46 *Case Western Reserve Law Review*. 695.

Geronimus, A.T. (1992) 'Teenage Childbearing and Social Disadvantage: Unprotected Discourse', *Family Relations*, vol 41, no 2, pp 244–8.

Geronimus, A.T. (1997) 'Teenage Childbearing and Personal Responsibility: An Alternative View', *Political Science Quarterly*, vol 112, no 3, pp 405–30.

Gershenson, H.P., Musick, J.S., Ruch-Ross, H.S., Magee, V., Rubino, K.K. and Rosenberg, D. (1989) 'The Prevalence of Coercive Sexual Experience among Teenage Mothers', *Journal of Interpersonal Violence*, vol 4, no 2, pp 204–19.

Gordon, L. (1976) *Woman's Body, Woman's Right: A Social History of Birth Control in America*, New York, NY: Grossman.

Heuser, R.L. (1976) *Fertility Tables for Birth Cohorts by Color: US, 1917-73*, Washington, DC: US Department of Health, Education and Welfare, Public Health Service, Health Resources Administration, National Center for Health Statistics, Division of Vital Statistics.

Jenks, C. (1995) 'Do Poor Women have a Right to Bear Children?', *The American Prospect*, vol 6, no 20, available at: www.americanprospect.com

Jones, E.F., Darroch Forrest, J., Goldman, N., Henshaw, S.K., Lincoln, R., Rosoff, J.I., Westoff, C. and Wulf, D. (1985) 'Teenage Pregnancy in Developed Countries: Determinants and Policy Implications', *Family Planning Perspectives*, vol 17, no 2, pp 53–63.

Kaplan, E.B. (1997) *Not Our Kind of Girl*, Berkeley, CA: University of California Press.

Kirby, D. (1997) *No Easy Answers: Research Findings on Programs to Reduce Teen Pregnancy*, Washington, DC: National Campaign to Prevent Teen Pregnancy.

Kirby, D. (2001) *Emerging Answers: Research Findings on Programs to Reduce Teen Pregnancy*, Washington, DC: National Campaign to Prevent Teen Pregnancy.

Kirby, D. (2002) *Do Abstinence-only Programs Delay the Initiation of Sex among Young People and Reduce Teen Pregnancy?*, Washington, DC: National Campaign to Prevent Teen Pregnancy.

Kirby, D., Coyle, K. and Gould, J.B. (2001) 'Manifestations of Poverty and Birthrates among Young Teenagers in California Zip Code Areas', *Family Planning Perspectives*, vol 33, no 2, pp 63-9.

Kozol, J. (1991) *Savage Inequalities: Children in America's Schools* (1st edition), New York, NY: Crown Pub.

Levitan, S.A. (1969) *The Great Society's Poor Law: A New Approach to Poverty*, Baltimore, MD: Johns Hopkins Press.

Levy, F. (1998) *The New Dollars and Dreams: American Incomes and Economic Change*, New York, NY: Russell Sage Foundation.

Littlewood, T.B. (1977) *The Politics of Population Control*, Notre Dame, IN: University of Notre Dame Press.

Lundberg, S. and Plotnick, R. (1990) 'Effects of State Welfare, Abortion, and Family Planning Policies on Premarital Childbearing among White Adolescents', *Family Planning Perspectives*, vol 22, no 6, pp 246-51.

Maynard, R.A., Trenholm, C., Devaney, B., Johnson, A., Clark, M.A., Homrighausen, J. and Kalay, E. (2005) *First-year Impacts of Four Title V, Section 510 Abstinence Education Programs*, Washington, DC: Mathematica Policy Research, Inc.

Michaels, G. (1988) 'Motivational Factors in the Decision and Timing of Pregnancy', in Michaels, G.Y. and Goldberg, W.A. (eds) *The Transitions to Parenthood: Current Theory and Research*, Cambridge, and New York, NY: Cambridge University Press, pp 23-61.

Musick, J. (1993) *Young, Poor, and Pregnant*, New Haven, CT and London: Yale University Press.

Orloff, A.S. and Skocpol, T. (1984) 'Why not Equal Protection? Explaining the Politics of Public Social Spending in Britain, 1900-1911, and the US, 1880s-1920', *American Sociological Review*, vol 49, no 6, pp 726-50.

Plotnick, R. (1999) 'Welfare and Out-of-wedlock Childbearing: Evidence from the 1980s', *Journal of Marriage and the Family*, vol 52, no 3.

Quadagno, J.S. (1988) *The Transformation of Old Age Security: Class and Politics in the American Welfare State*, Chicago, IL: University of Chicago Press.

Quadagno, J.S. (1994) *The Color of Welfare: How Racism Undermined the War on Poverty*, New York, NY: Oxford University Press.

Quadagno, J.S. (2005) *One Nation, Uninsured: Why the US has no National Health Insurance*, Oxford: Oxford University Press.

Rank, M. (1989) 'Fertility among Women on Welfare: Incidence and Determinants', *American Sociological Review*, vol 54, no 2, pp 296-304.

Rector, R. (2002) *The Effectiveness of Abstinence Education Programs in Reducing Sexual Activity among Youth*, Washington, DC: The Heritage Foundation.

Roosa, M.W., Tein, J.-Y., Reinholtz, C. and Angelini, P.J. (1997) 'The Relationship of Childhood Sexual Abuse to Teenage Pregnancy', *Journal of Marriage and the Family*, vol 59, no 1, pp 119-30.

Saul, R. (1999) 'Teen Pregnancy: Progress Meets Politics', *The Guttmacher Report on Public Policy*, vol 2, no 3, pp 6-9.

Singh, S., Darroch, J. and Frost, J. (2001) 'Socioeconomic Disadvantage and Adolescent Women's Sexual and Reproductive Behavior: The Case of Five Developed Countries', *Family Planning Perspectives*, vol 33, no 6, pp 251-8, 289.

Sonfield, A. and Gold, R.B. (2001) 'States' Implementation of the Section 510 Abstinence Education Program, FY 1999', *Family Planning Perspectives*, vol 33, no 4, pp 166-71.

Tucker, M.B. and Mitchell-Kernan, C. (1995) *The Decline in Marriage among African Americans: Causes, Consequences, and Policy Implications*, New York, NY: Russell Sage Foundation.

UNICEF (United Nations Children's Fund) (2001) *A League Table of Teenage Births in Rich Nations*, Florence: UNICEF Innocenti Research Centre.

Ventura, S., Matthews, T.J. and Hamilton, B.E. (2001) *Births to Teenagers in the US, 1940-2000, National Vital Statistics Reports*, vol 49, no 10, Hyattsville, Maryland, MD: National Center for Health Statistics.

Waller, M.R. (2001) *Unmarried Parents, Fragile Families: New Evidence from Oakland*, San Francisco, CA: Public Policy Institute of California.

Wilson, W.J. (1987) *The Truly Disadvantaged: The Inner City, the Underclass, and Public Policy*, Chicago, IL: University of Chicago Press.

THREE

Teenage pregnancy in New Zealand: changing social policy paradigms

Georg Menz

Introduction

The high rates of teenage pregnancy among Anglophone countries are striking and New Zealand is no exception in this regard. Three quarters of all 760,000 births to teenage mothers are accounted for by the six Anglophone Organisation for Economic Co-operation and Development (OECD) countries. In 1998, there were 29.8 births to women below the age of 20 per 1,000 15- to 19-year-olds, which is the third highest rate among the OECD countries, behind the UK (30.8) and the US (52.1) (UNICEF, 2001). Meanwhile, Western and especially Northern European countries record rates between one half and one fifth of this. Equally striking is the stark divergence between teenage pregnancy rates among Maori New Zealanders (74 per 1,000) and non-Maori 'Kiwis' (18 per 1,000). Yet even this much lower rate compares unfavourably with the record of most of Western Europe.

There are a number of general international trends in teenage pregnancy that apply to New Zealand. The first one is the great paradox, alluded to in a UNICEF study on the phenomenon (UNICEF, 2001), that teenage pregnancy as an empirical phenomenon has actually decreased since 1970 – in New Zealand, the rate has more than halved from the 1970 rate of 64.3 per 1,000 births. Meanwhile, the average age of mothers at first birth has increased. Thus, while the phenomenon itself has decreased in magnitude over time – although remaining at constant rates in New Zealand since the early 1980s – it has increasingly become considered socially deviant and regarded as a social policy problem. Similarly, while out-of-wedlock births have increased across Western societies as more couples have embraced non-conventional forms of partnership, the fact that most teenage mothers are unwed seems to contribute to their portrayal as engaging in irresponsible behaviour. Thus, in 1998, 58% of all New Zealand mothers were married against only 6% of new teenage mothers. Just as elsewhere, overall fertility has also decreased rapidly since 1960, from 4.24 children per woman in 1960 to 1.92 in 1998 (Castles, 2004). Finally, comparative studies highlight the fact that higher rates of teenage pregnancy among minority ethnic communities are not unique to New Zealand (Cheesbrough et al, 1999; Dickson et al, 2000).

This chapter consists of four sections. First, an outline of the phenomenon of teenage pregnancy in New Zealand is provided. Second, the public policy regulation of the phenomenon since 1970 is examined. The key argument developed here is that the phenomenon of teenage pregnancy and related public policy responses can be studied as representative case studies of larger paradigm shifts. Teenage pregnancy is thus treated as a social problem by contemporary New Zealand policymakers not least due to the continuing predominance of the workfarist paradigm in social policy design. In this sense, teenage pregnancy and social service provision for (young) single mothers can serve as a litmus test of broader trends in social policy formation: influenced by feminist activists seeking to correct the paternalistic assumptions of traditional New Zealand welfare policy in the 1970s, questioned by the more aggressively neoliberal conservative National Party returning to power in 1990, and finally redesigned as an issue of 'access' and 'social exclusion' under Labour since 2000. These debates have been strongly shaped by policy and ideational transfer from abroad, principally from the UK and the US. The third section provides a brief review of recent policy developments and evaluation, while the fourth section contains a concluding discussion.

Teenage pregnancy as an empirical phenomenon

In line with international trends, the average age at first birth has increased significantly since the 1970s in New Zealand. While in 1978 most recorded births corresponded to mothers between the ages of 20 and 29, by 1998, the age range had risen and encompassed mainly women aged 25 to 34, extending even slightly beyond. This general pattern is applicable both to the total population and Maori New Zealanders, comprising 20% of the country's population (Statistics New Zealand, 1999).[1]

In considering patterns of teenage pregnancy over time, it is also clear that the phenomenon reached its peak in New Zealand in the early 1970s and decreased significantly throughout that decade to reach a level by the early 1980s that has remained stable since. While in the early 1970s, the fertility rate for the age cohort of 15- to 19-year-olds was 70 per 1,000, this decreased to 30 per 1,000 by the mid-1980s, remaining stable until 1997 and decreasing slightly to 25.6 per 1,000 in 2002. Time series data suggest that while one third of the post-war cohort of women born in 1953 had given birth on or before their 19th birthday, this rate fell to one sixth for generations born after 1965 and thus closer to the rate for women born prior to 1925 of one in nine (Statistics New Zealand, 2003, p 2). The relative stability of the phenomenon between the early 1980s and the mid-1990s demonstrates that attempts by governments during this period to limit 'incentives' for teenage pregnancy by reducing transfer payment provisions were not particularly successful.

An important factor affecting the teenage pregnancy rate is access to abortion. The total number of abortions more than doubled between 1982 and 1999, increasing from about 7,000 to more than 15,000. Young women are more likely than older women to undergo an abortion. In 1999, women in the age groups 15-19, 20-24 and 25-29 years had respective abortion rates of 21.7, 34.8 and 24.5 per 1,000 women. The most highly represented group – women between the ages of 20 and 24 – accounted overall for approximately 30% of all abortions. Broadly based ethnic data reveal a somewhat higher rate of abortions among the non-European population of New Zealand, with Asians (298 per 1,000), Pacific Islanders (255 per 1,000) and Maori (247 per 1,000) women all being more likely to receive abortions than either the national average (212 per 1,000) or descendants of Europeans (202 per 1,000) (Statistics New Zealand, 1999). According to one study, poorer women are particularly likely to seek abortions: 43% of women undergoing them had a family income of less than £10,000 (NZ$22,000) in the early 1990s (Young et al, 1994). The relatively higher rates of abortion among young women, including teenagers, suggest that the somewhat easier availability of abortion acts to decrease occurrences of teenage pregnancies, which might otherwise amount to somewhat higher levels. In 2000, the national abortion rate for women between the ages of 15 and 44 stood at 19 per 1,000 (Ministry of Health, 2001, p 18). Among women between the ages of 15 and 19 it reached 22.5 per 1,000 in 1998 (UNICEF, 2001, p 20). Legislative restrictions on abortion are not pronounced, with women of any age having the right to a termination if two doctors agree that the pregnancy would seriously impair the mother's mental or physical health or that the baby would be affected by a serious disability. Incest is also recognised as legitimate grounds for a termination. The 1977 Contraception, Sterilisation, and Abortion Act provides the general legislative framework, while the 1961 Crimes Act (amended in 1977 and 1978) lays out the reasons for abortion deemed legitimate.

But not only has teenage pregnancy changed in quantitative terms, it has also assumed new qualitative characteristics. The teenage mothers of the 1970s were more likely to be married, while this was no longer true at the end of that decade. In 1971, 5,100 of the total of teenage mothers were married, while 3,700 were not. By 2002, only 200 teenage mothers were married, while 3,400 were not (Statistics New Zealand, 2003, p 3). Henceforth, contemporary teenage mothers are more likely to live in more informal relationships or indeed in no stable relationship.

There is also a persistent difference in fertility patterns between the indigenous Maori population and migrant communities and their descendants from neighbouring Pacific Islands on the one hand and descendants of European migrants on the other. When comparing the fertility rates of teenagers aged 13-17, the difference between the non-Maori population (4.9 births per 1,000 teenagers), the Maori population (26.2 per 1,000) and Pacific Islanders (17.0 per 1,000) becomes more apparent (1998 values, cited in Ministry of Health, 2001, p 16). Although it should be mentioned that the total fertility of the Maori population (having fluctuated between 2.3 and 2.9 births per 1,000 since 1970 is higher than that of the non-Maori population (ranging from 2.1 to 2.3 births per 1,000), the predominance of teenage pregnancy among Maori and Pacific Islander women needs to be noted. While recent changes to the methodology employed by governmental agencies undoubtedly make a difference, permitting the individuals concerned to identify their ethnic identity themselves, this persistent gap between New Zealand's ethnic groups cannot be ignored.

There are two additional factors, mentioned in the comparative literature, which may be correlated to rates of teenage pregnancy, namely use of contraceptives and average age at first sexual intercourse. Darroch et al (2001) argue that the low use of contraceptives among US teenagers is a crucial factor behind the high rate of pregnancies in the US. It has often been argued that early sexual activity is linked to greater likelihood of teenage pregnancy (Marsault et al, 1997; Dickson et al, 2000; Woodward et al, 2001; Ellis et al, 2003). In New Zealand, a number of studies have suggested that the median age for first sexual intercourse is 17 for males and 16 for females (Fenwick and Purdie, 2000). Studies on the use of contraceptives report rates fluctuating between 88% and less than 50% (for a summary, see Jackson, 2004). This wide range obviously reflects data validity problems, but relatively high rates of sexually transmitted diseases among young people (Ministry of Health, 2001) would seem to suggest relatively low use of condoms.

Both of these factors are related to the level and degree of sexual education provided for teenagers. Earlier work has argued that sexual education in secondary school, easy access to contraceptives, and societal openness to sexual matters affect teenage sexual conduct, use of contraceptives and teenage pregnancy rates (Dickson et al, 2000; Darroch et al, 2001; UNICEF, 2001). On this count, public policy initiatives in New Zealand have not led to a truly sustained nationwide effort at improving levels of sexual education and the availability of contraceptives. Jackson (2004, p 133) reports that there is no nationwide evaluation research of educational efforts. Practitioners representing the New Zealand Family Planning Association (interview, Family Planning Association of New Zealand, Wellington, 2005) also note that since schools enjoy relative autonomy in delivering teaching and parents wield considerable influence, the provision of sexual education is often limited in rural areas or among socially conservative minority ethnic groups. While the government's action plan (Ministry of Health, 2001) has recently led to a colourful advertising campaign endorsing the use of condoms, using a multitude of media and transmission channels, including the internet, it is too early to tell whether such efforts will prove effective in the long term.

Before proceeding, it is worth mentioning the link established between the likelihood of teenage pregnancy and lower socioeconomic status. Evidence from Western Europe suggests that, depending on the country, between 24% and 80% of all teenage mothers belong to the poorest 20% of the population. The so-called lifecourse adversity model posits that 'familial and ecological stress provokes earlier onset of sexual activity and reproduction' (Ellis et al, 2003, p 801). Teenage pregnancy seems to be correlated strongly with poverty and/ or low levels of educational achievement and expectations (Coley and Chase-Landsdale, 1998; Cheesbrough et al, 1999; Dickson et al, 2000; Ferguson and Woodward, 2000). This suggests that stigmatisation of teenage pregnancy may be related to this phenomenon's current concentration among poorer women. It should be mentioned in passing that low expectations of future professional trajectories cannot always be readily dismissed and may even be quite realistic – henceforth, the choice for a child may indeed be a rational one and the opportunity cost of lost earnings can be minimal.

The regulation of teenage pregnancy in New Zealand

New Zealand's welfare state in its original shape was universalist and comprehensive. It made few specific provisions for teenage mothers at first; however, a category was created in the 1970s for which teenage mothers could be eligible for social assistance under certain circumstances. It came under strong attack from the Right for providing wrong 'incentives'. While chronologically pre-empting many of its European cousins, in many ways it combined liberal and Bismarckian elements, being based on employment status and a male breadwinner model. Near full employment throughout the *trente glorieuses* did not test its capacity significantly. Welfare state structures attracted significant criticism from feminists due to its gendered and often heavily paternalist assumptions. In practice, applications for social assistance by females were arduous and single mothers needed to demonstrate that the male component of the family was absent due to no fault of the female. The reform measures of the 1970s sought to address some of these points of contention by making social assistance more widely and more easily available for female applicants, including notably single parents. The so-called domestic purposes benefit (DPB), introduced in 1975 following policy recommendations by the 1972 Royal Commission of Inquiry into Social Security (Rudd, 1997, p 257), was aimed at extending the social net to individuals raising children on their own, those caring for sick or older people, or those previously simply not having been catered for. Most of these new beneficiaries were female. The DPB was thus created as an alternative category to social assistance that was more easily available and better targeted at a demographic group that had previously been neglected.

As will be analysed in more detail below, the DPB has created considerable controversy over the years. For the New Right, it provided incentives for young females to 'choose' pregnancy, presumably a rational choice to the extent that a high proportion of recipients appear to possess low levels of formal qualifications. The numbers of recipients has risen from 10,000 at the time of inception to 110,067 as of 30 June 1999 and thus accounted for 14% of all recipients of social transfer payments, compared to 22% (or 164,530) accounted for by the so-called community wage, the heavily reformed former category comprising unemployment compensation (Statistics New Zealand, 1999).

Family benefits were abolished in 1991 and replaced with the so-called 'Family Support' programme, comprising effectively a negative income tax. However, a closer examination of the demographic composition of DPB beneficiaries reveals that since 1991 only between 18,000 (in 2000) and 20,000 (in 1991; the 1996 value is approximately 19,000) of the total recipients (hovering around the 100,000 mark) were young females between the ages of 15 and 24. Only 2,805 (or roughly 2.8%) of DPB recipients are actually teenage parents (Statistics New Zealand, 2004). What is more striking is the high level of poorly educated and women of Maori origin among the recipients. Although the level of formal education has to be inferred indirectly by examining the profile of those women also registered as jobseekers, it does become apparent that since 1991, between half and two thirds of all recipients do not hold a secondary school diploma. The correlation between low levels of education and a higher probability for reliance on the DPB is further substantiated by Statistics New Zealand data indicating that better-educated single mothers are more likely to work full or part time. Thus, only 48% of women with a secondary school diploma (24% of women with a tertiary education diploma) were not part of the labour market in 1996. Meanwhile, in 1991, 44% of all women between the ages of 20 and 35 receiving the DPB identified themselves as being of Maori origin, despite Maori constituting only 17% of this sub-group in the general population. These figures have not changed much in relative proportions over the years. Strikingly, Maori women also accounted for 49% of individuals among DBP recipients without a secondary school diploma, highlighting the dual nature of this ethnic group's over-representation (Statistics New Zealand, 2004).[2]

In this chapter it is being argued that social policy regulation is crucially shaped by larger paradigmatic changes. Examining the regulatory public policy approach towards teenage pregnancy, we thus find significant change since the 1970s. Teenage pregnancy is not truly a new empirical phenomenon but it is portrayed as social policy problem and socially deviant behaviour and dealt with differently in concrete policy terms as a result of macro-level ideological shifts.

Following important strides in the social policy literature in the 1990s (Pierson 1994; Rudd, 1997; Boston et al, 1999; Pierson, 1999, for New Zealand) that examined empirically the politics of 'retrenchment' associated with 1980s neoliberalism ('Rogernomics' in New Zealand), recent important work by Bonoli (2005) has attempted to grapple with the theoretical implications of welfare regimes coping with 'new social risks' of atypical patterns of employment, work–life balance, child care duties, and family responsibilities towards older people. However, few scholarly efforts have hitherto attempted systematically to assess the theoretical implications of what I shall refer to as the *second wave* of welfare state redesign that was carried out by the centre-left governments of the 1990s. Following the 1980s wave of welfare state retrenchment, most pronounced in the liberal welfare regimes, the 'reformed' Third Way social democratic parties of the 1990s and 2000s, have continued the restructuring and redrawing of labour and social market policy. However, while critics may accuse these policies of continuing the neoliberal logic of Thatcherism, unlike the 1980s retrenchment efforts, the target, discourse and ambition of these reforms were not primarily geared at 'rolling back the state', but rather aimed at creating enabling or 'active' labour market policy. This approach, often informed by policy transfer from the US (Daguerre, 2004), combines carrots with sticks. The often mandatory character of job (re)training measures imposed on transfer payment recipients by social democratic state managers is presumably sweetened by the prospect of labour market integration.

The advent of this workfarist paradigm is of pivotal importance to comprehending and making sense of welfare state restructuring in the late 1990s and early 2000s. Its underlying ideological basis is neither primarily the neoliberal belief in reduced state interventionism to avoid overburdened and deeply challenged social welfare systems nor the normative antipathy towards weaker members of society that surfaced during the first wave of retrenchment in the 1980s. Second-wave retrenchment is instead informed by a near missionary belief inherent in the 'Third Way' social democracy of the late 1990s that labour market participation is a panacea in resolving social problems, while reducing social welfare expenditure in the long term. However, the policy implications of this ideological obsession with raising labour market participation, prominently embedded in the Lisbon Agenda, for example, may indeed be highly significant for recipients and users of transfer payments and social services. This is because workfarism seeks to re-commodify labour, destroy welfare niches and prod and cajole individuals into the labour market who were previously exempted from such pressures, including single mothers.

This ideological shift bears on the phenomenon of teenage pregnancy to the extent that it is perceived as an impediment to labour market participation in later life by impairing educational opportunities. Teenage mothers are thus chastised for jeopardising their career potential and 'employability' – rather than accused of presumed moral deficiencies as during the 1980s. Yet stigmatisation remains a constant. Governmental efforts to reduce teenage pregnancy rates may be influenced by genuine normative concerns over public health and poverty reduction, but they are just as strongly coloured by the purported requirements to remain competitive and thus 'internalise globalisation' (Cerny et al, 2005). The second wave of welfare state reform and workfarism addresses two issues: designing social policy that contributes to a neo-mercantilist business-friendly *Standortpolitik* – deregulated labour markets, structurally weak or acquiescent trades unions, precarious and insecure work conditions – *and* a supply-side approach to the so-called socially excluded that can be rhetorically marketed as more caring and humane (hence reflecting a social democratic imprint) than first-wave retrenchment.

It is important to note that new social risks may consist of partly empirically new phenomena, but analytically they often result either directly from the implications of embedded neoliberalism and the prioritising of raising labour market participation rates or, at the very least, they need to be regarded through the analytical prism of a radically changed welfare state philosophy throughout the OECD that places the internalisation of globalisation above the more defensive priorities of the Keynesian welfare state. Without such a theoretical basis, descriptive attempts to chart new social risks remain analytically shallow.

While the phenomenon of teenage pregnancy has actually declined in purely quantitative terms since 1970, it has attracted the stigma of social delinquency. In the process of the average age of first-time mothers increasing, early motherhood has become socially constructed as deviant behaviour (Uttley, 2000; Cherrington and Breheny, 2005). In the following, the nature of teenage pregnancy public policy regulation since 1984 will be traced and analysed.

Analysts of the comprehensive neoliberal restructuring process that unfolded between 1984 and 1996 (Kelsey, 1997; Menz, 2005) have pointed to the slight peculiarity of a Labour government commencing this onslaught. Generally speaking, Labour's Lange government and Finance Minister Douglas in particular were responsible for the first wave of neoliberal reform measures, enacted between 1984 and 1990, and entailing financial deregulation, economic liberalisation, cuts to state subsidies, privatisation of public enterprises and experiments with monetarist policy. The right-wing National government that took over power continued in a similar vein, but concentrated on the legislative castration of the trades union movement, the significant undermining of labour legislation and, most crucially for our purposes, enacted major cuts to social policy spending and a comprehensive overhaul of the welfare state in general.

As elsewhere, the liberalisation of the economy led to a major increase in unemployment, causing a significant rise in social expenditure. The unemployment rate rose from 3.8% in 1985 to 7.7% in 1990. Meanwhile, the total number of individuals receiving welfare benefits rose from 179,964 in 1984 to 318,651 in 1990 (Kelsey, 1997, p 279). Among Maori, the impact was even more pronounced, with unemployment peaking at 27%. While Labour had consciously alienated the rural and farming clientele of the National Party by abolishing agricultural subsidies, the National Party retaliated by attacking the trades unions and social transfer recipients. Labour had hesitated to do so, although the blueprint of New Zealand's neoliberal reform programme contained advice towards that end. In the 1987 document *Government Management*, authored by a team of economic policy advisors within the Treasury, the following recommendations were made:

> We also believe that wage regulations in a number of areas affecting the labour market are acting to restrict employment opportunities.... We consider that a basis now exists for sustained improvements in New Zealand's overall economic performance. To secure this, though, it seems vital that the disinflation process is maintained; that it be supported by further fiscal consolidation, a further evening out of assistance structures across the economy and an ongoing process of regulatory reform. [...] [Ways need to be identified to ensure] ... that individuals face incentives that align their interests with those of others. (New Zealand Treasury, 1987, pp 172-3)

Labour's hesitancy to mimic Thatcherite welfare state 'reform' partially owed to Lange's reluctance, eventually leading to the dismissal of Roger Douglas, both Minister of Finance and chief architect of the controversial reform programme. But in its failure to expand the welfare state or address the needs of the rapidly rising unemployed, combined with neoliberal fiscal policy focusing on indirect taxation, changes to benefit indexation and minor cuts in unemployment benefit eligibility, the seeds were sown for future reforms. It was the conservative National Party that acted on these recommendations in the form of the April 1991 benefit cuts and the 1993 Social Welfare Reform Bill. The Bill's main aim was to curtail social expenditure both by·cutting absolute benefit levels and by curtailing eligibility. Both goals were also carried out with respect to the DPB. Its level was cut by 16.7% for single recipients and by 8.9% for sole parents with two children (Kelsey, 1997, p 276). Yet despite stricter eligibility criteria, lower levels of benefits and a rhetorical assault on DPB recipients, the overall level of recipients remained stable and has even increased marginally between 1994 and 1997. Given the rises in unemployment and the recession produced by economic liberalisation, this was perhaps unsurprising.

The discourse espoused by the Right during this period emphasised 'traditional' moral values and attempted to depict teenage pregnancy as socially deviant behaviour that constituted a conscious attempt to exploit welfare transfer payment structures. The National Party's Social Welfare Minister, Jenny Shipley, claimed: '... the welfare state itself, through its mechanisms, produces young illiterates, juvenile delinquents, alcoholics, substance abusers, drug addicts and rejected people at an accelerated speed' (*New Zealand Herald*, 20 July 1992, quoted in Kelsey, 1997, p 333). Similarly, Alan Gibbs (1994), associated with the neoliberal think tank and advocacy group 'New Zealand Business Roundtable' declared that:

> a practice that for thousands of years societies have said was fundamentally important to make sure that men did their cultural duty and took responsibility for a woman and her children we largely threw out. We decided we wouldn't bother with men, we'd get the state to do it for us. So we swapped husbands for benefits. (Gibbs, 1994, pp 264-5)

Such rhetoric – as indeed much of New Zealand's reform process – was heavily influenced by ideas and policy transfer from abroad. The rhetorical attacks against teenage mothers 'sponging off' the welfare state closely resembled the mythical Cadillac-driving US welfare queen, an image designed with no verifiable empirical basis by the Reagan government, and bore close resemblance to the campaign against single mothers by the Conservative governments of the 1980s in the UK. This line of reasoning is still regularly deployed by associates of the ultra-neoliberal far-right Association of Consumers and Taxpayers (ACT) Party, who argue that the DBP has created a persistent welfare-dependent underclass (*New Zealand Herald*, 25 July 2001) and encourages young women to get pregnant deliberately so as to secure themselves a stable income (*New Zealand Herald*, 30 June 2000).

Aside from alluding to mythical moral values, the Right was keen to clothe its attacks in pseudo-economic language, by arguing that benefit cuts encouraged re-entry into the labour market by providing stronger 'incentives' for this 'choice'. Decreasing or stagnating real wages in the 1990s meant that in order to maintain a gap to constitute such 'incentives', benefits needed to be cut. Indeed, *Government Management* (New Zealand Treasury, 1987, p 404) contained the following advice: 'The likelihood of undertaking paid employment is inevitably reduced by the offer of income support for those without paid employment'.

Minister of Social Welfare (and later National's Prime Minister) Jenny Shipley agreed in her 1991 legislative package entitled 'Welfare that Works' that:

> the levels of support offered in the forms of benefits and other social assistance are a major factor in our fiscal costs. They are also critically important in terms of the incentives and choices they offer to people. If assistance is poorly designed, the costs are measured not solely as extra state spending, but also as a major factor damaging our economy and undermining social behaviour. (cited in Kelsey, 1997, p 279)

Similar rhetoric was also espoused in reference to teenage pregnancy, portraying it as a 'choice' that would then incur further choices down the line. It is worth quoting National's Finance Minister Richardson at length in this context, following Kelsey (1997, pp 281-2), who went public in 1988 to proclaim:

> If the 16 year old engages in sexual adventure and there's an unintended pregnancy, she has to make choices. If she chooses to have and keep the child that must be a family decision. A 16 year old is a dependent child, not an

independent adult. If her family doesn't want her and if she is not able to get her partner (who is liable to be the same age) to support her economically, she must look at other choices, which is [sic] abortion. That is not a forced choice, it's the choice young women made before the domestic purposes benefit was available as of right. (cited in Kelsey, 1997, pp 281-2)

Here, the DPB is portrayed in pseudo-economic theoretical terms as creating a wrong incentive or a moral hazard that previously did not exist. Similar language can be found in a Business Roundtable statement on this subject, which claimed that the DPB 'weakens the incentives of individuals to consider the implications of family responsibilities in advance and to individuals to provide for caregivers and their children' (Kelsey, 1997, p 282).

Concurrently, the National Party stepped up its efforts to force 'shirking dads' to contribute to the cost of raising children. However, it would appear as though this measure was more aimed at opening up new channels for public revenue raising rather than by any real concerns over the standard of living of the children concerned (*New Zealand Herald*, 17 June 2001).

A major welfare reform was enacted in 1997. In her 17 February 1998 declaration to Parliament (Department of Social Welfare, 1998, p 3 ff), Prime Minister Jenny Shipley had laid out her so-called six principles of welfare. The first one held that 'everyone has a responsibility', while according to the third, 'work expectations and income support obligations should be linked to a person's capacity and ability to work'. The fourth one proclaimed that 'government social assistance must be designed to encourage people to help themselves'. These announcements foreshadowed the legislative package introduced into Parliament during the marathon session of 14-16 May 1998. Without any public hearings, parliamentary select committees or other forms of scrutiny, legislative instruments were rushed through Parliament that shifted the emphasis towards US-style workfarism and would appear clearly inspired by the US 22 August 1996 Personal Responsibility and Work Opportunity Reconciliation Act (PRWORA). Many of the previous categories of welfare recipients were now obliged to perform unpaid community work in exchange for their benefits, including DPB beneficiaries. While teenage pregnancy was not directly addressed by these measures, the overall aim was to force DPB recipients – thus including eligible teenage mothers – into the labour market.

In addition to this so-called 'community wage', transfer recipients now had to routinely demonstrate efforts to (re)join the labour force. Concurrent with this shift, the DPB was based upon the need to demonstrate a willingness to partake in annual 'planning meetings' to 'help ... set goals for ... [the] future', which culminates in the creation of a 'Personal Development and Employment Plan', outlining, to reproduce the rather menacing language of New Zealand's Ministry of Social Development (2005), 'goals for the future and the things you will do to reach these goals' and the 'need to show us that you are committed to reaching your goals'. These requirements follow those imposed on other transfer payments and mirror the so-called Job Seeker Agreement that is a conditionality imposed on income support recipients. However, while for sole parents with children below the age of 14 (later changed to seven), attendance at these meetings was the chief requirement, legislative changes introduced in 1997 meant that recipients with children above the age of 14 (later changed to between 7 and 14) must seek part-time work, while a later change requires all those with children above the age of 14 to seek or be in full-time employment. Non-compliance with these requirements could attract sanctions in the form of benefits cuts of 20% per registered 'offence'. Labour has since abolished the work-test requirement for DPB recipients (in 2003).

As in the case of earlier reforms, inspiration came from abroad, in this case principally from the US. In March 1997, the Department of Social Welfare headed by Margaret Bazley organised a policy conference at the Auckland Sheraton Hotel entitled 'Beyond Dependency' that granted the opportunity for US policy advisors to introduce workfarist US measures to a New Zealand audience. Jean Rogers introduced the particularly punitive 'Wisconsin Works' programme (*New Zealand Herald*, 18 March 1997) that much impressed Bazley notwithstanding the very contingent nature of its 'success'.

To the extent that an active labour market policy approach has influenced policy design with regards to young mothers, a persistent model of inspiration is the UK. This is particularly evident when assessing the record of the Labour government of Prime Minister Helen Clark. The approach taken has abolished the work requirement imposed by the conservative National government, but maintains that active labour market policy leading to labour market participation is the prime avenue for societal integration. In its manifesto, the Labour Party of New Zealand argues that:

> Our social development approach recognises that, while
> for most families the best form of security is a well-paying
> job, many people need to gain additional skills to get that
> job and positive income support is required in the
> meantime. [...] Our vision is of a social security system
> that supports people in times of need and helps them to
> improve their situation through skill development and
> employment or, if work is not currently an option due to
> childcare or disability, increases their ability to participate
> in their community and improve their future prospects.
> (New Zealand Labour, 2002)

The social policy approach taken therefore generally reverses some
of the decisions taken by the National government during its
reforms, by reintroducing separate unemployment and sickness
benefits, abolishing the so-called 'Community Work Scheme' and
increasing funding on case management. The Labour government
has also placed increased focus on motherhood by offering higher
child benefits, facilitating the labour market participation of women
by offering improved and more comprehensive child care facilities
as well as subsidies for child care, and easing the financial burden
for low-income parents by negative income tax programmes (Family
Support and Family Tax credits). Regarding the latter, the intention
has been to reduce or possibly abolish any punitive tax implication
of moving from welfare transfer payment receipt to labour market
participation as part of the 'Working for Families' programme.

This New Labour-style change in policy direction marks the most
recent shift in social policy paradigms and exemplifies once again
how the treatment of early motherhood can serve as a highly
representative and indicative case study of broader trends in policy
patterns. Of course, the right-wing opposition parties have been quick
to criticise Labour's stance. In rhetoric plainly reminiscent of 1980s
Thatcherism, leader of the opposition Don Brash claimed in a 2005
speech:

> Our welfare system is contributing to the creation of a
> generation of children condemned to a lifetime of
> deprivation, with limited education, without life skills, and
> without the most precious inheritance from their parents,
> a sense of ambition or aspiration. Nothing can be more
> destructive of self-esteem. (Brash, 2005)

The National government proposes to reintroduce the work requirement and apply pressure on mothers to reveal the identity of their children's father, so as to force the latter to contribute to the cost of raising the children.

A major public policy initiative relevant to the regulation of teenage pregnancy is the Sexual and Productive Health Strategy that commenced in 2001. Its four main goals are to modify societal attitudes, promote personal knowledge and skills, encourage and improve available sexual health services, and support research and information efforts. It led to the establishment of a comprehensive sexual education programme in 2002. It is arguably underfunded and does not always provide sufficient resources for teacher training (interview, Family Planning Association of New Zealand, Wellington, 2005). More seriously still is the dependence of local schools on the approval of parents who may block the delivery of sex education, thus increasing the likelihood of non-exposure to this education especially among conservative rural areas and inner-city areas with high concentrations of Pacific Islanders and Asian people.

Evaluation

The recent policy initiatives launched by the Labour government attempt to pursue three goals: first, to eliminate the clearly exclusively punitive aspects of the early 1990s National welfare reforms; second, to design more comprehensive policies that combine public health campaigns on sexually transmitted diseases with the use of contraception; and third, to copy aspects of US and especially UK 'Third Way'-style active labour market policy in prodding and cajoling welfare recipients into the labour market.

The academic literature on teenage pregnancy identifies a number of factors positively correlated to the issue: 'life adversity', early sexual development, lack of sexual education, limited access to contraception, and low educational achievements (Coley and Chase-Landsdale, 1998; Dickson et al, 2000; Darroch et al, 2001; Wellings et al, 2001; Ellis et al, 2003). It is not clear that successive New Zealand governments have invested sufficient efforts into addressing these issues. Sexual education and access to contraceptives in particular are areas in which there is a significant gap in comparison to Western Europe. While difficult to operationalise, cultural factors, combining elements of a traditional, often socially very conservative settler society with the accompanying macho tendencies may play a role among New

Zealanders of European descent. Sexuality is an issue that is associated with taboos among Maori and indeed South Pacific island cultures more generally. One piece of evidence for deficiencies in the areas of sexual education and contraceptives with respect to Maori – and Pacific Islanders – is the higher than average infection rate with sexually transmitted diseases such as gonorrhoea and chlamydia (Ministry of Health, 2001, p 19 ff).

Indeed, public policy efforts on teenage pregnancy are sometimes met with scepticism. Some Maori leaders have criticised public policymakers for lacking sensitivity to non-European concepts of family units, arguing that more extended families can easily accommodate children born to young mothers. In some quarters there is also some suspicion that efforts to combat teenage pregnancy may reduce fertility rates among the Maori population, thus jeopardising the long-term demographic future of New Zealand's first people. Maori Party co-leader Tariana Turia has rejected the characterisation of fertility among young Maori as a 'problem' and engaged in a public dispute over this issue with the Minister for Race Relations Trevor Mallard (*Television New Zealand*, 5 November 2004).

With the disproportionately high rates of teenage pregnancy among Maori women, the issue touches upon questions of inter-racial relations and national identity for post-colonial New Zealand/Aotearoa. Public policymakers need to ensure that their efforts to address teenage pregnancy do not assume undertones of population control or even eugenecism. Instead, the efforts need to focus on ensuring that high-quality sex education is provided on a comprehensive and nationwide basis, a perennial weakness in New Zealand secondary education and arguably one of the root causes of high teenage pregnancy rates.

With the abolition of the most punitive aspects of the policy towards DPB recipients and the embrace of Third Way-style active labour market policy, Labour has described a very modest shift to the political Left and has abandoned the straightforward politics of 1980s retrenchment. Instead, Labour is (re)discovering employment and emphasises entry or return into remunerated employment as the normative goal that should inform all social policymaking. This process of labour commodification thus generally conceives of transfer payments of temporary benefits, not general entitlements. It is only against the backdrop of the 1980s retrenchment policy, that such initiatives may appear progressive – they remain informed by designing welfare state programmes as temporary safety nets. The fact that teenage pregnancy rates have stagnated in recent years in New Zealand and, more pertinently, seem to have developed independent of social policy initiatives demonstrates that easy generalisations about public policy 'incentives' are incorrect.

Conclusion

The issue of teenage pregnancy can be analysed as a fascinating case study both of how social problems are constructed – often to justify subsequent public policy attempts to re-regulate, monitor and control them – and how greater paradigm shifts in social policy have evolved since 1970. As can be ascertained from reviewing statistical trends, fertility rates have decreased and the age at first motherhood has significantly increased since 1970. However, this only means that teenage pregnancy can be construed as socially deviant behaviour that is outside current societal norms. Given the concentration of DPB recipients among Maori and Pacific Islander groups and not highly educated women, such stigmatisation may also assume racial undertones.

Pressure from feminist groups in the 1970s led to the relaxation of previous assumptions of conventional male-led families and encouraged taking the particular needs of females into consideration. In constructing the DPB, policymakers have created the institutional basis for a welfare category that previously did not exist and covered scenarios that may have otherwise led to destitution. However, this protective net became the subject of New Right polemique and the purported mythical welfare-dependent underclass. Spared from a comprehensive attack by Lange's decision to dismiss Roger Douglas, the architect of New Zealand's 1980s neoliberal reform programme, substantial cutbacks to welfare spending and a restructuring of welfare transfer payments were undertaken by the conservative National government of the early 1990s. The Right was convinced that by applying a more punitive approach with respect to welfare recipients and by eliminating certain categories of welfare transfer, total numbers of recipients could be reduced and a deregulated labour market would be able to absorb these newly commodified individuals. The approach taken by Labour since 1999 is somewhat different. Informed by developments both in the US and the UK, Labour has implemented workfarism with a slightly leftish colouring. This meant.abolishing the work requirement for DPB recipients, but generally committing to prodding and cajoling transfer recipients into the labour market. Recent policy developments would indicate that the government has understood the importance of education in ensuring that youth pregnancies are indeed the result of informed and voluntary choices.

A more pragmatic stance may result in a further decrease in the total level of teenage pregnancies, but to the extent that the syndrome is a combination of persistent poverty, lack of education, social exclusion and deprivation, major changes would appear unlikely. In its re-commodification of welfare transfer recipients, the New Zealand government embraces a return to a safety-net conception of the welfare state, in line with a workfarist approach typical of the second wave of retrenchment. The extent to which US-style workfarism is both idiosyncratic and a fair-weather model seems to have bypassed advocates of rapid policy transfer. In adopting – or at least being strongly inspired by – UK-style active labour market policy, New Zealand once again remains dedicated to copying major policy paradigms from the former colonial power, just like during the 1980s.

Teenage pregnancy remains a relatively controversial and often hotly debated issue, not least due to its often potentially racial undertones. To the extent that the government is realising the need for increased educational efforts, such efforts may trigger positive policy change. However, the strikingly reactionary rhetoric still fashionable among the political Right demonstrates that old myths about 'incentives' and 'dependency creation' still continue to influence policy design in some circles.

Notes

[1] New Zealand Maori are strongly represented among the lower socioeconomic strata of society, owing to a history of discrimination, confiscation of Maori land and repeated violations of the country's founding document between Maori Iwi and the English Crown, the 1840 Treaty of Waitangi. Misguided attempts at assimilating Maori in the 1950s was accompanied by urban relocation of state housing tenants, contributing to the decline of rural Maori settlements. Maori were also strongly represented among unskilled workers, with 40% leaving secondary school with no formal qualifications. Economic restructuring and the privatisation of ancient Maori land during the 1980s thus exacerbated poverty and unemployment. In the early 1990s, the average Maori household received only 79.2% of the average nationwide household income. Concurrently, Maori remain strongly represented among the unemployed and recipients of social welfare transfer payments (see also Pool, 1991).

[2] The current rate of DPB is NZ$241.47 per week (= £95 or €139), implying a total annual cost of approximately NZ$1,275,738,167 (= £502,461,536 or €736,026,688) using the 1999 number of beneficiaries and the 2005 rate of benefit.

References

Bonoli, G. (2005)'The Politics of the New Social Policies: Providing Coverage against New Social Risks in Mature Welfare States', *Policy & Politics*, vol 3, no 3, pp 431-49.

Boston, J., Dalziel, P. and St John, S. (1999) *Redesigning the Welfare State in New Zealand*, Auckland: Oxford University Press.

Brash, D. (2005) 'Welfare Dependency: Whatever Happened to Personal Responsibility?', Speech to the Orewa Rotary Club, 25 January, available at www.national.org.nz.

Castles, F. (2004) *The Future of the Welfare State: Crisis Myths and Crisis Realities*, Oxford: Oxford University Press.

Cerny, P., Menz, G. and Soederberg, S. (2005) 'Different Roads to Globalization: Neoliberalism, the Competition State and Politics in a More Open World', in S. Soederberg, G. Menz and P. Cerny (eds) *Internalizing Globalization: The Rise of Neoliberalism and the Decline of National Varieties of Capitalism*, Basingstoke: Palgrave/Macmillan, pp 1-33.

Cheesbrough, S., Ingham, R. and Massey, D. (1999) *A Review of the International Evidence on Preventing and Reducing Teenage Conceptions: The United States, Canada, Australia, and New Zealand*, London: Health Education Authority.

Cherrington, J. and Breheny, M. (2005) 'Politicizing Dominant Discursive Constructions about Teenage Pregnancy: Re-locating the Subject as Social', *Health: An Interdisciplinary Journal for the Social Study of Health, Illness & Medicine*, vol 9, no 1, pp 89-111.

Coley, R.L. and Chase-Landsdale, P.L. (1998) 'Adolescent Pregnancy and Parenthood: Recent Evidence and Future Directions', *American Psychologist*, no 53, pp 152-66.

Daguerre, A. (2004) 'Neglecting Europe: Explaining the Predominance of American Ideas in New Labour's Welfare Policies since 1997', *Journal of European Social Policy*, vol 14, no 1, pp 25-39.

Darroch, J., Singh, S. and Frost, J. (2001) 'Differences in Teenage Pregnancy Rates among Five Developed Countries: The Roles of Sexual Activity and Contraceptive Use', *Family Planning Perspectives*, vol 33, no 6, pp 244-50 and p 281.

Department of Social Welfare (1998) *Towards a Code of Social and Family Responsibility*, Wellington: Department of Social Welfare.

Dickson, N., Sporle, A., Rimene, C. and Paul, C. (2000) 'Pregnancies among New Zealand Teenagers: Trends, Current Status and International Comparisons', *New Zealand Medical Journal*, vol 113, pp 241-5.

Ellis, B., Bates, J.E., Dodge, K.A., Fergusson, D.M., Horwood, L.J., Pettit, G.S. and Woodward, L. (2003) 'Does Father Absence Place Daughters at Special Risk for Early Sexual Activity and Teenage Pregnancy?', *Child Development*, vol 74, no 3, pp 801-21.

Fenwick, R. and Purdie, G. (2000) 'The Sexual Activity of 654 Fourth Form Hawkes Bay Students', *New Zealand Medical Journal*, vol 113, pp 460-4.

Ferguson, D.M. and Woodward, L.J. (2000) 'Teenage Pregnancy and Female Educational Underachievement: A Prospective Study of a New Zealand Birth Cohort', *Journal of Marriage & the Family*, no 62, pp 147-61.

Gibbs, A. (1994) 'The Impact of the Changing Economy on Families', *Transcript of the International Year of the Family Conference*, New York: United Nations, Nov/Dec, pp 264-5.

Jackson, S. (2004) 'Identifying Future Research Needs for the Promotion of Young People's Sexual Health in New Zealand', *Social Policy Journal of New Zealand*, no 21, March, pp 123-36.

Kelsey, J. (1997) *The New Zealand Experiment: A World Model for Structural Adjustment?* (2nd edition), Auckland: Auckland University Press.

Marsault, A., Poole, I., Dharmalingam, A., Hillcoat-Nalletamby, S., Johnstone, K., Smith, C. and George, M. (1997) *Technical and Methodological Report: New Zealand Women: Family, Employment and Education Survey*, Hamilton, New Zealand: Population Studies Centre, University of Waikato.

Menz, G. (2005) 'Making Thatcher Look Timid: The Rise and Fall of the New Zealand Model', in S. Soederberg, G. Menz and P. Cerny (eds) *Internalizing Globalization: The Rise of Neoliberalism and the Decline of National Varieties of Capitalism*, Basingstoke: Palgrave/Macmillan, pp 49-68.

Ministry of Health (2001) *Sexual and Reproductive Health Strategy – Phase One*, Wellington: Ministry of Health.

New Zealand Labour (2002) 'Social Security Policy 2002', available at: www.labour.org.nz/policy/families/2002policy/socialsecuritypol/index.html.

New Zealand Ministry of Social Development (2006) 'Brief to the Incoming Government, Wellington: Treasury', available at: www.workandincome.govt.nz/get-assistance/main-benefit/domestic-purposes-widows.html#can-i-get-dpb.

New Zealand Treasury (1987) *Government Management*, Wellington: The Treasury.

Pierson, C. (1999) *Beyond the Welfare State? The New Political Economy of Welfare* (2nd edition), Cambridge: Polity Press.

Pierson, P. (1994) *Dismantling the Welfare State? Reagan, Thatcher, and the Politics of Retrenchment*, Cambridge: Cambridge University Press.

Pool, I. (1991) *The Iwi Maori: A New Zealand Population Past, Present, and Projected*, Auckland: Auckland University Press.

Rudd, C. (1997) 'The Welfare State', in R. Miller (ed) *New Zealand Politics in Transition*, Auckland: Oxford University Press, pp 256-68.

Statistics New Zealand (various years).

UNICEF (United Nations Children's Fund) (2001) *A League Table of Teenage Births in Rich Nations*, Innocenti Report Card No. 3, Florence: Innocenti Research Centre.

Uttley, S. (2000) 'Lone Mothers and Policy Discourse in New Zealand', *Journal of Social Policy*, vol 29, no 3, pp 441-58.

Wellings, K., Nanchahal, K., Macdowall, W., McManus, S., Erens, B., Mercer, C.H., Johnson, A.M., Copas, A.J., Korovessis, C., Fenton, K.A. and Field, J. (2001) 'Sexual Behaviour in Britain: Early Heterosexual Experience', *The Lancet*, no 358, 9296, pp 1843-50.

Woodward, L., Fergusson, D.M. and Horwood, L.J. (2001) 'Risk Factors and Life Processes associated with Teenage Pregnancy: Results of a Prospective Study from Birth to 20 years', *Journal of Marriage & the Family*, vol 63, no 4, pp 1170-84.

Young, L.K., Farquhar, C.M., McCowan, L.M., Roberts. H.E. and Taylor, J. (1994) 'The Contraceptive Practices of Women Seeking Termination of Pregnancy in an Auckland Clinic', *New Zealand Medical Journal*, vol 107, no 978, pp 189-92.

FOUR

Teenage pregnancy and parenthood in England

Anne Daguerre

Introduction

England has the highest teenage pregnancy rate in Western Europe, standing, in 2003, at 42.1 conceptions per 1,000 girls under the age of 18. England has been called a 'baby factory' by some sections of the media. The issue of teenage pregnancy was highlighted in May 2005 by the case of three sisters in Derby (North England). One sister became pregnant at the age of 12 and the other two at ages 14 and 16 respectively. The Minister for Children and Families, Beverley Hughes, described the case as 'a tragic loss of opportunity' (*The Guardian*, 26 May 2005).

Teenage pregnancy has been portrayed as a major social problem since the early 1980s. The Conservative government traditionally played on negative stereotypes towards lone parents in general and teenage mothers (aged 15-19) in particular. Public hostility towards early motherhood reached a peak in the mid-1990s but has become much more subtle in recent years, especially since Labour's return to power in 1997. Indeed, the Prime Minister Tony Blair himself raised the political profile of the issue when he commissioned the Social Exclusion Unit to produce a report on teenage pregnancy (SEU, 1999). Because the occurrence of teenage motherhood is strongly linked with educational, economic and social disadvantage, the government integrated prevention of early pregnancies and support to young parents in its overall pledge to improve the well-being of children. Thus, the Teenage Pregnancy Strategy introduced in 1999 as part of a wide range of policy programmes that aim to address the twin problems of social exclusion and child poverty. Moreover, the government has paid increased attention to the issue of youth access to contraceptive and reproductive health services. New Labour policies represent a radical break with previous practices in the sense that successive Conservative governments made very few attempts to address the issue. The Tories' approach can be described by the paradoxical combination of an aggressive rhetoric regarding young mothers and the absence of any significant policy initiatives in this area.

In contrast to its predecessor, the current government no longer accuses young mothers of becoming become pregnant in order to obtain council housing. There is some recognition that teenage motherhood is a consequence of material and educational deprivation as well as poor access to confidential sexual health services. But progress remains slow and uneven. Current policies are being criticised for failing to address the root causes of early motherhood, namely social exclusion and high income inequality (Hoggart, 2002; Kidger, 2004). Sex education is improving tremendously but British public attitudes continue to hold negative views about teenage sex, something that is reflected by the Teenage Pregnancy Strategy.

This chapter focuses on England within the four individual countries that compose the UK (Scotland, Northern Ireland, England and Wales) and is divided into five sections. First, I identify the reasons why teenage pregnancy has been constructed as a social problem since the 1970s. Second, I analyse policy developments and debates in the period 1980–2004 and show that Labour's return to power in 1997 enabled the emergence of a more progressive agenda for teenage parents. The third section argues that the Teenage Pregnancy Strategy lacks some strategic coherence as a result of the great deal of political unease regarding two controversial issues: sex education and social disadvantage. The fourth section provides an assessment of the teenage pregnancy strategy. To conclude, the fifth section identifies the lack of political ambition to tackle social and educational disadvantage as the main impediment for substantially reducing teenage pregnancy.

Teenage pregnancy: a social problem?

What makes teenage pregnancy particularly challenging to investigate is its multidimensionality and moral ubiquity. The reasons why political actors identify teenage pregnancy as a source of public concern vary. Teenage pregnancy has four potentially problematic dimensions from a public policy perspective. The first, most fundamental component is the sexual dimension. The contentious questions can be formulated as follows: should young people have sex? What are the acceptable conditions under which they can engage in sexual activities? Although even babies can be physically aroused, sex, notably penetrative intercourse, continues to be seen as an adult activity. Public attitudes towards teenage sex vary across countries, some being much more accepting than others. In a quantitative opinion survey conducted by Widmer et al (1998), the authors designed 'sex regimes' clusters depending on national attitudes towards teenage sex. The US, Ireland and Poland were described as 'sexually conservative' countries: respectively 71% of US, 84% of Irish and 77% of Polish interviewees held negative views about teenage sex. At the other end of the spectrum, only 27% of East German and 34% of Swedish interviewees condemned sex before the age of 16. Britain, with 67% of respondents describing teenage sex as wrong, belonged to the 'Moderate Residual' cluster. However, British attitudes towards teenage sex were closer to US views (67% against 71%) than Norwegian (55%), Spanish (59%) and Italian (58%), Italy and Spain being part of the 'Moderate Residual' regime. In short, British attitudes towards teenage sex remain fairly conservative, at least in a comparative perspective. These findings explain why sex education is still a controversial issue in Britain although the levels of controversy are by no means comparable to the recurrent episodes of moral panic in the US (see Chapter Two, this volume).

The second dimension is the financial cost to the welfare state. Teenage mothers are most likely to be single and poor, just like adult lone mothers. As noted by Reekie (1998, p 10), there is an overlap between teenage pregnancy, lone parenthood and illegitimacy (births outside of marriage). An increase in single parenthood is likely to lead to a rise in public expenditure (Ford and Millar, 1998). Poor lone parents, who are predominantly women, need social assistance to provide for their children. As a result, lone parents can suffer from social stigma because of their alleged 'welfare dependency'. This is even more relevant for young mothers who are by definition financially dependent on their families and less likely to be able to provide for their child. The problem of the financial cost to the taxpayer is linked to well-known controversies surrounding the underclass debate developed by Murray (1984) and experts from the Institute of Economic Affairs (Murray et al, 1990). In 2000, Murray argued that out-of-wedlock births were happening mainly among the unskilled and the unemployed. Murray is a powerful advocate of the moral backlash against feminism and self-indulgence. Because 'sex without commitment can be lots of fun' and 'because marriage gets in the ways of sex without commitment, we have conveniently concluded that what we enjoy is what we should do' (*The Sunday Times*, 13 February

2000). There is clearly an overlap between the underclass, the illegitimacy and the teenage pregnancy debates. In many cases, the pregnancy actually increases the young mother's reliance on her family as a main source of financial and emotional support, thus lengthening the transition towards adulthood, at least in the financial sense of the word.

The third dimension is social exclusion and poverty. Existing literature has shown the strong correlation between experience of poverty in childhood and the occurrence of teenage pregnancy (Hobcraft and Kiernan, 1999; SEU, 1999). Teenage mothers are likely to have experienced poverty in their childhood but early motherhood reinforces pre-existing social disadvantage. Teenage pregnancy is declining in most Western industrialised countries, but is now strongly correlated with social and educational disadvantage, which is the reason why all governments are trying to reduce it (UNICEF, 2001).

The fourth element is the public health dimension: teenage mothers and their children experience significant health deficits (SEU, 1999). Young mothers' babies are more exposed to cot deaths and domestic accidents and are also more likely to be born premature and/or have a low birth weights (see Chapter One, this volume).

The key indicator for assessing the scope of teenage pregnancy is the under-18 conception rates that result in either births or legal abortions (illegal abortions and miscarriages are not included). The most striking characteristic of teenage pregnancy rates in the UK is how different they are to the rest of Europe: through the 1980s and 1990s teenage pregnancy rates remained relatively unchanged in the UK while most of Northern and Western Europe witnessed a steady decline in rates.

However, in the UK, as in the rest of Europe, there has been a decline in teenage pregnancies since the 1970s. This decline largely mirrored similar trends in the adult population: indeed, live birth rates to women of reproductive age started to decline in the mid-1960s. Nevertheless, as noted by Kane and Wellings (1999, p 58), live birth rates for women aged 15-19 'did not decline until the early 1970s. The live birth rate to women aged 15-19 levelled off around 1978 after a steady decline between 1972 and 1978'. Data show a reduction of 8.6% in England's under-18 conception rates between 1998 and 2001 (TPU, 2004). However, this rate increased by 0.2% from 42.5 conceptions per 1,000 girls aged 15-17 to 42.6 per 1,000 in 2002. The under-18 conception rate fell from 46.2 per 1,000 in 2002 to 42.1 per 1,000 in 2003. The under-16 conception rate fell from 8.9

per 1,000 in 1998 to 8 per 1,000 in 2003. However, there has been a slight increase between 2002 and 2003, from 7.9 per 1,000 in 2002 to 8 per 1,000 in 2003 (ONS, 2004).

Teenage conception rates and live birth rates vary considerably in England, with rates tending to be higher in the North of England and lower in the South. This geographical variation is mostly due to socioeconomic characteristics of different parts of the country. The poorest areas in England have teenage conception and birth rates up to six times higher than the most affluent areas (SEU, 1999, pp 20-1; Turner, 2004). Turner notes that women from disadvantaged areas 'are more likely than those from advantaged areas to reject abortion and perceive fewer negative implications of becoming a mother' (Turner, 2004, p 237). According to the Social Exclusion Unit (SEU) report, 'the risk of becoming a teenage mother is almost ten times higher for a girl whose family is in social class V (unskilled manual) than those in social class I (professional)' (SEU, 1999, p 17). Other factors also come into play, such as a history of teenage pregnancy in the family, low educational attainment, child sexual and/or physical abuse, or having been looked after by a local authority. Low educational achievement, coupled with low social expectations, is clearly one of the strongest causes underlying teenage pregnancy (Cheesbrough et al, 1999; SEU, 1999, ch 2; UNICEF, 2001).

Ethnic origin also plays a role, as shown by Berthoud (2001, p 12) although the importance of ethnic and cultural factors seems to be declining since the late 1900s. Berthoud's study showed that among South Asian groups, Pakistani teenagers (41 per 1,000) and Bangladeshi (93 per 1,000) were most fertile in the 1980s. They were much more likely to have children than young white women (29 per 1,000) and Indian teenagers (17 per 1,000) in 1983-89. Caribbean teenagers' birth rates (40 per 1,000) were similar to the birth rates of Pakistani young women. However, by the late 1990s ethnic differences in teenage birth rates were much less significant. In particular, there had been a marked fall in early fertility among South Asian women. Indeed, Pakistani teenagers' birth rates (30 per 1,000) were similar to white teenagers' birth rates (31 per 1,000) in 1996. Young Bangladeshi women remained more fertile (53 per 1,000) than Pakistani and white teenagers but they too showed signs of a strong fall between the 1980s and the mid-1990s (53 per 1,000 in 1996 compared to 93 per 1,000 in 1989). By contrast, the pattern of early motherhood for Caribbean women seemed stable, with 47 per 1,000 in 1996 compared to 40 per 1,000 in 1989. White teenagers' birth rates remained similarly stable (29 per 1,000 in 1989 compared to 31 per 1,000 in 1996). Young Asian women were likely to be married when giving birth whereas white and Caribbean young women tended to be single at the time of the birth.

Assuming that delaying the age at first sexual intercourse is desirable from a public health point of view, England does not stand out in comparison to other European countries. The mean age at first sexual intercourse is 14.1 years for English girls, 14.7 years for Polish girls, 14.5 years for Italian girls and 13.9 for French girls. However, the percentages of 15-year-olds who report having had sexual intercourse is 40.4% for English girls compared to 18.6% in France, 30.9% in Sweden and 33.5% in Germany (WHO, 2002).

The fact that teenage pregnancy has been constructed as a social problem by the Conservative and Labour governments in the UK alike is surprising since the teenage birth rate has fluctuated between fairly narrow bands since 1978 (Kane and Wellings, 1999, p 66). More specifically, in England the under-18 birth rate fell between 1971 and 1981 and rose again between 1981 and 1991. Since then, rates have fluctuated.

Teenage pregnancy is made up of four problematic dimensions that are picked up by different policy entrepreneurs and actors at various times. For instance, in the 1980-90s the campaign against single mothers launched by the Conservative Party picked up the second dimension of the problem, that is, the financial cost to the welfare state. However, the Conservative government became increasingly aware of the public health dimension and pledged to halve the rate of teenage pregnancies, a vow renewed by Tony Blair in 1997 when Labour returned to power. Thus, policy developments in this field display a pattern of rupture and continuity along the four problematic dimensions identified earlier. The Labour government developed a specific Teenage Pregnancy Strategy for England and Wales from 1999 onwards. This strategy attempts to address the three principle dimensions – sexual, medical and social – of teenage pregnancy.

Policy developments 1980-2004

England was a pioneer in relation to sexual health policy in the 1960s and 1970s. Liberal legislation was passed in 1967 and influenced policy developments in the rest of Europe later in the 1970s. The 1967 Abortion Law Reform Act ended the terrible plight of women whose last resort was clandestine abortion when they wanted to end their pregnancy. In Britain, under section 1 of the

1974 Family Planning Act, health authorities had to provide contraceptive services to all. In 1974, family planning clinics had to provide contraceptives free of charge (Burtney et al, 2004, p 39). However, in the mid–1980s evidence of a Conservative backlash began to appear in England. Debates principally concerned sex education in primary and secondary schools. Of central concern was children's right to confidentiality vis-à-vis parental involvement. Second, teenage mothers were increasingly portrayed as a financial burden to the welfare state, especially in the mid–1990s.

Until 1986, sex education in English schools was ad hoc. Responsibility was placed in the hands of the governing body of the school. Governing bodies could consider whether or not to include sex education in the secular curriculum. They could decide to accept or reject parents' requests for their children to be withdrawn from sex education. The 1986 Sex Education Act was very much in tune with the Thatcher agenda: the 1986 Act 'specified that school sex education should encourage pupils to have due regard to moral considerations and the value of family life' (Haydon, 2002, p 183). Guidance suggested that children should be cautioned against the risks associated with promiscuity and casual sex. This moralistic approach was dominant until the mid–1990s. However, the 1993 Sex Education Act made sex education in secondary schools mandatory. But the most important event during this time was the *Gillick* case, which illustrated the tensions between parental and children's rights. In 1981 Victoria Gillick mounted a legal campaign claiming that prescriptions of contraceptives by a doctor would encourage unlawful sex. In 1986, a House of Lords judgment rejected this argument. Nonetheless, the judgment defined safeguards for doctors to prescribe contraceptives without parental consent. The doctor's intervention would be justified if 'it was in the girl's best interests; she understood the advice; she could not be persuaded to tell her parents; without treatment her health would suffer; and she would continue having sex' (Haydon, 2002, p 186).

There has been a high level of policy interest in teenage pregnancy since the 1990s. In 1992, the Department of Health set the target of reducing the rate of pregnancy among the under–16s which stood at 9.4 per 1,000 in 1989 to 4.8 per 1,000 by the year 2000. The Department of Education's guidance recommended that sex education should be integral to the learning process and provided for all children, young people and adults. Young people's rights prevailed in English law but the negative publicity of the *Gillick* ruling had long-lasting consequences. Moreover, health professionals were unsure about where to stand in relation to teenagers' access to contraception, which reinforced the young people's distrust in adult authorities since confidentiality is a key criterion for assessing service provision.

Attitudes towards teenage mothers took a turn for the worse in the 1980–90s. In contrast to the US where the problem was framed in terms of illegitimate access to cash aid, in England the problem was portrayed as illegitimate access to scarce social housing rather than access to benefits per se. Teenage motherhood became the symbol of the underclass reproducing themselves at the nation's expense. As noted by Reekie (1998), these views are not new: in his famous *Essay on the Principle of Population* (1803), Malthus condemned illegitimacy as morally wrong and costly. To prevent the poor from reproducing at the nation's expense, he recommended abolishing the Poor Law because public assistance encouraged indolence and lack of responsibility for one's child. Two centuries later, similar arguments were made by Conservative ministers and Labour Members of Parliament such as Frank Field (1995). Teenage mothers were regularly targeted by some sections of the Conservative Party and by the tabloid press. Public hostility to young mothers reached a peak in the 1990s. In October 1992 the Social Security Secretary Peter Lilley declared at the Tory Party conference: 'I have a little list of young ladies who got pregnant just to jump the housing list' (quoted in Selman, 1998, p 142). In 1993 the Minister of Housing declared: 'How do we explain to the young couple who want to wait for a home before they start a family that they cannot be re-housed ahead of the unmarried teenager expecting her first, probably unplanned, child' (*The Guardian*, 9 November 1993). These declarations 'were accompanied by a hostile press campaign culminating in 1995 with reports linking teenage mothers to the collapse of family life in Britain' (Selman, 1998). In October 1998, Margaret Thatcher recommended sending young mothers to convents, declaring 'that it is far better to put the children in the hands of a very good religious organisation, and the mother as well, so that they will be brought up with family values' (BBC News, 1998).

However, such attacks were ill-informed because social security legislation became much less lenient with regards to young people aged 16-19 in the 1980s, especially under the 1988 Social Security Act, which raised the minimum age of entitlement to Income Support from 16 to 18. One of the explicit objectives of the legislation was to save money. In fact, young people's entitlement to social security and housing benefits were progressively reduced under Margaret

Thatcher and John Major (Pascall, 1997). Harris notes that 'unemployed lone parents have not been left in a particularly advantageous situation under the Income Support reforms: and there is still no extra help for pregnant women (of whatever age) until they have had their babies apart from the social fund maternity allowance' (Harris, 1989, p 100).

When Labour came to power in 1997, the new government was committed to addressing the pressing issues of social exclusion and inequalities in health. This signalled a radical break from the Conservative agenda. Teenage pregnancy was no longer seen through the prism of welfare dependency and illegitimacy. Instead, it was portrayed as a public health and social exclusion problem. The first indicator of this new thinking was the so-called Acheson Report. In July 1997, the Minister for Public Health, Tessa Jowell, commissioned an Independent Inquiry into Inequalities in Public Health. The Report (Acheson, 1998) noted that 'it is possible that reducing inequalities in some socioeconomic risk factors – for example, poverty or educational attainment – would reduce inequalities in unwanted teenage pregnancies' (Acheson, 1998, part 2). The government's health strategy: *Saving Lives: Our Healthier Nation* was published in July 1999 (DH, 1999) and drew upon the Acheson Report's recommendations. Indeed, Prime Minister Tony Blair had decided to make the fight against social exclusion a governmental priority. The Prime Minister's SEU was commissioned to issue a report on teenage pregnancy. The SEU consulted various lobby groups and non-governmental organisations (NGOs), such as the Family Planning Association, the National Children's Bureau and Brook, a powerful advocate of children's right to access free, confidential sexual health services. Although the consultation exercise was carried out with extreme care, no NGO was directly involved in the drafting of the report. In the words of one commentator, 'the SEU started from scratch. They talked to everybody and then they produced their report. There was never a collective approach to it. The government did not want to give the issue to a lobby with an axe to grind'.[1] Teenage pregnancy being by definition a 'hot potato', the government took special precautions to prevent new policy initiatives from getting negative media coverage, especially in the tabloid press such as the *Daily Mail* and *The Sun*. The report of the SEU (1999) entitled *Teenage Pregnancy* aimed 'to develop an integrated strategy to cut rates of teenage parenthood, particularly under-age parenthood, towards the European average, and propose better solutions to combat the risk of social exclusion for vulnerable teenage parents and their children' (p 2).

In his foreword to the report, the Prime Minister, while reaffirming his moral opposition to teenage sex, also called for a more pragmatic stance towards the phenomenon:

> Let me make one point perfectly clear. I don't believe young people should have sex before they are 16. But I also know that no matter how much we might disapprove, some do. We should not condone their actions. But we should be ready to help them avoid the very real risks that under-age sex brings. (SEU, 1999, p 4)

The report introduced a major break with the moralistic philosophy in vogue under the Conservative era. The SEU report, in line with the Sex Education Forum, the Family Planning Association and Brook, adopted a pragmatic stance towards teenage sex and pregnancy.

The report's recommendations must be seen in the light of the government's overarching goal of reducing poverty and exclusion through the promotion of employment and training opportunities. At the heart of the governmental strategy is the will to ensure young people's participation in training, education and, as a last resort, paid work. The fact that young mothers are highly likely to drop out of school is presented as a particular cause for concern. This concern is in line with New Labour's focus on education and paid work as the best route out of poverty. Thus, teenage parents are potential targets of the New Deal for Lone Parents and the Sure Start Plus Programme, a cross-departmental programme that aims to 'address all areas of social and economic inequality and limited choice experienced by teenage parents and their children' (TPU, 2002).

The Teenage Pregnancy Unit (TPU) was set up in 1999. An Independent Advisory Group (IAG) composed of 25 experts was also created in 2000 in order to monitor the TPU's strategy. The IAG published its first annual report in 2001. The TPU pledged to reduce the under-18 conception rate by 50% by 2010. This target is a joint Department of Health and Department for Education and Skills Public Service Agreement.

The government published a Green Paper entitled *Every Child Matters* in September 2003, in which the Teenage Pregnancy Strategy is cited as a key policy area. The 2004 Children Act places a duty on local authorities to achieve the goals of the Green Paper through the creation of a Children's Services Department. The aim is to improve coordination between various programmes and services. At the local level, every top-tier local authority area has a 10-year

Teenage Pregnancy Strategy in place. A Teenage Pregnancy Local Implementation Grant is paid to every top-tier local authority. In 2003/04 the grant was £27.39 million. In 2004/05 the grant increased to £32.39 million (TPU, 2004, p 5).

All areas have agreed local conception reduction targets of between 40% and 60% by 2010 with the greatest reductions sought in the highest rates areas (TPU, 2005, p 8). The TPU also aims to increase the participation of teenage mothers in education, training or work to 60% in 2010 to reduce the risk of social exclusion. The integration of anti-poverty and sexual health policies, with the aim of reducing social inequalities in sexual health, indicates a shift towards a more holistic approach in government thinking. The Teenage Pregnancy Strategy must be seen in the light of the promotion of paid work and participation in training programmes as the best route out of poverty and social exclusion. The strategy is thus in tune with the promotion of an active welfare state, where every citizen is expected to become self-sufficient in exchange of temporary and conditional assistance.

The first dimension of the strategy focuses on sex education. The TPU launched a national media campaign in 2000, which targets boys and girls aged 13-17 with advertisements in teenage magazines and on local independent radio. In addition, the government has developed a framework for Personal, Social and Health Education (PSHE). Sex education is part of the national curriculum and is compulsory in secondary schools, but not in primary schools. Parents have the right to withdraw their children from sex and relationship education (SRE) courses although the Department of Education guidance recommends that they should consult the child and the teachers before taking any drastic steps. The guidance states that 'SRE does not encourage early sexual experimentation'. Delayed sexual activity is preferable: 'Secondary pupils should learn to understand human sexuality, learn the reasons for delaying sexual activity and the benefits to be gained from such delay' (DfEE, 2000, p 4). There is an underlying value judgement about teenage sex in the governmental guidance. The SRE guidance promotes a comprehensive approach based on the Dutch model. This model encourages discussion about sex and relationships in an open and warm atmosphere while encouraging teenagers to wait until they are ready for sex (UNICEF, 2001; Young, 2004, p 181). Recommendations concerning confidentiality preserve the rights of the pupils. Since SRE should help pupils identify what constitutes acceptable behaviour, teachers may have to disclose information for child protection purposes (in the case of sexual harassment or child sexual abuse, for instance). However, pupils have no unconditional right to confidentiality and should be made aware of this by the teacher (Haydon, 2002, p 190).

The TPU has made a tremendous effort to ensure that teenage mothers are no longer excluded from schools. The primary emphasis is to help teenage parents to get back into secondary education. The total amount of the Vulnerable Children Grant – which helps support school-age teenage parents and other vulnerable groups – was £84 million in 2003/04. Half of the grant is provided by central government and local education authorities are required to provide match funding. The TPU has established reintegration officers and specialist units to enable teenage parents to continue with their education. Extra child care and support is being provided through Sure Start Plus and Connexions, the government's support service for all young people aged 13 to 19 in England. In addition, all low-income pupils under 16 are eligible for the Education Maintenance Allowance (EMA), a weekly payment up to £30, if they want to continue in further education. Twenty Sure Start Plus pilots are providing a personal advisor to support teenage mothers. The advisors help pregnant girls make a decision about their pregnancy and provide advice about contraception. Sure Start programmes are funding specialist midwifery and health visitors to provide advice to teenage parents on topics such as smoking cessation and nutrition on a limited budget (DH, 2004).

The contradictions of the Teenage Pregnancy Strategy

The TPU is responsible for implementing the Teenage Pregnancy Strategy in England. This unit includes a mix of civil servants and those drawn from outside the civil service for their particular expertise. The unit, composed of 12 people, was originally located within the Department of Health and, from June 2003, within the newly established Children, Young People and Families directorate in the Department for Education and Skills. The TPU is directly accountable to the Minister for Children and Families, Beverley Hughes. The strategy can be seen as understaffed in the light of the ambitious target to halve teenage pregnancy rates by 2010. This is especially true at the local level, where there are clear indications of labour shortages, especially in relation to teenage pregnancy advisors (see TPU, 2004; IAG, 2004).

The first contradiction of the strategy concerns sex education policies. Attitudes towards teenage sex and teenage pregnancy remain globally negative in Britain. This explains why the government is always extremely careful about the issue, especially at election times. The TPU must respond to the concerns expressed by liberal campaign groups such as Brook Advisory Centres (Brook), the Family Planning Association and the National Children's Bureau while at the same time avoiding being pilloried in the right-wing press such as the high-circulation *Daily Mail*. In February 1999, Professor John Guillebaud, medical director of the London-based Family Planning Centre, argued that teenagers could be implanted with a highly effective hormonal device in order to help reduce teenage pregnancies since they are even more likely than older women to forget to take the pill. Although the Family Planning Association and Brook criticised Guillebaud's proposal on the grounds that the method was too coercive, the proposal gave rise to a public outcry by family group campaigners. In particular, the anti-abortion charity, Life, called for Guillebaud to be arrested for promoting unlawful sex (BBC News, 1999). Likewise, when the SEU recommended to extend sex education in primary schools, the Education Secretary immediately backtracked, 'saying that he did not want children under ten to have their age of innocence taken away from them' (Slater, 2000).

Moreover, the TPU must strike a difficult balance between the demands expressed by liberal NGOs and the criticisms of an extremely vocal lobby composed of the Conservative Party and family values campaigners such as the Family Education Trust and Family and Youth Concern – referred to as the 'antis' by liberal charities. Although family campaigners are not successful when they try to challenge sex education measures through the courts, 'they do have an influence on the climate. There is always a big outcry in the media, which reinforces government's sensitivity'[2] explains a representative from the Family Planning Association. Parental lobby groups regularly criticise the TPU for being too permissive. Not only does the issue of sex education remain highly controversial in British society, it proves to be equally divisive within the Labour Party and the government itself. In particular, there are intergovernmental battles between the Department of Health, which tends to have a pragmatic stance towards teenage sex, and the Department for Education and Skills, which tends to be much more moralistic in relation to sex education. These battles started in 1997 and have continued ever since.

It should therefore come as no surprise that sex education guidance sends mixed messages to teachers and teenagers alike, as pointed out by the IAG's last report (2004). The IAG recommends that 'the national media campaign should be broadened to promote a more open discussion on teenage pregnancy and sexual health' (IAG, 2004, p 17). Likewise, the IAG recommends that government should make PSHE a statutory part of the curriculum, which is currently not the case for primary schools. The TPU's response is that 'at the moment making PSHE statutory is not on the cards, because the DFES is trying to reduce the statutory elements of the curriculum across the board. But the government wants to improve the training of teachers and health professionals who have to deal with teenagers on a day-to-day basis. We are really trying to implement a cultural shift in this country'.[3]

The IAG's recommendations somehow confirm the assessment of British sex education by Lewis and Knijn (2002). Indeed, sex education continues to emphasise the risks associated with 'under-age sex' to the detriment of the positive dimensions of sexual intercourse. Teenagers are well aware that sex can be a pleasurable activity; otherwise adults would not be so interested in it. By overemphasising the very real risks of unsafe sex, current messages run the risk of losing credibility in the eyes of young people.

The inconsistencies of the Teenage Pregnancy Strategy are also striking in the area of confidentiality, especially in relation to child protection issues. The proposed 2003 Sexual Offences Bill, whose primary imperative was to protect young people from abusive and exploitative relationships, had the potential to criminalise under-age sex between teenagers. The legislation oscillates between the need to protect young people from potentially abusive situations and the need to provide them with confidential advice about contraception. A senior official acknowledges that this was indeed the case but adds that 'it was never the intention of the legislator to criminalise consensual sex between the under 13 teenagers. An amendment was made which made clear that consensual sex between teenagers would not be considered unlawful'.[4] Under the 2003 Sexual Offences Act, anyone providing contraceptive or sexual health advice or treatment to the under-16s, including the under-13s, will not be committing an offence if they act to protect the young person from pregnancy or sexually transmitted infections, to protect their physical safety or to promote their emotional well-being. However, the IAG remains concerned that 'some confusion exists about the provision of confidential advice to under 13s' (IAG, 2004, p 12). When asked about how the TPU is addressing this concern, a TPU representative responded that 'we have already produced an enormous amount of work in this area'.[5]

The Teenage Pregnancy Strategy: an assessment

The Teenage Pregnancy Strategy has produced mixed results, both in terms of the prevention of teenage pregnancies and support to teenage parents. In relation to sex education, the national campaign has produced positive results since it has made young people more aware of the risks associated with unsafe sex (TPU, 2005, p 16). There is little doubt that the TPU is genuinely committed to implementing a cultural shift that would allow teenagers to talk about sexuality and relationships in an open, non-judgemental climate, with highly trained professionals. However, it is equally clear that the strategy does not engage far enough in this direction mainly because of the wider political and societal pressures analysed in this chapter. The current concern with under-age sex seems to be slightly out of proportion in light of the evidence, since the median age at first intercourse is 14 years old in Europe and is not significantly higher in England than elsewhere in Europe, with the notable exception of Poland and Portugal. Yet, officials at the TPU want to encourage teenagers to delay the age at first sexual intercourse. The rationale behind this concern is that the earlier the sexual experience, the more likely young people, especially girls, are likely to express regret (Wellings et al, 2001). Yet the study by Wellings et al also suggested that during the 1990s a higher proportion of young women had sexual intercourse before the age of 16 but stated 'that the trend towards earlier heterosexual experience may have stabilised for women.... At the same time, there is evidence of increasing adoption of risk reduction practices' (Wellings et al, 2001, p 1849). The government's concern seems therefore relatively ungrounded, or at least based on contradictory evidence. What matters most is the interpretation of this evidence and here the current message is less liberal than might been expected. In the words of a representative from the TPU: 'We are concerned that young people are being bombarded with very explicit sexual messages in the media and therefore do not wait when if they delayed having sex it would be probably a better experience for them. But this has nothing to do with the sexual abstinence message coming from the US; the TPU is absolutely not going down that route'.[6] Although officials describe the abstinence message from the US as a counter-model, they have endorsed a moralistic attitude towards teenage sex. In May 2005, shortly after the victory of the Labour Party in the 2005 parliamentary elections, the new Minister for Children and Families, Beverley Hughes, appealed to parents to educate their children about sex. She said that current sex education policies had 'reached a sticking point' and that parents had to initiate a dialogue about sex with their children (*The Guardian*, 26 May 2005).

Similarly, the government's attitudes towards abortion remain ambivalent, as pointed out by Hoggart (2002). The increase in abortions among very young teenagers, that is, girls aged under 14, should be good news. The government's response to this, however, is typically cautious: 'From a social exclusion perspective, yes, it is probably better, but this remains a public health issue'.[7] However, there is no indication that abortions can damage teenagers' sexual health or reduce their likelihood of having a successful pregnancy when they are older. What is at stake is the quality of the procedure and the stage at which the termination is performed. Late abortions pose significantly higher risks to all women regardless of their age than early terminations, and teenagers are more likely to report their pregnancies later than adult women, partly as a result of inexperience and fear. Indeed, abortion continues to be seen as a 'dirty secret' in all cultures, as demonstrated by the French sociologist Luc Boltanski (2004). In this context, teenagers are even more likely than adult women to express deep ambivalence about their pregnancies and fear stigmatisation. These fears can alas be well-grounded and again explain why teenagers may have later terminations than their older counterparts.

In relation to supporting to teenage parents, the Teenage Pregnancy Strategy has been relatively successful. Support to teenage parents has markedly improved. According to the TPU, 26.3% of teenage parents were in education, training or work in 2003 compared with only 16% in 1997. However, benefit levels remain far too low. According to a survey conducted on behalf of the Food Commission and the Maternity Alliance in 2003, benefits for 16- to 17-year-olds are complex and depend on the young woman's circumstances. For a pregnant 16- to 17-year-old living at home, her parents can claim £38.50 per week. If she is eligible to claim benefit in her own right she can claim £32.90 a week or in some circumstances, including where she can show she is estranged from her parents, £43.25. Some young women aged 16-17 may not be eligible for any benefit, even if they are pregnant and live independently. The benefit rate for women aged 18-24 is £43.25 while women aged 25 or over are entitled to £54.65. For most pregnant teenagers, this allowance is available after the 29th week of pregnancy. Thus, young pregnant single women who lack family support do not receive adequate financial help at a time when they need a highly nutritious diet (Food Commission and Maternity Alliance, 2003).

The government has launched a consultation process with relevant NGOs following the publication of a Treasury-led review investigating the benefit and support system for young people (HM Treasury, 2004). Housing provision for pregnant teenagers remains inadequate. In the words of the latest evaluation of the Teenage Pregnancy Strategy: 'Interviews revealed no major improvements in housing provision. Waiting times were long and mobility was high. There were reports of frequent moving upsetting the routine of the babies....' (Teenage Pregnancy Strategy Evaluation Team, 2002, p 24). Moreover, benefit levels remain too low to sustain a pregnant young woman.

Overall the biggest problem remains social deprivation and educational attainment. In 1998-2003, around four in five local authorities experienced an overall decline in their under-18 pregnancy rate. Around a fifth of local authorities had an overall increase in their rates (TPU, 2005, p 8). Variations in teenage pregnancy rates largely mirror the pattern of poverty across England, with high teenage pregnancy rates overwhelmingly concentrated in areas of high deprivation. Teenage pregnancy rates for 2000-02 in the most deprived 20% of local authorities in England averaged 56 pregnancies per 1,000 girls aged 15-17, compared to 25 per 1,000 in the 20% least deprived local authorities. This strong association between teenage pregnancy and deprivation has persisted despite the decline in the national teenage pregnancy rate since 1998 (see Figure 4.1).

Typically, wards that have high pregnancy rates are among the most deprived 20% in England, are in towns and large urban areas and have poor educational outcomes. At-risk teenagers live in large public housing estates, especially in multicultural areas concentrated in the North East of England and the South East of London. Young people in these areas live in weak family structures, and are typified by low aspirational but status-seeking behaviour (TPU, 2005, p 4).

Conclusion

The progress of the Teenage Pregnancy Strategy has remained slow and uneven. As Hoggart (2002, p 149) argues, part of the slow results

Figure 4.1: Under-18 pregnancy rates in England by deprivation quintile, 1997-99 and 2002-02

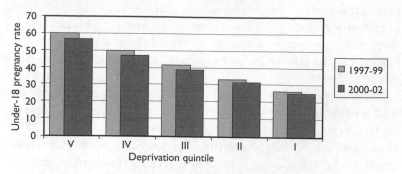

Sources: ONS (2004); TPU (2004); ODPM Deprivation Index (2004)

of the strategy can be attributed to the government's 'unwillingness to tackle the social inequalities central to teenage sexual behaviour and decision-making'. Indeed, the major problems in deprived areas are low educational achievement and extremely poor social aspirations of young people. The government does not really address the problem of income inequality, which contributes to perpetuating the cycle of social deprivation in extremely disadvantaged local areas. The governmental mantra according to which education is the best way out of poverty has simply not been implemented in those areas. Moreover, the persisting rise in income inequality contributes to perpetuating pockets of poverty and social disadvantage in the sense that families move out of these areas as soon as they can afford to move to another area, thus unwillingly contributing to the circle of low expectations and educational disadvantage that prompted them to move out of the area in the first place. In this respect the uneven progress of the Teenage Pregnancy Strategy is explained by the structure of the policy itself, which primarily targets age groups rather than social disadvantage. An approach less targeted on age groups and more focused on eliminating the root causes of poverty and social exclusion might be more effective than the narrow focus chosen by the New Labour government. This is linked with the first hypothesis of the book, which posits that there is a strong link between income inequality, social disadvantage and teenage pregnancy. It is partially because New Labour has been reluctant to address the structure of educational disadvantage and poverty that its ability to halve teenage conception rates remains open to question.

Notes

[1] Interview with a representative from the Family Planning Association, London, January 2005.

[2] Interview with a representative from the Family Planning Association, London, January 2005.

[3] Interview with a representative from the TPU, London, February 2005.

[4] Interview with a representative from the TPU, London, February 2005.

[5] Interview with a representative from the TPU, London, February 2005.

[6] Interview with a representative from the TPU, London, February 2005.

[7] Interview with a representative from the TPU, London, February 2005.

References

Acheson, D. (Chair) (1998) *Independent Inquiry into Inequalities in Health Report*, London: The Stationery Office.

BBC News (1998) 'Thatcher stirs up single parents', available at: http://news.bbc.co.uk/1/hi/uk/197963.stm

BBC News (1999) '"Forgettable" teen contraceptive sparks fury', available at: http://news.bbc.co.uk/hi/english/health/newsid_270000/270374.stm

Berthoud, R. (2001) 'Teenage Births to Ethnic Minority Women', *Population Trends*, Summer, no 104, pp 12-17.

Boltanski, L. (2004) *La condition foetale*, Paris: Gallimard.

Burtney, E., Fullerton, D. and Hosie, A. (2004) 'Policy Developments in the United Kingdom', in E. Burtney and M. Duffy (eds) *Young People and Sexual Health*, Basingstoke: Palgrave Macmillan, pp 38-59.

Cheesbrough, S., Ingham, R. and Massey, D. (1999) *Reducing the Rate of Teenage Conceptions: A Review of the International Evidence on Preventing and Reducing Teenage Conception*, London: Health Development Agency.

DfEE (Department for Education and Employment) (2000) *Sex and Relationship Education Guidance*, Nottingham: DfEE.

DH (Department of Health) (1999) *Saving Lives: Our Healthier Nation*, London: HMSO.

DH (2004) *National Service Framework for Children, Young People and Maternity Services*, London: HMSO.

Field, F. (1995) *Making Welfare Work*, London: Institute of Community Studies.

Food Commission and Maternity Alliance (2003) *Good Enough to Eat: The Diet of Pregnant Teenagers*, available at: www.foodcom.org.uk.

Ford, R. and Millar, J. (1998) 'Lone Parenthood in the UK: Policy Dilemmas and Solutions', in R. Ford and J. Millar (eds) *Private Lives and Public Responses*, London: Policy Studies Institute, pp 1-21.

Green Paper (2003) *Every Child Matters*, Cm 5860, London, HMSO.

Harris, N. (1989) *Social Security for Young People*, Aldershot: Avebury.

Haydon, D. (2002) 'Children's Rights to Sex and Sexuality Education', in B. Franklin (ed) *The New Handbook of Children's Rights*, London: Routledge, pp 182-95.

HM Treasury (2004) *Supporting Young People to Achieve: A New Deal for Skills*, London: HM Treasury.

Hobcraft, J. and Kiernan, K. (1999) *Childhood, Early Motherhood and Adult Social Exclusion*, London: Centre for Analysis of Social Exclusion, London School of Economics and Political Science.

Hoggart, L. (2003) 'Teenage Pregnancy: The Government's Dilemma', *Class and Capital*, no 79, pp 145-65.

IAG (Independent Advisory Group) (2001) *First Annual Report*, London: Department of Health.

IAG (2004) *Annual Report 2003/04*, London: Department for Education and Skills.

Kane, R. and Wellings, K. (1999) *Reducing the Rates of Teenage Conceptions: An International Review of the Evidence: Data from Europe*, London: Health Education Authority.

Kidger, J. (2004) 'Including Young Mothers: Limitations to New Labour's Strategy for Supporting Teenage Parents', *Critical Social Policy*, vol 24, no 3, pp 291-311.

Lewis, J. and Knijn, T. (2002) 'The Politics of Sex Education Policy in England and Wales and the Netherlands since the 1980s', *Journal of Social Policy*, vol 11, no 4, pp 669-94.

Malthus, T.R. (1803) *An Essay on the Principle of Population*, London: J. Johnson.

Murray, C. (1984) *Losing Ground*, New York, NY: Basic Books.

Murray, C. (2000) 'The British Underclass: Ten Years Later', *The Sunday Times*, 13 February.

Murray, C. with Field, F., Brown, J.C., Deakin, N. and Walker, A. (1990) *The Emerging British Underclass*, Choice in Welfare Series no 2, London: Institute of Economic Affairs Health and Welfare Unit.

ONS (Office of National Statistics) (2004) *Health Statistics Quarterly 24*, Winter, London: The Stationery Office.

Pascall, G. (1997) 'Women and the Family in the British Welfare State: The Thatcher/Major Legacy', *Social Policy and Administration*, vol 31, no 3, pp 290-305.

Reekie, G. (1998) *Measuring Immorality*, Cambridge: Cambridge University Press.

Selman, P. (1998) *Teenage Pregnancy, Poverty and the Welfare Debate in Europe and the United States*, available at: www.cicred.org/Eng/Seminars/PAUVRETE/ACTES/selman.pdf

SEU (Social Exclusion Unit) (1999) *Teenage Pregnancy*, Cm 4342, London: The Stationery Office.

Slater, J. (2000) 'Britain: Sex Education under Fire', in *UNESCO Courier*, July/August, available at: www.unesco.org/courier/2000_07/uk/apprend.htm

Teenage Pregnancy Strategy Evaluation Team (2002) *Annual Synthesis Report*, London: Teenage Pregnancy Unit.

TPU (Teenage Pregnancy Unit) (2002) *Sure Start Plus*, available at: www.dfes.gov.uk/teenagepregnancy/dsp_content.cfm?pageid=73

TPU (2004) *Implementation of the Teenage Pregnancy Strategy, Progress report, December 2004*, available at: www.dfes.gov.uk/teenagepregnancy/dsp_content.cfm?pageid=255

TPU (2005) *Targeting Vulnerable Groups and High Rates Neighbourhoods*, Teenage Pregnancy Strategy Discussion Paper, London: TPU.

Turner, K. (2004) 'Young Women's Views on Teenage Motherhood: A Possible Explanation for the Relationship between Socio-Economic Background and Teenage Pregnancy Outcome?', *Journal of Youth Studies*, vol 7, no 2, pp 221-38.

UNICEF (United Nations Children's Fund) (2001) *A League Table of Teenage Births in Rich Nations*, Innocenti Report Card No. 3, Florence: Innocenti Research Centre.

Wellings, K., Nanchahal, K., Macdowall, W., McManus, S., Erens, B., Mercer, C.H., Johnson, A.M., Copas, A.J., Korovessis, C., Fenton, K.A. and Field, J. (2001) 'Sexual Behaviour in Britain: Early Heterosexual Experience', *The Lancet*, no 358, 9296, pp 1843-50.

WHO (World Health Organization) (2002) *Young People's Health in Context: Health Behaviour in School-Aged Children (HBSC) Study: International Report from the 2001/2002 Survey*, Geneva: WHO, pp 153–61.

Widmer, E., Treas, J. and Newcomb, R. (1998) 'Attitudes towards Non Marital Sex in 24 Countries', *Journal of Sex Research*, vol 35, no 4, pp 349–58.

Young, I. (2004) 'Exploring the Role of Schools in Sexual Health Promotion', in E. Burney and M. Duffy (eds) *Young People and Sexual Health*, Basingstoke: Palgrave, pp 172–89.

Part Two
Continental and Scandinavian welfare states

FIVE

Approaches to teenage motherhood in Québec, Canada

Johanne Charbonneau

Introduction

A number of recent Québec policy initiatives in such areas as vocational integration, school attendance, social services and family support services have targeted young mothers under the age of 20. The circumstances of those young women contrast sharply with those of older women, who are opting to start a family later or even forego children altogether. Indeed, the low fertility rate among Québec women stirs regular debates. Why then, does early parenthood pose a problem in need of special attention?

This is the question that this chapter seeks to address. It provides a discussion of early pregnancy and motherhood as a 'social problem' through an exploration of the literature and of the latest statistics.[1] The analysis will be set in the broader framework of changing social policies in Canada and Québec. It will be shown that early motherhood cuts across a set of specific issues and circumstantial factors, creating a novel situation that largely accounts for the interest it creates.

Teenage pregnancy and motherhood: a social problem?

Does becoming pregnant in adolescence and keeping the child represent a problem? The literature on teenage pregnancy and motherhood published year after year yields no simple answer to this question.

Three lines of argument fuel the debates over teenage pregnancy and motherhood in Québec. First, there is the two-pronged debate between those who interpret the statistics as a cause for concern on the ground that the situation shows no signs of significant subsiding over time and those who emphasise other survey findings that reveal a set of problem behaviours associated with this phenomenon. Second, questions arise as to causality and consequences, that is, are these events the cause of subsequent problems or simply occurrences along a predetermined walk of life? Third, there are attempts to allocate rights and responsibilities, particularly those that fall to the adolescent female and society. This discussion is part of the broader process of redefining family and work values in Canadian and Québec society, which is reflected in the evolution of social policy.

Alarming statistics

The Canadian province of Québec has a total population of 7.5 million inhabitants. In 2001, close to 9,400 females under the age of 20 became pregnant, with the older age group (18-19) accounting for most of those pregnancies (ISQ, 2003).[2] The total number of pregnancies among girls under the age of 20 has been variable over the years. It reached a peak in 1998 of 10,500. Since the early 2000s, it has dropped back to the early-1990 level. The pregnancy rate for females under the age of 20 is lower in Québec than in other parts of Canada (Rochon, 1997; Roy and Charest, 2002). Internationally, Canada's teenage pregnancy rate is in line with other Anglophone countries such as the UK, the US, New Zealand and Australia.

In 2003, Québec females under the age of 20 gave birth to 2,560 children; 76% of these females were aged 18-19. Births in this particular age group are declining (there were 4,132 in 1990). During the period 1990-98, they accounted for a growing proportion of all births (from 4.1% in 1991 to 4.8% in 1998), but the trend reversed course in 1998, and they now represent only 3.5% of all births. According to the Québec Bureau of Statistics (ISQ, 2004), the fertility rate of Québec females between the ages of 15 and 19 has steadily dropped since the early 1990s (from 1.81% in 1990 to 1.13% in 2003). Québec teenage girls have the lowest fertility rate in Canada (Roy and Charest, 2002).

Elective abortions in Québec reached 2.29% in 2002 among females aged 15-19, after a steady rise for almost three decades (up from 0.45% in 1976). Statistics Canada (2004) reports that at the turn of the 20th century, almost 64% of pregnancies among Québec females aged 15-19 ended in an elective abortion, by comparison with 53% for all pregnancies in the same age group for Canada as a whole.

These facts and figures have led to concerns over the rise in pregnancies, and over the failure of contraceptive distribution and poor access to abortion. It should be added that the percentage of young females under the age of 20 using oral contraceptives did not grow between 1992 and 1998, despite a new drug insurance plan that makes them more widely available (ISQ, 2000b). According to the results of the latest social and health survey (Government of Québec, 2002), about 60% of males aged 16 and older reported having used a condom the first or most recent time they had sexual relations. However, 15% of boys and 18% of girls used no contraception during their first or most recent sexual encounter.

More optimistic commentators have pointed out that the birth rate is holding quite steady, considering that sexual activity is beginning earlier than in the past (ISQ, 2000b). In Québec, the legal age of consent to sexual activity is 12 years old (for relations with someone not more than two years older). A survey of 3,700 young people aged 9, 13 and 16 found that less than 5% of young people aged 13 or under and less than 50% aged 16 had experienced sexual relations (Government of Québec, 2002).

As regards fertility, no recent analysis – and especially none of those conducted in the institutional sector – has uncovered any change in the trend prevailing since 1998. This challenges the alarmist discourse concerning the magnitude of this 'social problem'. One analysis of dropping fertility rates in the regions of Québec between 1998 and 2002 shows that the decline is specific to a few regions, although the reasons are not all that clear (Duchesne, 2003). Significant declines in fertility are posted in such varied regions as the highly urbanised Montréal area, the Montréal suburb of Laval and hinterland areas (Saguenay, Gaspé Peninsula and Abitibi). The exception is Northern Québec, where the rate of 8.59% raises no eyebrows and in fact seems fairly stable for a region occupied mostly by Aboriginal communities.

The construct of early motherhood as a social problem arises from a second statistical exercise that consists of taking an age factor (roughly 14–19), an event (pregnancy or birth) and various situations socially regarded as problem situations, and then observing correlations between those inputs (Côté, 1997; Carataga,1999). The problem situations most often mentioned include single parenthood, school dropout and entry into the cycle of welfare dependency and long-term poverty. Some studies, stemming mostly from the US, have pointed to highly negative consequences of teenage motherhood, both with respect to the young girl's vocational path and the attendant social costs (see Maynard, 1997). The social cost argument is often raised to justify government intervention aimed at reducing 'the risk' of teenage pregnancy and motherhood.

A survey conducted in Toronto in the 1980s (Turner et al, 2000) followed a cohort of 200 teenage mothers over an eight-year period. It shows that by comparison with women who had a child when older, the teenage mothers encountered more stressing events, including in the years following childbirth: conjugal violence, sickness and accident or close proximity to someone with a drug or alcohol problem. The probability of experiencing a larger number of stressful events is examined here as a factor explaining their emotional problems and economic hardship. According to Roy and Charest (2002), mothers under the age of 20 are more exposed to health problems, such as anaemia, hypertension, kidney diseases, eclampsia and depressive disorders.

While some surveys tie early childbearing to several potential problems for the mother, the most negative prognosis concerns her children. Mothers under the age of 20 appear to be more likely to have premature babies, low birth-weight babies or infants with a congenital abnormality (Roy and Charest, 2002). Certain US surveys show that teenage mothers are usually considered to be at-risk parents who are quicker to punish their children than older mothers. Their children are said to run a higher than average risk of behavioural and adjustment problems (Chase-Lansdale et al, 1991). The biggest risk factors in this regard are the mother's age and her immaturity, low schooling levels and welfare dependency. The risks are all the greater, it is argued, if the mother lives alone in an underprivileged environment. These factors are said to affect the child's physical living conditions and mental development. Abuse and neglect are also to be expected (Buchholz and Korn-Bursztyn, 1993; Hanson, 1990). This reading of the phenomenon carries a great deal of weight in Québec.

The hypothesised negative consequences of teenage motherhood have been challenged in the light of long-term life paths more favourable than those commonly cited (Charbonneau, 2003; Hoffman, 1998). But such analyses are rare, and not all their conclusions are positive. Furthermore, while a mother's circumstances may improve far down the road, this says little about the early living conditions of her child.

In Canada and Québec, it is mostly feminist researchers who oppose a pathological reading of the consequences of early motherhood. They assert that over and above statistical assessments, what is considered 'problematic' changes in light of how social and political issues regarding women, sexuality and procreation are defined and evolve (Nathanson, 1991; Côté, 1997; Hacking, 1999; Kaufman, 1999; Charbonneau, 2002). In a review of feminist writings on this subject, Kelly (1999) states that 'cultural relativity' is propounded especially by feminists who identify with the culturalist and identity streams that tend to favour recognising the importance of motherhood for women. This creates tensions with the radical feminist school, which has urged women to cast off the traditional constraints associated with maternal obligations (Descarries and Corbeil, 1994; Côté, 1997). In any case, statistical correlations should be used with caution to avoid the all too common slippage from correlation to causality.

Motherhood: cause or consequence?

The second debate considers the chain of events over a broad time frame. Is early motherhood the cause of the hard paths these mothers might walk after the birth of their children? Analyses that demonstrate this view abound, including studies on the alleged link with school dropout. Close scrutiny of the real chain of events – not found in surveys based on synchronic data – shows a far more subtle relationship between motherhood and schooling, refuting the somewhat mechanistic link between teenage childbearing and dropout. Instead, it highlights the importance of weighing other factors, such as a young girl's plan to become a 'stay-at-home mother' like her own mother, a model some teenage mothers still see as valid in a society bemoaning its low birth rate (Charbonneau, 2003). Additional factors are the unpreparedness of the schools to accommodate these young mothers and the subtle pressure on them to leave the schooling environment, partly out of fear that they set a 'bad example' for other teenage girls.

The most frequent counter-argument against the theory of motherhood as the ultimate cause of a life marked by hardship looks elsewhere for the causes, in childhood or the poverty in which these mothers grew up. Instead of stigmatising these young women, already victimised by an underprivileged background, they argue that the problems of poverty and inequality of living conditions must be solved (Davies et al, 1999), a position that Québec feminists on early pregnancy and motherhood are very much in line with (Carataga, 1999). This approach emphasises the predominant influence of social determinisms beyond individual control. It is argued that since society as a whole is responsible for the inequality, the welfare state must take responsibility for its consequences by providing the resources that mothers and their children need.

However, the focus on pre-pregnancy conditions also prompts early intervention intended to 'break the generational cycle of hardship', as stated by the time-honoured formula. Many studies have in fact uncovered predisposing factors for teenage pregnancy (for an overview of Québec, see Cournoyer, 1995), and their conclusions serve to identify the at-risk groups in need of intervention to forestall the risk of pregnancy and motherhood. Once the risk factors are identified, measures can be taken to prevent pregnancy or, with even earlier intervention, to ensure that children born through teenage pregnancy do not themselves become teenage parents.

Responsibility and maturity

The third area of debate concerns individual rights and responsibilities. It addresses the motivations and desires of teenage girls, as well as their ability to foresee the consequences of their actions. Recent Québec studies have delved deep into this issue (Manseau, 1998; Letendre and Doray, 1999; Dufort et al, 2000). American researchers seem to find that teenage girls are irresponsible in choosing to become mothers and lack parenting skills. They hold that maturity bespeaks the ability to make a rational decision after analysing the long-term consequences (Musick, 1993; Budd et al, 1998). In the US, teenage girls who choose abortion or adoption are found to be more mature than those who keep their child (Leynes, 1980).

Some Québec and Canadian researchers, especially those associated with feminist movements, are not altogether comfortable with their American colleagues' line of reasoning. They tend to argue the contrary, namely that young women who choose to become mothers show great maturity and a real sense of responsibility – the responsibility of an adult who makes sound decisions (Kaufman, 1999) and of a 'good mother' who always attends to her children's well-being (Davies et al, 1999; Kaufman, 1999; Kelly, 1999). The argument of desire for a child is used by those calling for unconditional respect for a young girl's personal decision about her pregnancy outcome (Manseau, 1998; Davies et al, 1999; Kaufman, 1999). This squares with the thinking of feminists of the 'gynergy' school, who present motherhood as an assertion of identity and an invitation for self-fulfilment, although they tend to obscure the concrete, practical aspects of the consequences (Descarries and Corbeil, 1994). They hold that society should become 'responsible' for ensuring that women have the means to satisfy their maternal desire and can exercise their right to community support in order to satisfy that desire.

A close analysis of the events leading to teenage pregnancy suggests that the phenomenon cannot be reduced to the notion of desire or lack of desire (Charbonneau, 2003). In some cases, previous miscarriages may have awakened a fear of sterility, and that fear was laid to rest by carrying a pregnancy to term. In other cases, teenage motherhood seems simply to represent generational repetition of a particular behaviour.

In short, there is a strong opposition between those who side with the teenage girls and respect their decision to keep the child they wanted, and those who side with government experts and policymakers, pointing to the resulting hardships. This does not prevent the government from marshalling numerous resources to prevent teenage motherhood. What, then, accounts for this sustained interest?

How social policy has evolved in Québec

Several schools of thought have influenced social policymaking in Québec. Since Québec is located in a country with a liberal welfare system, the movements emerging from civil society, including feminist lobby groups, play an important role in charting new directions for employment and family policies. The recent trend in Canadian and Québec social policies suggests, however, that these policies are steadily converging on common objectives. Emerging from this scenario is the dominant figure of parent–producer against the backdrop of war on poverty, especially child poverty. These new directions go a long way in explaining why teenage motherhood is a prime target for intervention.

Québec: a hybrid welfare regime

Esping-Andersen's proposed categorisation of welfare states (1990) associates Canada with the liberal model predominant in Anglophone countries. Under the liberal system, the marketplace is the prevailing institution on which all must rely to cater for their needs. In countries associated with the liberal model, the state plays a residual role in social policy matters. Each family member, each individual, is encouraged to work and make the most of market opportunities. Compared with the other systems, liberal societies tend to invest less in social policies.

Saint-Arnaud and Bernard (2003) used statistical analyses to confirm that Canada's was a liberal welfare system. Although not conducted specifically for Québec,[3] the tracking of social policy trends suggests that this province is closer to the social democratic model than are Canada's other provinces. This is especially true when one considers the process of 'defamilialisation'[4] and not only 'decommodification', on which Esping-Andersen's first analysis was based. Québec has often developed pioneering social policy programmes and can be regarded as an exception on the North American continent with regard to its comprehensive family policy system (Morel, 2002a). Nonetheless, several of the principles underlying the institution of new social policies in Québec are fully in line with the dynamics of a liberal system as it has evolved since the 1980s in all countries using this model. Thus, Québec's welfare system can be regarded as a hybrid form.

Social policy trends in Canada and Québec

According to Jenson (2000), Canada's post-war social policies definitely drew on liberal values, but originally they also entertained equality issues aimed at alleviating the injustice and inequalities associated with the vicissitudes of life. The unemployment insurance and family allowance plans are the best-known examples. The public assistance, pension and health insurance plans were added in the 1960s. Some of these schemes enforced a degree of socioeconomic equality for all. Others, such as unemployment insurance and public assistance, were intended to prevent family poverty when adult workers could not be self-sufficient through salaried employment.

Under the post-war regime, families were still free to decide whether the mother could stay at home to rear the children. Family allowances and a few tax breaks provided minimal support for that choice. Women's family responsibility was first acknowledged with the 1937 introduction of an assistance programme for needy mothers, which qualified widows for a small benefit. Prior to the 1970s, mothers without spouses had to rely mainly on their families and religious charities (Dandurand and St-Pierre, 2000). Access to assistance for needy mothers was restricted to widows and women separated from husbands who were institutionalised in prisons or asylums and to women whose husbands had abandoned the family.[5]

Given that meagre government support, it is not surprising that until the mid-1960s a large proportion of unwed mothers put their babies up for adoption. Québec's Social Aid Act came into effect in 1969. Underlying that legislation was the principle that all citizens were entitled to a minimum standard of living regardless of the root causes of their need for social assistance. Access to benefits was not limited by the children's age, providing they were minors. The Act cancelled the 'good morals' eligibility criterion for public assistance. Many women in difficult circumstances achieved financial independence through the programme. Several decades later, it was observed that single-parent families were its longest-term beneficiaries.

Family policy until the 1960s was built on principles that valued stay-at-home mothers. The next decades witnessed many changes, however. Spurred by the mobilisation of the feminist movement, which was very active in Québec in the 1970s, demands seeking to facilitate women's access to the workforce indirectly diminished the role of stay-at-home mothers. Feminists demanded day care services and parental leave, as well as measures in favour of gender equality and against discrimination in recruitment (Jenson, 2000). But there was a paradox: should the demands call for consolidating job-related rights or for acknowledging the unrecognised role of women through entitlement to government assistance (Morel, 2002b)? The question became all the more pressing when social policies began shifting owing to a neoliberal ideology that promoted the concept of an 'active society' in which each individual must fulfil their needs through paid employment (Dufour et al, 2003).

The 1980s were marked by fiscal crisis and a government credibility gap, although that gap was never as serious in Québec as in Canada's other provinces (Morel, 2002a). Against that backdrop, the neoliberal ideology tried to impose the concept of a residual role for the state. Thus began a time of redefining the responsibilities of the state and private citizens, which in turn spurred the idea that individuals should bear the primary responsibility for their well-being (Jenson, 2000). Since the state could no longer assist all those in need, priorities for social redistribution had to be set. Universal access to some social measures was called into question, with emphasis on means-testing for the groups most at risk (Dandurand and St-Pierre, 2000).

Pressured by the fiscal crisis, the federal government was quick to restrict access to its unemployment insurance programme.

However, the pretext of a budget crisis was not the only impetus for redefining social policy in Canada. For political debate soon turned to the design and delivery of new social policies (Jenson, 2000).

Promoting an active society

It was ultimately the active society concept that dominated the debate, promoting the idea of a residual role for the state in tandem with the predominant role of the marketplace (Dufour et al, 2003). Individual autonomy became the priority, and the state was expected to provide everyone with the means to participate in paid work. Non-participation became suspect: it was thought to mean tenacious dependency on the state. Even mothers' joblessness was frowned upon, and family policies were redesigned so as to facilitate their entry into the workforce.

The Canadian and Québec governments embarked upon three kinds of measures to promote an active society: first, they cut benefits to make assistance programmes less attractive and concomitantly raised benefits for low-income workers to keep them in the workforce; second, they made programme eligibility criteria tougher and took measures to rapidly get people off those programmes, the idea being to reduce the number of beneficiaries. Third, they developed new policies focused on prevention in order to solve the problems at source and avoid future demand for assistance.

The eligibility criteria in the Canadian employment insurance and the Québec income security systems have undergone a phased tightening. In Canada, assistance programmes were communicating vessels, and restricted access to employment insurance sent applicants into the arms of the provincial welfare system. During the 1990s, however, extensive reform also altered the eligibility criteria for Québec's welfare programme. Means-testing was introduced to target those who could be offered incentives such as training and apprenticeship to enter or re-enter the labour market. Moreover, a 'mild' version of US-style workfarism based chiefly on voluntary job re-entry measures was adopted (Dandurand and McAll, 1996; Dufour et al, 2003). Voluntary compliance was replaced by stricter obligations for certain groups deemed to be at greater risk, for example young people aged 18-24, the intention being to ward off any initial contact with the welfare system.[6]

According to Dufour et al (2003), the workfare principle took the offensive against the culture of dependency, which led to a loss of abilities, demotivation, development of a habitual low standard of living that limited the search for employment, and a weakened work ethic. Its opponents usually decried its punitive flavour. Welfare recipients were seen as potential fraud artists who had to be kept under surveillance, not as victims of economic vicissitudes (Boismenu and Dufour, 1998).

The long-term dependency of single mothers on Québec's welfare programme was often mentioned, so it comes as no surprise that they were among the groups targeted by those reforms (Dandurand and McAll, 1996). Little by little, the promotion of an active society, which limited parental freedom of choice, demolished the idea that single mothers on welfare might be exempt from the obligation to seek work on the ground that their childrearing role outweighed the obligation to earn a wage (Jenson, 2000). Debates began in 1988 on a proposal to restrict the right of mothers of young children to be considered 'incapable of work' and thus not obliged to participate in job re-entry schemes. The government wanted to rule that only mothers with children under the age of two could be declared incapable of work. After feminists protested, the age limit was set at six years or under. Ten years later, after further reform during which the government again tried to bring in the two-year-old rule, the age limit was set at five years. The government also wanted mandatory registration of single mothers considered fit to re-enter the workforce (on pain of having their benefits reduced), but backed off when lobby groups opposed the move (Morel, 2002a).

An analysis of the use of job re-entry measures conducted four years after the implementation of the 1988 reform showed that single mothers were willing to work, but experienced many limitations owing to a lack of work–life balance initiatives, including adequate child care provision (Dandurand and McAll, 1996). This observation was not forgotten, for the latest reform attempted to eliminate those constraints.

Such debates, however, often tend to confuse teenage motherhood and single parenthood. True, some teenage mothers are single mothers. In our day and age, raising a child alone is sufficiently common to be socially acceptable. But today, teenage motherhood is more of a deviation from the social norm than in former times when adolescent girls often married and started a family early – as some teenage mothers still do. There are also other reasons for the confusion. First, teenage motherhood outside of marriage is the development showing the most spectacular growth since the 1960s. Furthermore, individualistic analyses of teenage motherhood tend to disregard the presence of the males (Descarries and Corbeil, 1994). Males enter the thinking on teenage pregnancy and motherhood at very specific points – the time of the first sexual relations (Kelly, 1999), which tend to repeat a situation of violence and domination often decried by feminists. The males' absence when comes the time to assume paternal responsibilities is also pointed out (Kaufman, 1999). Still, there are many instances of early motherhood when the mothers are not alone (Government of Québec, 2002; Charbonneau, 2003). This type of teenage motherhood goes unnoticed by social services. It is also a fact that whether alone or not, teenage mothers often live in poverty.

Social policy reform challenged the universality of several social measures and advocated selectivity towards 'at-risk' groups. Low-income families were the prime target of the new policies, which encouraged them to stay in the workforce. A further idea was soon to emerge from the redefinition of social policies, namely, the need to break the generational cycle of poverty (Jenson, 2000; Dufour, 2002). To ease the demand for welfare assistance in the long term, is it not better to take preventive action aimed at those who might become future applicants, that is, today's poor children? In choosing to focus on 'investments' to guarantee equal opportunities for citizens of the future, the Canadian government developed a residual model of intervention reflecting the expectations of a liberal welfare state.

The child as the centrepiece of social policy

In the 1990s, the preventive approach emerging from that strategy and focused on teenage mothers translated into three related developments: (1) the straddling of family and employment policies, (2) the convergence of public debate and government initiatives around the issue of poverty, especially child poverty, and (3) the sustained interest in child development measures to provide children with the best preparation for taking their place in society.

Since the parent-producer is a key figure in liberal systems, all social policies must seek to facilitate the gainful employment of all adults, including those who might once have been legitimately considered 'inactive', for example stay-at-home mothers. Change at the federal level began in the 1980s (Dufour, 2002). The National Child Benefit (1992) was designed to promote work attachment for low-income parents by allowing them to continue receiving the services to which they were entitled while on welfare. The war on poverty remained an objective when the National Child Benefit System was introduced in 1998, but the primary focus shifted to child poverty. In Québec, the adoption of a strategy to fight poverty in 2002 closely followed a massive popular mobilisation, albeit driven by a different rationale (Noël, 2002).

According to Dufour (2002), Québec developed universal measures while adhering to liberal thinking. The new child care services, for instance, are accessible to all parents, even those not working, and to all income classes. Low-cost child care provision was not intended solely to make life easier for working parents. The other aim was to persuade non-working mothers in underprivileged circumstances to put the education of their young children in the hands of child development 'experts'. This reasoning became even more explicit in programmes developed specifically for young mothers.

The focus on children began in the mid-1980s at the federal level (Dufour, 2002). Several civil society groups formed a national coalition in the early 1990s to lobby the federal government to end child poverty.[7] Because of its constitutional status, Québec could choose to develop its own family policy, which nevertheless pursued the same objectives as the Canadian strategy: to give more assistance to working parents and promote child development.

In the 1990s, prevention became the key word of the Québec government's policy action in the areas of health and welfare, as well as family and education (Dandurand and St-Pierre, 2000; Jenson, 2000). Some scientific studies conclude that children's experiences in early childhood have a lifelong effect on their health and well-being. Several programmes were thus introduced for child protection, antenatal care, school achievement, screening for at-risk children, and improvement of parenting skills and day care services. There were also specific programmes for single mothers on welfare, as teenage mothers often are.

Teenage pregnancy and motherhood: a prime target for action

According to Dandurand and McAll (1996), the conservative Right generally resists the idea of working mothers, but is also opposed to single mothers receiving welfare benefits. The welfare Left, for its part, is keenly sensitive to the fate of poor children. Liberal feminists advocate primarily for women's financial independence through salaried employment and pregnancy prevention. Feminists of other stripes champion increased recognition for housework. When it comes to hammering out specific action plans for pregnant teenagers and teenage mothers, these positions are no longer as far apart as they seemed at first, especially since the different groups often rub shoulders in a small society the size of Québec. The design of Québec social policies often grows out of social mobilisation, expert consultation or the creation of mixed taskforces comprising academics, government department representatives and selected associative groups.

As regards pregnancy prevention, sex education is the first area in which the government can move and is in fact among the most popular means of prevention in social democratic welfare systems. After years of representations by women's groups, Québec's first sex education programme was introduced in 1984 as part of personal and social training in the high school curriculum. Although the schools had to comply with the Department of Education's mandatory frame of reference, the organisational rules allowed them some room for tailoring the programmes as they saw fit. Studies uncovered major shortcomings in the sex education programme and showed that although the intention was to take a broad positive approach to sexuality, it actually focused on activities for preventing such problems as AIDS, violence, harassment and pregnancy. On the initiative of school nurses, some school boards created activities such as the Flour Baby Project (adapted for Québec from a California project). The scheme consists of entrusting a baby (a bag of flour) to each young person, who has to take care of it 24 hours a day for 11 days and also to attend information sessions.

In 2002, the elementary and high school curricula underwent sweeping reform based on the generic skills approach to learning. The new sex education programme continues the government's intention to take a broad positive approach to the matter (Government of Québec, 2002). Consistent with the general philosophy of the reform, the new programme cuts across several streams (ethics, art, French, history, physical education) and is no longer tied to one specific course. The biggest change may be that this training will begin in early childhood (age five) and continue through high school, with objectives tailored to the different age groups. This new approach to sex education, still in the implementation stage, has elicited no negative reaction from experts or the public at large. Furthermore, despite the shortcomings of the previous programmes, it is important to bear in mind that teenage pregnancy and fertility in Québec are still among the lowest in Canada.

Actual pregnancy is the second moment when the government can intervene. When the time comes to choose between keeping the child, having an abortion or giving the child up for adoption, pregnant teenagers can seek counselling from social and health services personnel (nurses and social workers), who show great respect for the young women's personal choices, an approach influenced by the feminist ideology that promotes a woman's right to take control of her own body and not experience social pressure when deciding on the outcome of her pregnancy (Charbonneau, 2003). For teenage girls who choose to keep their child and become mothers, a first misunderstanding has already been created because this approach suggests that they will be offered support for their plan to become a parent, even if a young girl decides to be a stay-at-home mother. Once her decision has been made, the future teenage mother will face another type of discourse and be entrusted to other professionals dealing with school dropout or assistance programmes.

The approaches that frame the teenage motherhood issue are directly influenced by neoliberal ideology, which promotes the active society and the parent-producer figure. Their aim is to get teenage mothers back into the labour market as soon as possible. There are several reasons for this. First, parenthood is no longer a valid reason not to participate in employment. Teenage motherhood is regarded as a risk factor for school dropout, meaning that it jeopardises the ability to develop job entry skills – an unacceptable risk in an active society. In addition, teenage motherhood is almost inescapably a shortcut to welfare dependency, even before the teenager has had her first job. If the government has created obstacles to prevent young people from developing this dependency mentality even before entering the workforce, this also concerns young mothers.

As was mentioned earlier, a proportion of teenage mothers are also single parents (ISQ, 2000b). Since single mothers remain on welfare the longest, it is not surprising that the government tries to discourage them from having a second child, a situation that would further confirm their status as stay-at-home mothers on welfare. This means encouraging them to map out a plan for attending school or taking up a vocational course. Feminists, academics and representatives of community organisations promoting women's financial independence generally agree with these objectives.

Institutional intervention aimed at teenage mothers is influenced by another of the new social policy thrusts – promotion of the war on poverty – not only because these mothers are often poor, but even more so because the generational poverty cycle must be broken. Promoting workforce integration for teenage mothers means preventing their children from growing up in a culture of poverty. This idea has spread in Québec since the early 1990s in the wake of a major report (Bouchard, 1991) by a taskforce[8] created by the Minister of Health and Social Services to propose ways to forestall the onset of serious problems among children. The report was one of the mainsprings of Québec's Health and Welfare Policy (1992). It alerted the general public early on to the worrying rise in the teenage pregnancy rate and its subsequent problems, and recommended early intervention with children.

Ten years later, the new social policy directions included a sustained focus on child development. One case in point is the will to persuade teenage mothers to place their children in public day care facilities, not only because they reside in disadvantaged areas targeted by those services or because it will then be easier for them to balance family and work, but also because they are perceived as immature and lacking in parenting skills.

In practice, teenage mothers first have access to Québec's new child support payment programmes. Single mothers with a yearly income under CAN$30,000 (£14,950) will receive CAN$2,700 (£1,345). The allowance increases by CAN$1,000 for each additional child. If they are employed, they qualify for the new 'employment bonus', an initiative designed to encourage low-income parents to keep their job (the CAN$2,190 bonus for a single-parent family is four times higher than for a person living alone). After successive rounds of welfare reform, they now have access to this programme until their child is five years old. Specific programmes have also been created to promote rapid job re-entry for teenage mothers. In the late 1990s, an interdepartmental committee coordinated by Québec's Status of Women Secretariat,[9] was formed to draft an action plan to prevent early pregnancy and support teenage mothers.

In 2000, the job-entry programme *Ma place au soleil* (my place in the sun) offered certified training together with the provision of child care and transport facilities to single mothers on welfare under the age of 21. Its stated objective was to break the generational poverty cycle and teach the skills needed to be financially independent. In the first year, 1,000 young mothers reportedly went back to school, but the number who went off welfare was minimal: 60 to be precise.

A more comprehensive strategy was then developed, and a new Young Parents Support Programme was introduced in September 2002 (Government of Québec, 2002). The government called on outside experts to design this initiative. The task was entrusted with Richard E. Tremblay, a psycho-educator who sat on the youth taskforce back in the early 1990s. He enlisted the help of co-workers and used a broader consultative process organised by the Public Health Branch. This researcher, who favours early intervention to prevent problems of physical aggression, propounds the idea that children are aggressive by nature and that mothers under the age of 20 lack the skills needed to control that aggressiveness. The programme follows up young families from the time the teenager becomes pregnant until the time their child enters school. It takes an empowerment approach wherein the state serves as a companion for individuals who must themselves find answers to their needs. The programme literature suggests an approach that, albeit much more authoritarian, is entirely consistent with an individual accountability approach. According to the government documents, this programme offers support to (1) promote the child's overall development, (2) prevent or alleviate social inadequacy problems and (3) remedy situations in which young children are neglected or abused. It is aimed at improving family living conditions, accessibility to services, social and vocational integration and overall child development, as well as developing wholesome lifestyles and educational skills for young parents. This comprehensive and preventive approach entails ongoing individual follow-up by a social worker (for example a nurse or psycho-educator) through home visits.[10] It also involves collaboration with local community organisations providing a range of services (breastfeeding support, advice about nutrition, social and vocational integration activities, and so on). All aspects of daily living are likely to be addressed during the visits (living conditions, social integration, child development, lifestyle, health problems, marital relations). These visits must also include stimulation and modelling activities for the child.

A group of community organisations that serve teenage mothers has denounced the approach advocated by the Young Parents Support Programme (Laurin and Stuart, 2004). After a few informal meetings, the group called on a number of university researchers to examine the matter. The *Groupe d'étude critique sur la prévention précoce* (critical study group on early prevention) has organised several activities to discuss the purposes of this programme, which it sees as exerting undue social control over teenage mothers, based on exaggerated generalising and on stigmatising and condemning people experiencing social hardship. According to the study group, this type of programme 'reduces the specificity of parenthood to a matter of managing unwholesome forms of behaviour as defined by experts' (translation) (2002, p 31). It also claims that it resembles the old-style moral education rather than recognising how complex social situations have now become. Preventive approaches are seen as a means of reinforcing the experts' control over social life and providing access to an individual's private life. At the same time, they show little concern for actions that would improve people's living conditions. In brief, the goals set for parents are too high and in its blind pursuit, the programme appears to be fully in line with the general social policy frame found in liberal welfare states.

Conclusion

Each year, 2,600 Québec females under the age of 20 become teenage mothers, and the trend has been dropping for more than five years. In July 2005, 2,808 mothers under the age of 21 were receiving welfare assistance from the Québec government. The figure represents 2.8% of all of the welfare population unable to work for health or other social reasons that are of a temporary nature, and 22% of the people under the age of 21 receiving welfare assistance. Alongside certain social problems (for example, conjugal violence, pathological gambling and drug use), these numbers represent a tiny group of people, considering all the attention they receive. Still, they typify a group considered at high risk of not taking part in the new 'active society' and not giving their children the ability to lead successful lives. Teenage mothers often demand a freedom of choice that no longer exists – the freedom to stay at home to raise their children – and are therefore completely outside the social norm. Promotion of the active society is still on the Québec government's agenda and became even more explicit when the Québec Liberal Party came back to power in 2003, after nine years of absence. One of its first actions was to dismantle the Department of Family and Childhood, which was replaced by the Department of Employment, Social Solidarity and Family.

Because teenage mothers are at risk of school dropout, poverty, lack of parenting skills and long-term welfare dependency, they find themselves at the juncture of some of the issues addressed by the new Canadian and Québec social policies such as child poverty and entrapment in the dual culture of poverty and dependency. Clearly, a strong pathological reading forms the present basis for policies aimed specifically at teenage mothers, even under the cover of an empowerment approach. Although Québec is now governed by a new political party, which apparently wanted to clear the slate of all initiatives taken by the previous administration, the 2004-05

Budget speech nevertheless reconfirmed the Young Parents Support Programme through additional public funding. As regards schooling, the Department of Education has invited tenders for research projects to take stock of school achievement among teenage mothers and make new action proposals.

This approach to teenage motherhood leaves little room for a more subtle analysis showing that three quarters of these young mothers are actually adults (18–19 years old), that some have less troubled life stories and that others are even in stable conjugal relationships.

Looking again at the argument of cultural and historical relativism sometimes raised by Québec feminists, it seems obvious that as a family form, teenage motherhood currently represents a serious contender to liberal governments' preferred model of parent-producer.

Notes

[1] It is not easy to paint a precise picture of the situation since not all the data are Canadian census figures, but may also be compiled by provincial government departments, which do not necessarily use the same base years.

[2] Teenage pregnancy and pregnancy outcome data usually pertain to the 15–19 age group. Data for that group include data for adolescents under the age of 15.

[3] The reader should know that Canada's two levels of government (provincial and federal) divide up jurisdictions over different matters and that family policies are mainly a provincial responsibility. Other policies, for example those pertaining to insurance and labour management, are shared by both levels of government. For the remainder of our analysis, we will always identify which government level we are referring to.

[4] 'Defamilialisation' is a process that measures the emancipation of women from family-related constraints. It refers to government initiatives that acknowledge the value of women's unpaid work by providing a range of public services and tax benefits as compensation for the work traditionally done within the family (Esping-Andersen, 1990).

[5] This assistance was not available to divorced or single mothers. Beneficiaries had to agree to devote themselves full time to family

obligations and vouch for their parenting skills under the watchful eye of a notary, church pastor or bank manager (Baillargeon, 1996; Dandurand and McAll, 1996). According to Morel (2002a), this shows that differential treatment based on principles distinguishing 'decent' poor folk from others is not such a new idea, contrary to what some would seem to believe.

[6] The sanctions were officially abolished by the Québec Liberal Party in 2004, but new restrictions on access were introduced, and benefits are only partially indexed to the cost of living for welfare recipients who are deemed 'fit' to work but do not 'voluntarily' participate in those measures.

[7] In the wake on the 1989 United Nations Convention on the Rights of the Child, the United Nations took Canada to task and urged it to do more to eradicate child poverty.

[8] This taskforce, chaired by psychologist and UQAM professor Camil Bouchard, was comprised of academics, professionals and executive staff from youth protection, health, education and justice services and community organisations. It exemplifies a fairly widespread Québec government initiative that consists of taking stock of a social issue to then develop specific policies and encourage experts in various fields to set up forums to address this issue.

[9] The committee included representatives of the Departments of Health and Social Services, Education, Family and Childhood, Employment and Social Solidarity (which manages the public assistance programme), and Citizen Relations and Immigration, as well as the Youth and Native Affairs secretariats.

[10] The programme provided for a minimum of 12 prenatal home visits, one weekly visit during the first three months after childbirth and one bi-weekly visit during the next three months. Although the frequency of subsequent visits was not established, it was supposed to help maintain a significant link with the family. The programme's outcomes have yet to be assessed.

References
Baillargeon, D. (1996) 'Les politiques familiales au Québec: une perspective historique', *Lien social et politiques*, no 36, pp 21-32.

Boismenu, F. and Dufour, P. (1998) 'Nouveaux principes de références et différenciation des arbitrages politiques: le cas des politiques à l'égard des sans-emploi', *Revue canadienne de science politique*, vol 31, no 1, pp 113-42.

Bouchard, C. (1991) *Un Québec fou de ses enfants. Rapports du Groupe de travail pour les jeunes*, Québec: Ministère de la Santé et des Services Sociaux (Ministry of Health and Social Services).

Buchholz, E.S. and Korn-Bursztyn, C. (1993) 'Children of Adolescent Mothers: Are they at Risk for Abuse?', *Adolescence*, vol 28, no 110, pp 361-82.

Budd, K.S., Stockman, K.D. and Miller, E.N. (1998) 'Parenting Issues and Interventions with Adolescent Mothers', in J.R. Lutzker (ed) *Handbook of Child Abuse Research and Treatment*, New York, NY: Plenum Press, pp 357-76.

Carataga, L. (1999) 'The Construction of Teen Parenting and the Decline of Adoption', in J. Wong and D. Checkland (eds) *Teen Pregnancy and Parenting: Social and Ethical Issues*, Toronto: University of Toronto Press, pp 99-120.

Charbonneau, J. (2002) 'Grossesse et maternité adolescentes: débats idéologiques et nouvelles perspectives d'analyse', in F. Descarries and C. Corbeil (eds) *Espaces et temps de la maternité*, Montréal: Éditions du Remue-Ménage.

Charbonneau, J. (2003) *Adolescentes et mères: Histoires de maternité précoce et soutien du réseau social*, Québec: Presses de l'Université Laval.

Chase-Lansdale, P.L., Brooks-Gunn, J. and Paikoff, R.L. (1991) 'Research and Programs for Adolescent Mothers: Missing Links and Future Promises', *Family Relations*, vol 40, no 4, pp 396-403.

Côté, J. (1997) 'Brève généalogie de discours sur les mères adolescentes', *Anthropologie et sociétés*, vol 21, no 2-3, pp 287-301.

Cournoyer, M. (1995) *Grossesse, maternité et paternité à l'adolescence: Recueil de recension d'écrits*, Québec: Institut québécois de recherche sur la culture.

Dandurand, R. and McAll, C. (1996) 'Welfare, workfare, wedfare: faut-il encore assister les mères seules?', *Lien social et politiques*, no 36, pp 79-91.

Dandurand, R. and St-Pierre, M.-H. (2000) 'Les nouvelles dispositions de la politique familiale québécoise: un retournement ou une évolution prévisible?', in M. Simard and J. Alary (eds) *Comprendre la famille*, Québec: Presses Universitaires du Québec, pp 59-80.

Davies, L., McKinnon, M. and Rains, P. (1999) 'On my Own: A New Discourse of Dependence and Independence from Teen Mothers', in J. Wong and D. Checkland (eds) *Teen Pregnancy and Parenting: Social and Ethical Issues*, Toronto: University of Toronto Press, pp 38-51.

Descarries, F. and Corbeil, C. (1994) 'Entre discours et pratiques: l'évolution de la pensée féministe sur la maternité depuis 1960', *Nouvelles questions féministes*, vol 15, no 1, pp 69-93.

Duchesne, L. (2003) *La situation démographique au Québec: Bilan 2003: Les ménages au tournant du XIXe siècle*, Québec: Institut de la statistique du Québec.

Dufort, F., Guilbert, É. and Saint-Laurent, L. (2000) *La grossesse à l'adolescence et sa prévention: au-delà de la pensée magique*, Research Report, Québec: Conseil Québécois de la Recherche Sociale.

Dufour, P. (2002) 'L'État post-providence: de nouvelles politiques sociales pour des parents-producteurs: une perspective comparée', *Revue canadienne de science politique*, vol 35, no 2, pp 301-22.

Dufour, P., Boismenu, G. and Noël, A. (2003) *L'aide au conditionnel: La contrepartie dans les mesures envers les personnes sans emploi en Europe et en Amérique du Nord*, Montréal: Presses Universitaires de Montréal.

Esping-Andersen, G. (1990) *The Three Worlds of Welfare Capitalism*, Cambridge: Polity Press.

Government of Québec (2002) *Programme de soutien aux jeunes parents: Document initial pour la première phase de l'implantation*, Québec: Ministère de la Santé et des Services Sociaux.

Groupe d'étude critique sur la prévention précoce (2002) *De l'intervention précoce à la prévention féroce ?*, Montréal: Université du Québec à Montréal.

Hacking, I. (1999) 'Teenage Pregnancy: Social Construction?', in J. Wong and D. Checkland (eds) *Teen Pregnancy and Parenting: Social and Ethical Issues*, Toronto: University of Toronto Press, pp 71-80.

Hanson, R.A. (1990) 'Initial Parenting Attitudes of Pregnant Adolescents and a Comparison with the Decision about Adoption', *Adolescence*, vol 25, no 99, pp 631-43.

Hoffman, S.D. (1998) 'Teenage childbearing is not so bad after all ... or is it? A review of the new literature', *Family Planning Perspectives*, vol 30, no 5, pp 236-40.

ISQ (Institut de la statistique du Québec) (2000a) *Étude longitudinale du développement des enfants du Québec (ELDEQ, 1998-2002): Milieux de vie: La famille, la garde et le quartier*, volumes 1 and 2, Québec: ISQ.

ISQ (2000b) *Statistiques démographiques: Les naissances et la fécondité*, available at: www.bdso.gouv.qc.ca

ISQ (2003) *Calculs: Unités d'études et d'analyse* Québec: Ministère de la Santé et des Services Sociaux (Ministry of Health and Social Security), Direction de l'évaluation, de la recherche et de l'innovation (Directorate for evualation, research and innovation).

ISQ (2004) *Naissances et taux de fécondité selon l'âge de la mère, Québec, 1998-2003*, available at: www.stat.gouv.qc.ca/donstat/societe/demographie

Jenson, J. (2000) 'Le nouveau régime de citoyenneté du Canada: investir dans l'enfance', *Lien social et politiques*, no 44, pp 11-23.

Kaufman, M. (1999) 'Day-to-day Ethical Issues in the Care of Young Parents and their Children', in J. Wong and D. Checkland (eds) *Teen Pregnancy and Parenting: Social and Ethical Issues*, Toronto: University of Toronto Press, pp 25-34.

Kelly, D.M. (1999) 'A Critical Feminist Perspective on Teen Pregnancy and Parenthood', in J. Wong and D. Checkland (eds) *Teen Pregnancy and Parenting: Social and Ethical Issues*, Toronto: University of Toronto Press, pp 52-70.

Laurin, C. and Stuart, C. (2004) 'Programme soutien aux jeunes parents: contre qui, contre quoi?', *Nouvelles pratiques sociales*, vol 16, no 1, pp 215-21.

Letendre, R. and Doray, P. (1999) *L'expérience de la grossesse à l'adolescence*, Montréal: Conseil québécois de recherche sociale.

Leynes, C. (1980) 'Keep or Adopt: A Study of Factors Influencing Pregnant Adolescents' Plans for their Babies', *Child Psychiatry and Human Development*, vol 11, no 2, pp 105-12.

Manseau, H. (1998) *La grossesse chez les adolescentes en internat: Le syndrome de la conception immaculée*, Research Report for the Québec Centre of Scientific Research, Montréal: Department of Sexology, Université du Québec à Montréal.

Maynard, R.A. (ed) (1997) *Kids Having Kids: Economics Costs and Social Consequences of Teen Pregnancy*, Washington, DC: Urban Institute Press.

Morel, S. (2002a) *Modèle du workfare ou modèle de l'insertion? La transformation de l'assistance sociale au Canada et au Québec*, Ottawa: Condition féminine Canada.

Morel, S. (2002b) 'La transformation des obligations de travail pour les mères touchant l'assistance sociale: quels enseignements pour les féministes?', *Lien social et politiques*, no 47, pp 171-86.

Musick, J.S. (1993) *Young, Poor and Pregnant: The Psychology of Teenage Motherhood*, New Haven, CT, and London: Yale University Press.

Nathanson, C.A. (1991) *Dangerous Passage: The Social Control of Sexuality in Women's Adolescence*, Philadelphia, PA: Temple University Press.

Noël, A. (2002) 'Une loi contre la pauvreté: la nouvelle approche québécoise de lutte contre la pauvreté et l'exclusion sociale', *Lien social et politiques*, no 48, pp 103-14.

Rochon, M. (1997) *Taux de grossesse à l'adolescence, Québec, 1980 à 1995, régions sociosanitaires de résidence, 1993-1995 et autres groupes d'âge*, Québec: Service de la recherche, direction générale de la planification et de l'évaluation, Ministère de la Santé et des Services Sociaux (Ministry of Health and Social Security).

Roy, S. and Charest, D. (2002) *Jeunes filles enceintes et mères adolescentes: un portrait statistique*, Québec: Ministère de l'Education du Québec.

Saint-Arnaud, S. and Bernard, P. (2003) 'Convergence ou résilience? Une analyse de classification hiérarchique des régimes providentiels des pays avancés', *Sociologie et sociétés*, vol 35, no 1, pp 65-93.

Statistics Canada (2004) *Grossesse chez l'adolescente, selon l'issue des grossesses, femmes de 15 à 19 ans, Canada, provinces et territoires, données annuelles*, available at: www.statcan.ca

Turner, R.J., Sorenson, A.M. and Turner, J.B. (2000) 'Social Contingencies in Mental Health: A Seven Year Follow-up Study of Teenage Mothers', *Journal of Marriage and the Family*, vol 62, no 3, pp 777-91.

SIX

Teenage pregnancy and reproductive politics in France

Corinne Nativel

Introduction

On 17 January 2005, France was celebrating the 30th anniversary of the Veil law. This landmark in contemporary French social history legalised the right to abortion, closely following the Neuwirth law on free access to the contraceptive pill.[1] The 'second contraceptive revolution' emerged in the midst of the 1968 feminist battles,[2] which paved the path for significant changes in the sexual reproductive behaviour of the French, including that of teenagers (Mossuz-Lavau, 2002; Jaspard, 2005). The existing consensus is based on two assumptions: first, that fertility is under control; and second, that childbearing is strongly associated with adulthood, a desire to have a child and an ability to 'take responsibility' (Leridon, 1995). Moreover, despite displaying higher fertility rates compared to many of their European counterparts, French women have increasingly delayed the birth of their first child (Prioux, 2004). In 2004, the fertility rate stood at 1.9 and the mean age at birthgiving for the first child was just below 30 compared to 26 in the early 1970s. Meanwhile, late pregnancies among women aged over 40 are on the rise (Daguet, 1999; Prioux, 2004). In this changing demographic context, it is therefore not surprising that births to teenagers are often portrayed as an anomalous case of deviant and immature behaviour (Le Van, 1998).

Drawing upon the case of France, this chapter provides a discussion of teenage reproductive politics, which is understood herein as a field encompassing public attitudes, laws and measures towards teenage sexuality, pregnancy and parenthood. The chapter shows that the low incidence of teenage motherhood in France compared to countries of the liberal welfare regime has been achieved in the absence of any targeted policy specifically designed to prevent births to teenagers. Rather, it appears that this phenomenon has been indirectly prevented through the comprehensive social policy framework that characterises France's republican version of the conservative-corporatist welfare regime. This framework comprises universal rights in the fields of public health, youth education, family and childhood protection. However, the deliberate wish to avoid considering teenage motherhood as a pathological social problem means that specialist provision remains weak in some French localities and that adequate governance models are still to be invented.

The chapter begins with a statistical and qualitative overview of the trends in teenage pregnancy and childbearing. The second section provides a conceptual framework for understanding teenage reproductive politics. The chapter then analyses sexual health policies and the development of reproductive rights. The fourth section reviews the social protection measures available to teenage mothers. The conclusion highlights some of the limitations in the provision made available to the stable core of female teenagers who have and are most likely to continue having children.

Teenage pregnancy and sexuality in France: an overview

International league tables of teenage pregnancy consistently rank France in an intermediary position, behind countries such as the Netherlands and Italy (Darroch et al, 2001; UNICEF, 2001). At the beginning of the 21st century, France displays birth rates that average 10 per 1,000 teenagers aged between 15 and 19. Teenage conceptions have significantly declined since the 1980s: while 20,710 cases were registered in 1980, by 1997, the figure had dropped to 13,192 (Kafé and Brouard, 2000). It is striking that if the decline was particularly steep in the 1980s, teenage conceptions began to reach a stable level in the early 1990s. The rate of live births to teenagers more than halved in this period: at the beginning of the 1980s, 28 per 1,000 adolescents had embraced motherhood compared to 14 per 1,000 a decade on. By 1997, they were 12 per 1,000 (Kafé and Brouard, 2000). In 2001, a slight increase occurred with a total of 14,998 conceptions to teenagers aged under 18 (see Figure 6.1). A further measure of the fall in teenage pregnancy since 1980 is the reproduction rate. According to the French Statistical Agency, the *Institut national de la statistique et des études économiques* (INSEE), this rate fell from 8.94% in 1980 to 3.93% in 2004.[3]

Against this trend, the proportion of births to teenagers aged

Figure 6.1: Births and abortions to teenagers aged under 18 in France

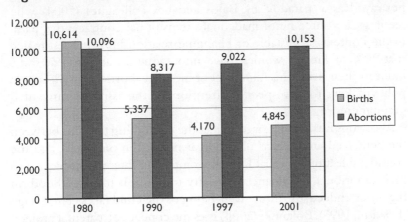

Sources: Institut National d'Études Démographiques (INED): Institut National de la Statistique et des Études Économiques (INSEE); Direction de la Recherche, des Études, de l'Évaluation et des Statistiques (DREES).

below 16 has steadily – albeit only modestly – increased since 1980: 8.6% of the total of births to teenagers (under 18) in 1980, 9.5% in 1990 and 11% in 2001. In absolute terms, in 2001 the figure corresponds to 521 live births to mothers aged below 16, which compares to 4,410 for the same year in England.[4]

One in two pregnancies ends in an induced abortion (Uzan, 1998). Nonetheless, abortion levels among pregnant teenagers have not declined since the early 1980s (see Figure 6.1). In 2002, there were just over 11,000 abortions among teenagers compared to a total of 206,000 in France, which means that they represent around 5% of the total (Vilain, 2004). The mass campaigns against the risk of HIV/ AIDS infection has spurred teenagers to use condoms when initiating sexual activity, with only 25% reporting having had unprotected intercourse (Lagrange and Lhomond, 1997). However, the switch from the use of condoms to the contraceptive pill occurs on average within a time span of six months from first intercourse, which suggests that teenagers face difficulties in seeking and obtaining parental advice (Kafé and Brouard, 2000). In January 2005, a polling institute, the TNS-SOFRES (*Société Française d'Enquête par Sondage*), carried out a survey of 31,500 young people aged 15 to 25 on behalf of the Ile-de-France regional authorities. The survey showed that only 8% felt ill-informed about condoms against 33% with regard to the contraceptive pill (TNS-SOFRES, 2005).

It is worth stressing that the stability of abortion rates concerns the whole female population, regardless of age. Given the widespread access to various contraceptive methods, this trend is portrayed as a 'paradox' by Bajos and her colleagues (2004) who see it as the outcome of inadequate transitional contraceptive paths in the context of unstable or changing relationships. It is estimated that 40% of French women have undergone an abortion at some point in their lives. This high level of induced abortion has prompted policymakers to pay specific attention to the issue of unwanted pregnancies.[5]

Abortions further appear to reflect the conflicting tensions between the perceived 'imperative' of childrearing on the one hand, and the considerable attention that French women and their partners grant to their emotional and financial capacity to commit to parenthood on the other. Indeed, the future well-being of the child takes centre stage (Leridon, 1995). Boltanski (2004) uses the concept of 'parental project' to describe the increasing disconnection between sexuality and childbearing in French society. Thus, one important question is whether the formulation of such a 'parental project' can apply to teenage pregnancy or whether the usual stereotypes (irresponsible victims versus devious misfits) that have led to the stigmatisation of this group in the public discourse (Musick, 1993; Charbonneau, 2003) can hold true.

Le Van's (1998) qualitative study based on 30 interviews with pregnant teenagers in the Pays-de-Calais – a northern county that has above-average rates of teenage pregnancy and low rates of induced abortions – mirrors these concerns. Drawing on the varying perceptions of maternal desire and attitudes to contraception, she underlines the heterogeneity of the phenomenon by distinguishing five categories of teenage pregnancy: (1) the pregnancy as a rite of initiation, (2) the 'SOS' pregnancy, (3) the 'insertion' pregnancy, (4) the 'identity' pregnancy and (5) the accidental pregnancy. The first corresponds to a planned and voluntary exposure to the risk of pregnancy as a means of putting the stability of the relationship to a test, or to a lesser extent, to attract parental attention. While interviewees expressed their childbearing desire, the majority decided to interrupt their pregnancy. Likewise, the 'SOS' pregnancy entails a voluntary exposure to risk but does not correspond to a defined parental project. It is clearly the expression of psychological difficulties, a 'cry for help', an attempt to obtain parental attention and comfort. By contrast, the 'insertion' pregnancy[6] is intrinsically bound up with motherhood as these young girls have consciously chosen not to use contraception. In this case, childbearing is a pathway to acquiring an approved social status, that of a mother. The 'identity' pregnancy concerns the most disaffected group and is defined by respondents as accidental. The pregnancy cannot be interpreted as a message to partners, parents nor to the community at large, but helps the teenager become conscious of her own existence. The final type of pregnancy is unambiguously accidental due to the absence or failure of contraceptive methods and its resulting interruption.

Le Van's study is helpful in debunking the myth that all teenage pregnancies are accidental and unwanted. Other authors show that 80% of pregnant teenagers are from lone-parent families with an average of five children and that two thirds are out of school and without qualifications (Marcault and Pierre, 2001). The ethnic dimension of teenage childbearing remains under-researched in France although further small-scale evidence, mainly from obstetricians and medical practitioners, highlights that young females from Turkish, North African (mainly Algerian and Moroccan) and South African (Malian, Congolese) backgrounds do, in certain instances, represent up to 40% of the pregnant teenage population (Uzan, 1998; Faucher et al, 2002).[7]

As in other countries, parallels have been drawn between teenage pregnancies and socio-demographic changes such as the rise of out-of-wedlock births from 6% in the early 1960s to 45% (and 57% for the first child) in 2001 (Barbier and Théret, 2004, p 44). Other explanations include the decline in the age of puberty and early sexual activity: female cohorts born in 1980 tend to have their first sexual intercourse a year and a half younger, at 17.4, than those born in 1950, who were just under 19 (Bozon, 2002, p 49). A major national study into teenage sexuality carried out in the mid-1990s showed that at the age of 16, just over 40% of French teenagers had lost their virginity against three quarters of those aged 18 (Lagrange and Lhomond, 1997). The early onset of sexual activity is recognised by the law, which has established the age of sexual consent at 15.

While the correlation between early entry into sexuality and teenage pregnancy is far from clear, as evidence from the Nordic countries shows, public authorities are increasingly admitting that young girls must be protected from sexist behaviour when discovering sexuality. However, the need to protect young girls from potentially abusive relationships entails a rather sensitive redrawing of the boundaries between the public and the private spheres.

Teenage pregnancy does not exist as a 'social problem' in the French public discourse, even if, as in other European countries, teenage childbearing has undoubtedly adverse outcomes for young women: aside from leaving the education system, three quarters of those who have a partner become single parents within five years

(Marcault and Pierre, 2001). Additionally, one in two mothers entrusts the child to either a foster family or to social services in the fourth year following its birth (Knibiehler, 1997, p 283). Nonetheless, in contrast to their British or American counterparts, French policymakers are not overly concerned with the costs of teenage pregnancy. Despite the growing influence of neoliberal ideas on French policymakers, attacks on welfare recipients and reference to the underclass have remained limited. Social policy still emphasises the importance of the mother's and the child's welfare to the exclusion of financial considerations. This caring ethos reflects the strong political value attached to childrearing and motherhood in French society.

Approaches to teenage sexuality and childbearing in France

An embodied governance

In France, the analysis of teenage pregnancy is meshed in a broad reflection on the interaction between the public and private realms. Instead of drawing upon risk management approaches for analysing contemporary sexual health policies, I would suggest that the 'embodied governance' paradigm (Fassin and Memmi, 2004; Iacub, 2004) is a useful heuristic device to explain public attitudes towards this phenomenon. This approach is rooted in the Foucaldian legacy, which shows how the longstanding genealogy of biopolitics of discipline and control (Foucault, 2001) has resulted in the production of a sophisticated legal and institutional apparatus framing how individuals can or cannot use their bodies to reproduce life through sexual activity. The fields commonly scrutinised include prostitution, gay sex or assisted medical procreation (see, for example, Mathieu, 2000; Fassin, 2001; Iacub, 2004). Teenage reproductive politics has received less attention, although Memmi (2003) finds that it has undergone a shift from a punitive control regime towards a surveillance regime. While old control regimes were based on the active involvement of the Church and the school in the regulation of sexual behaviour, the new regime could be described as rational and 'hygienic'. Indeed, the medical profession plays a crucial role. The technical competence of proximity networks replaces the role hitherto played by old neighbourhood communities. This is illustrated through the delivery of the morning-after pill, known as Norlevo. Since June 1999, Norlevo has been available from chemists who endorse the responsibility of informing and advising women about the benefits of a more traditional oral contraceptive (Memmi, 2003, p 41); in June 2001, access to Norlevo was extended to teenagers free of charge following major parliamentary battles, an issue that will be addressed later. As with other groups targeted by the new biopolitics, the key regulation mechanism lies in the verbal exchange and the production of a consensus between two parties, that is, between the professional 'expert' and the recipient. The responsibility of delivering Norlevo is left to two categories of professionals: school nurses and chemists. School nurses are the first profession involved. They are entitled to deliver Norlevo to school pupils following a preliminary interview with the teenage girl. Chemists represent the second profession entrusted with the regulation of teenage reproductive behaviour. They are also required to hold an 'interview' with the adolescent to ensure that the delivery of the morning-after pill does indeed correspond to urgency criteria and to inform her about the benefits of a medical follow-up. However, an experimental study based on 104 interactions between teenagers and chemists showed that the great majority of professionals did not dare extend their role as providers and venture into the moralistic terrain that they have been assigned to by the law. These control mechanisms are thus difficult to implement in big cities, which in turn facilitates the shift towards a less stringent control regime.

It is important to bear in mind that welfare capitalism does not solely incorporate institutional legacies in the sense used by Esping-Andersen, but that 'path dependency is often also based on a *longue durée* at the cultural level' (Pfau-Effinger, 2005, p 15). The rites of passages inherent in youth are certainly among the enduring anthropological aspects of human life overlooked by welfare regimes. Arguably, welfare regimes with high levels of labour commodification offer relatively more abrupt lifecourse transitions than others precisely because they place little value on the affective dimension of social life.

Following the path opened up by Giddens (1992), several French scholars have emphasised the importance of the discovery of love, intimacy and sexuality among teenagers (Duret, 1999; Lagrange, 1999; Maillochon, 2001; Maia, 2004). These authors explain that, unlike adults, teenagers are extremely emotional about their first sexual encounter and that there is a strong gendered dimension to entry into sexuality. Youth surveys consistently show that teenage girls are very unlikely to envisage sex without love (Galland and Lambert, 1993; Lagrange and Lhomond, 1997). Moreover, marriage remains a norm highly valued by French youngsters. A recent survey of some 5,000 young people aged between 16 and 18 established that 82% considered getting married later in life and 92% wished to have a child (Maillochon, 2001).

In this context, then, how does welfare capitalism fare in reducing the (natural) risks associated with transitions into adulthood? Aït el Cadi (2003) argues that public authorities have paid little attention to the risk behaviour of adolescent girls, possibly because compared to that of boys, this tends to be internalised and inflicted upon their own bodies. Girls were usually socially invisible but the opening in 2005 of several pilot centres for female teenagers experiencing anorexia and other forms of psychological distress suggests significant shifts. Other authors emphasise the continued significance of parental and community involvement in the sexual education of teenagers. Galland (1997) argues that the relationship between young people and adults increasingly entails the disappearance of authority and the growing display of 'affective negotiation' between parents and children, on children's autonomy and discreet parental guidance. According to the aforementioned survey by the TNS-SOFRES (2005), 85% of young people report having good relationships with their parents. Nonetheless, although parents have become more permissive, teenagers remain reluctant to confide in them about sexual matters (Galland, 1997, p 233). Moreover, a striking example of social control can still be found in the construction of gendered identities among young girls from second-generation North-African muslim families to whom abstinence is strictly imposed as a distinctive norm; in this normative framework, sexuality cannot be disconnected from endogamous – and often forced – marriages. Girls who fail to respect this contract are treated as whores (Lacoste-Dujardin, 1992; Amara, 2003). In several neighbourhoods, it is still common practice for families to call upon compliant doctors to establish certificates of virginity so as to satisfy would-be-husbands that their daughters are 'pure' (Amara, 2003, p 56).

These pressures are compounded by the changing relationships between girls and boys in the context of a growing exposure to erotised and pornographic material, and in particular the crisis of masculinity among teenage boys reported to be particularly strong in metropolitan suburbs (Duret, 1999; Lagrange, 1999). Verbal abuse – and in some instances physical violence – towards female teenagers has been on the rise in disaffected neighbourhoods, thus making the discovery of intimacy particularly challenging (Bellil, 2002; Amara, 2003). As a result, an escape route for many girls is to get married at the age of 16 or 17. With the resilience of patriarchy among North-African immigrants and polygamy for those originating from Sub-saharan Africa, pregnant mothers from minority ethnic backgrounds are less likely to be single when seen by obstetricians (Faucher et al, 2002), although this does not indicate that in the long run their relationships are more stable.

Lifecourse transitions remain relatively focused on the ideal-type of a three-pronged transition into adulthood starting with higher education, followed by entry into a professional career and completed with the establishment of a family (Galland, 1997). The education system is at the core of this transitional process; it is considered as a promise of equality and social integration. Thus, obtaining the *baccalauréat* (the equivalent of British A-levels) remains the main objective for young people: by the turn of the 21st century, 70% of 19-year-olds had successfully passed their *baccalauréat* and entered further and higher education, in contrast to 30% in the early 1980s (Brin, 2001). The educational achievement of young women is particularly striking: in 1991, 48% of young women aged between 20 and 24 had obtained their *baccalauréat*. Ten years later, 71% had obtained it, performing better than boys. For these new generations, entry in a professional career takes precedence over motherhood (Galland, 1997). However, this lifecourse model has been gradually eroded by macroeconomic conditions unfavourable to those cohorts born after the *Trente Glorieuses* period of economic prosperity, which creates a major cleavage, an erosion of the intergenerational reproductive consensus (Chauvel, 1998). Cichelli and Martin (2004) illustrate the resulting tensions as young people navigate between a dual process of increased autonomy and financial dependency on their parents. The delay in establishing autonomous households is mainly the result of persistent youth unemployment[8] and prolonged time spent in higher education, a phenomenon France shares with many other countries of the conservative-corporatist and Mediterranean welfare regimes (see Chapter Seven, this volume). Moreover, unless they have at least one dependent child, French citizens under the age of 25 are not entitled to the minimum income (*Revenu Minimum d'Insertion*), which aggravates the dependency on the family. The fact that parents with students aged up to 25 can avail themselves of fiscal relief and that students living on their own are entitled to relatively generous housing benefits implicitly places entry into adulthood around the age of 25 and sustains the youth 'educational project' in opposition to the youth 'parental project'.

The abundant literature on social and labour market exclusion among young people and on youth deviance (see, for example, Dubet, 1987; Rey, 2000) illustrates the important concern of the French with minimising the social risks associated with the increasingly difficult implementation of the aforementioned ideal-type. While much of the literature is focused on young males, Rubi (2005) highlights that deviant violent behaviour is also increasing among female teenagers. The growing failure of educational and labour market institutions to provide synchronised paths into adulthood has resulted in the transformation of the relationship between youth and the state. The state is increasingly playing the role of an intermediate body between the child and its family (Galland, 1997; Commaille et al, 2002). In the mid-1990s, it was established that French youngsters displayed one of the highest rates of suicide in Europe (Brin, 2001) and this *malaise* spurred public authorities to create several services to support youngsters experiencing psychological difficulties. Issues surrounding sexuality and pregnancy are tackled under this broad preventive umbrella.

One such initiative is known as the *Fil Santé Jeunes*. *Fil Santé Jeunes* is a free telephone hotline for young people aged between 11 and 25, although three quarters of those using the service are aged below 18. The hotline was created in 1995 and is managed by a voluntary sector organisation, the *École des Parents et des Éducateurs* (the School for Parents and Teachers), with funding from the Ministry for Employment and Social Affairs and a major foundation known as *Fondation de France*. Staff from the *Fil Santé Jeunes* handle, on average, 600 enquiries per day. These enquiries emanate less frequently from boys than from girls seeking information and advice on health, emotional and relationship matters.

The increasing concern with the provision of 'youth-friendly' public services is further reflected in the creation, in 1996, of flexible structures known as the *Points d'Accueil et d'Ecoute Jeunes* (PAEJ) that offer free and confidential advice for young people aged between 10 and 25 years who find themselves in situations of social distress in the parental home. By 2004, there were 174 PAEJ offices, generally comprising three to four permanent staff such as educational psychologists and social workers. The creation of another 300 offices was announced in the June 2004 Programme on Social Cohesion of Employment Minister Jean-Louis Borloo. A budget of €3 million has been allocated to this extension, which will lead to a full territorial coverage by 2007. While they share some of the operational principles of the Connexions service in the UK (provision of information and advice, and so on), these 'contact points' may be established in either the public or the voluntary sector and are partly funded by municipalities. In this field also, young girls who may wish to obtain advice on sexual and contraceptive matters can approach adult advisors in a less intimidating environment than medical surgeries or family planning associations.

Public policy towards sex education, family, health and reproductive rights

It is crucial to bear in mind that, in the first instance, childhood protection is located in the private sphere, which means that parents are responsible for ensuring the 'security, health and morality' of children aged under 18, which entails protecting them from risks, such as the risk of pregnancy. The Napoleonic Code (1804) set the foundations for parental responsibility in civil law (*code civil*). By establishing a set of rights and responsibilities that would apply to all individuals, the Napoleonic Code was central to the constitution of the family and indeed of the nation. For a long time, it remained highly patriarchal: not only did it serve to strongly ground the norm of procreation in the matrimonial regime, it also gave the male breadwinner full *paternal* authority. However, a series of amendments such as Article 371-2 (1972) introduced equal *parental* authority. The balance of rights and responsibilities was not only redrawn between the mother and father, but also between parents and children whose wishes were increasingly taken into account. For example, in 1974, Article 209-10 allowed pregnant teenagers to have a say with regard to abortion, to freely consult doctors and obtain medical contraceptives from chemists, and thus to exert autonomy over their own bodies.

The literature on teenage pregnancy prevention often underlines the important role of sex education in empowering young people to make informed decisions about their health and well-being (Lewis and Knijn, 2002; Harris and Meredith, 2005). In this regard, ministerial guidelines introduced in 1973 stipulate that information and education on sexual matters is to be dispensed in primary and secondary schools through at least three annual classes to same-age groups of pupils. These classes may draw on both teachers as well as external professionals. However, despite the existence of a legal framework, sex education in schools remains insufficient with an average of two contact hours per year (Gauthier, 2002, p 424). In addition, the focus on the biological and technical dimensions of reproductive sex remains disconnected from the affective dimensions of sexuality, although some efforts have recently been made through the introduction of experimental pilot projects, as will be shown later.

Since 1956, the *Mouvement Francais pour le Planning Familial* (MFPF) (the French Family Planning Movement)[9] has played a key activist role in the promotion of sex education and women's reproductive rights. Organised as a confederation with 120 regional, county and local branches throughout France, it offers free and confidential medical advice. Teenagers can attend weekly educational meetings to discuss a range of sexual and emotional matters. However, the MFPF remains under-used by teenagers, partly because of misinformation, but also because it suffers the image of a distant and stale institution.

The political climate in relation to reproductive politics has considerably changed since the mid-1970s. In 1972, a major event involving a 16-year-old teenager became the hallmark of a cultural and political revolution in this respect. Marie-Claire Chevalier was brought to the children's tribunal of Bobigny, a municipality situated near Paris, for having undergone a clandestine, illegal abortion. The case received significant media coverage and the teenager was subsequently released. This court decision implied that the law of 31 July 1920, which penalised women for undergoing abortion by making them liable to 10 years' imprisonment, had become outdated (Mossuz-Lavau, 2002, p 103).

As mentioned earlier, the law of 17 January 1975 devised by Simone Veil legalised abortion up until the 10th week of pregnancy. In 1982, the Roudy law authorised for the costs of induced abortions to be refunded by the State. In 1988, the RU 486, a drug allowing chemical abortion, was authorised while the Neiertz law of 1993 made any attempt to prevent a woman from terminating a birth a 'crime' that could be subject to two to three years of imprisonment. Under the socialist government of Lionel Jospin, further important steps were taken such as the Bill championed by the then Minister for Employment and Solidarity, Martine Aubry, in July 2001. Opposing Conservative claims that the Bill favoured eugenicism and female narcissism, it established the legal abortion time of 12 weeks into the pregnancy, bringing it in line with most other European countries and considerably reducing cross-border migration of women wishing to abort. One of its strongest opponents was Philippe de Villiers from the Conservative *Mouvement pour la France* (Movement for France) party who declared in Parliament that 'history will remember that under the impulsion of the national-socialists, State eugenics was introduced in our country.... We have reached the stage where children to be born are carefully selected. A new right is emerging: the right to antenatal euthanasia' (translation) (Mossuz-Lavau, 2002, p 399). The 2001 Aubry law suppressed the need to obtain parental consent for performing an abortion. The sole requirement is for the teenager to be accompanied by a 'refereeing adult' who may be, for example, a relative, a teacher or a doctor. Some Conservative Members of Parliament (MPs) opposed this measure on the grounds that the sovereignty of the family was undermined (Mossuz-Lavau, 2002, p 405).

Similarly, Segolène Royal, the then Minister for Education, faced fierce opposition when seeking to extend access to Norlevo (the morning-after-pill), which was made available to teenagers in June 1999. Her Green Paper of 29 December 1999 was first declared void by the *Conseil d'Etat*[10] and could only be adopted through an amendment of the 1967 law, which stipulated that the prescription of Norlevo was to be entrusted with medical doctors only. The legal amendment was seen as a 'fatal blow' to the family by Conservative MPs but the Bill was passed by Parliament in October 2000 (Mossuz-Lavau, 2002, p 395). Teenagers can thus obtain Norlevo from school nurses and chemists since 2001 but its use has not increased significantly to date (Jaspard, 2005, p 62). In addition, following consultations with parental organisations, Segolène Royal launched an educational campaign in schools, which consisted of disseminating a pocket guide to contraception. The guide sought to disseminate the message of responsibility and respect but many head teachers remained reluctant to distribute it to pupils (Gauthier, 2002, p 426).

Since 2002, under the leadership of the right-wing government of Jean-Pierre Raffarin, further steps have been taken in the field of women's reproductive rights. In November 2004, the then Health Minister, Philippe Douste-Blazy, encouraged the adoption of a Bill authorising the use of RU 486 at home as well as the implementation of an antenatal programme (*plan périnatal*) between 2005 and 2007. This initiative brings increased psychological support to pregnant women with a non-compulsory interview in the fourth month of their pregnancy. Its aims are to address personal and social issues faced by the mother and to improve levels of care during and after the birth of the child. To this end, local authorities are tasked with the creation of antenatal proximity networks of health professionals and social workers. In contrast to other social policy areas such as employment and labour market policies, there is a strong pattern of pragmatism and continuity in the politics of sexual health and reproductive rights.[11] However, parts of the 1920 law are still in existence, which remains a sensitive issue for many governments (Gauthier, 2002; Mossuz-Lavau, 2002).

Finally, the role of religious institutions deserves some attention. Returning to Pfau-Effinger's (2005) call for a greater recognition of cultural path-dependency, the analysis of Church–state patterns can reveal important insights into the outcomes of family and abortion policy. According to Minkenberg (2003, p 213), 'the French tradition of *laïcité*[12] and the high levels of secularisation in terms of conventional measures of church-going and religiosity have resulted in a cultural paradigm which severely restricts the room for manoeuvre of the Catholic Church'. This has allowed for the emergence of an innovative family policy, which it shares with the Protestant social democratic regime. Yet the latter has 'full establishment' features while France has 'separationist' features in which the Church is 'visible but not vociferous' (Minkenberg, 2003, p 212). In fact, the most vociferous groups are pro-life commandos, close to Jean-Marie Le Pen's National Front. These groups were particularly active in the early 1990s, seeking to implement the ideology of American evangelical movements in France (Mossuz-Lavau, 2002, p 391). Between 1987 and 1999, 127 such commandos forcefully made their way into maternity wards, thereby causing major disruption and delays (Gauthier, 2002, p 375).

Social protection mechanisms for teenage mothers

Welfare provision in France is characterised by a strong protective stance in relation to teenage mothers. The French welfare state seeks to offer holistic and non-discriminatory family rights regardless of age. Indeed, France is known to have one of the most advanced social protection systems towards the family (Commaille et al, 2002). In this context, teenage mothers are entitled to a range of social protection measures catering for their well-being and that of their child. These can be divided in two categories: '*aide sociale*' (social assistance) and '*action sociale*' (social action), the former providing a legal framework of welfare rights and benefits and the latter consisting of complementary, discretionary measures that actively support the parenting function in a decentralised and preventive fashion.

Non-discriminatory social protection

Under the French social security system, social benefits are administered by a powerful quango, the *Caisse Nationale des Allocations Familiales* (CNAF) (National Family Allowance Fund), which steers a network of 123 regional branches (*Caisses des Allocations Familiales* or CAF) directly responsible for managing social benefits and assistance to welfare recipients. In 2004, the CNAF's total budget was €59.3 billion, which was distributed to 10 million beneficiaries out of which €3.1 billion was spent on 'social action' services.

One of the benefits funded by the CNAF is the *Allocation de Parent Isolé* (API), a benefit for single parents introduced in 1976, 10 years before the *Revenu Minimum d'Insertion* (RMI) and with which it shares the general objective of protecting vulnerable individuals and their families from economic hardship through a guaranteed minimum income financed through tax revenues.[13] The single-parent allowance is usually paid for a period of 12 months and no longer than the third birthday of the child to ensure minimum living standards and protection in the early childhood period. Young single parents and pregnant teenagers, regardless of their living arrangements, are legible for the API.

Under the API, lone parents receive a monthly flat allowance of €530.39 per month. On average, 12 to 15% of API recipients were teenage mothers throughout the 1990s. The youngest recipient was 13 and a half years old and the average entitlement period was 25 months (Chaupain-Guillot and Guillot, 2004). The longitudinal follow-up of teenage API recipients shows that teenagers aged under 18 are more likely to become recipients of the RMI when exiting the API, or re-entering the API, than those aged between 18 and 20. However, at the same time, their employment rate rises progressively to reach a similar level to the older cohorts: 5% of teenagers were employed when entering the API compared to almost 20% at the end of its spell, which does not warrant the claim that early motherhood inevitably leads to a welfare dependency trap (Chaupain-Guillot and Guillot, 2004).

In addition, teenage mothers can claim the *Prestation d'accueil du jeune enfant* (PAJE), which since January 2004 replaces the *Allocation pour jeune enfant* (APJE) and which is generally paid to parents who give up work to bring up a child under the age of three (this is often described as a 'labour-shedding' benefit). The payment of this allowance is linked to two stringent requirements: first, the pregnancy must be declared within the first 14 weeks of the pregnancy; second, the mother must agree to undergo eight compulsory medical visits and three compulsory visits for her child at eight days, 10 months and 24 months. If these conditions are met, the teenage mother can claim the allowance from the third month of her pregnancy and until her child reaches its third birthday. The basic rate is €165 per month and teenage API recipients are entitled to draw the PAJE. If they or their partner/husband draws an income, the PAJE is means-tested and the amount is revised accordingly.

The decentralisation laws of 1982 and 2003 have led to the growing significance of the local welfare regime referred to as the '*département providence*' (welfare county) by Lafore (2004). For example, a free 'social action' service known as *Protection maternelle et infantile* (PMI) (maternal and childhood protection) – which is similar to the Sure Start service in the UK – is placed under the overarching responsibility of the Ministry of Health and Social Protection and devolved to county councils. The PMI carries out medical prevention, detection of medical conditions and health education for future parents with children under six years of age known as '*veille sanitaire*' (sanitary watch). These services are essentially targeted at vulnerable families and include home visits. Around 40% of toddlers are regularly seen by PMI staff. In disadvantaged neighbourhoods, PMI centres are run by voluntary sector organisations such as the Red Cross with varying coverage between localities.

In the context of rising local welfarism, one further important aspect for teenage mothers is related to the regime of child protection, which was set up after World War Two (Daguerre, 2000). This regime consists of a judicial and an administrative branch. First, the judiciary system towards children and teenagers is split between penal justice (for juvenile delinquency) and civil justice (for children and teenagers at risk). Second, the administrative social protection system towards children, *Aide Sociale à l'Enfance* (ASE) (Social Assistance to Children) (labelled '*Assistance Publique*' until 1959), falls under the remit of the Ministry of Social Affairs, Employment and Solidarity and from 1984, it was further devolved to county councils, that is, to the president of the *Conseil Géneral* of each French *département*. The legislation established that the ASE exerts a preventive social action amongst families whose living conditions are at risk of endangering the health, security and morality of their children. Measures established either through the magistrate or through the ASE involve, among other things, placements of children and teenagers in a host family or a community hostel. Likewise, the law establishes that each *département* of France must have a *centre maternel* (maternal centre) to house isolated mothers until their child reaches its third birthday. The proportion of teenage mothers in independent housing is almost nil as they are not entitled to claim housing benefits (Chaupain-Guillot and Guillot, 2004). Hence, for the minority who for various reasons cannot stay under the parental roof, the availability of maternal centres is paramount.

There are currently 120 maternal centres that cater for 4,200 teenage mothers throughout France (Carpentier, 2003). These centres are publicly funded and managed either by the county council or by a voluntary sector organisation. Maternal centres adopt a holistic approach providing accommodation on site and in some rare cases, in an independent furnished flat. Efforts are made not to mix the teenagers who have decided to terminate their pregnancy with young mothers. The maternal centre's protective environment helps the mother bond with her child. Interdisciplinary teams of social workers provide psychological counselling, parenting and social skills and seek to re-establish contacts with the mother's family whenever possible. For example, fathers are invited to attend to develop ties with the child. Staff assist mothers with the search for suitable employment, training courses and independent housing. Once again, mirroring the overall stance discussed earlier, the objective is to facilitate smooth transitions in adult life. Here the welfare state clearly acts as a substitute to the family.

A small fraction of these maternal centres are dedicated entirely to teenage mothers and have an average intake of 15, while others have a mixed population of up to 50. Smaller centres appear to be more successful in providing the necessary support as staff can devote more attention to young mothers. Social workers are often under immense pressure and lack the necessary skills due to inadequate training. Compounded with low salaries, this makes recruitment and retention difficult (Carpentier, 2003). Moreover, centres run by the voluntary sector, which have been specifically created for this population, are unequally spread geographically and subjected to a demand that cannot be satisfied. The director of such a centre claims that for an intake capacity of 24 young mothers, the centre receives approximately 100 requests each year.[14]

In September 2003, the County Council of Seine-Saint-Denis – which registers, on average, 90 births to teenagers each year – opened a new centre in the municipality of Saint-Ouen, located in the northern outskirts of Paris – the *Maison Colette Coulon*. This was created to cater for the needs of teenage mothers who, because of a lack of local amenities, used to be sent away to maternal centres in Lille or Nantes. According to the county council's director of services for single-parent families who designed this project:

> 'A pregnant teenager is confronted with the social gaze, with that of the family, the school, and of society. Delocalising her would represent yet another institutional violence, isolating her even more and reinforcing her existential anxieties.'[15]

The *Maison Colette Coulon* has a team of 17 staff catering for 15 teenage mothers, the majority of whom are from South Africa. Great care was given to the forging of links between the centre and the main local institutions such as the hospital, the college, the PMI and the job centre.

As social services to families are devolved and coordination mechanisms between counties remain weak, the latter must voluntarily seek to exchange information. The authorities of the Seine-Saint-Denis county reported that neighbouring counties had approached them to seek information on the *Maison Colette Coulon* and that they had developed a series of meetings to transfer their experience and knowledge.

Furthermore, the possibility of developing innovative methods of prevention through transnational policy learning has recently been explored. The lack of specialist provision spurred the authorities of the Somme county in the North of France, where rates of teenage pregnancy are twice the national average, to launch an INTERREG project partly funded by the European Regional Development Fund (ERDF) in partnership with Kent County Council in the UK. This innovative project with a budget totalling €755,966 was named '*Parlez-moi d'amour*' (Let's talk about love) and ran between 2004 and 2006. It sought to move away from the 'technical/educational paradigm' that had hitherto overwhelmingly characterised approaches to teenage pregnancy (Arai, 2003) to pilot new preventive methods, which may then be further mainstreamed. These include new educational programmes focused on teenage values and perceptions of life and on the early detection of risks through the establishment of networks of health, educational and social services professionals. There is currently an important gap in this area and the increased emphasis on new methods of educational communication is a step in the right direction.

Conclusion

This chapter has argued that, in contrast to countries of the liberal welfare regime, France does not have a normative framework that explicitly addresses the risk of teenage pregnancy. This is precisely due to the fact that early childbearing is not labelled a 'social problem'. Rather, it is indirectly and more subtly addressed through the country's wide-ranging state-sponsored family policy. There are, however, important tensions in this welfare intervention model since the post-Fordist labour market clearly relegates single mothers and youth to its periphery. The resulting 'new social risks' (Bonoli, 2005) have meant that public authorities have started to pay more attention to youth, including teenage pregnancy and childbearing. This new focus is to be welcomed since, as we have seen, there is a stable core of teenagers who choose to become mothers. The reconfiguration of France's traditional universalist approach to the family may well be underway: individualised services, proximity networks and local dialogue are among the new buzzwords as illustrated by recent initiatives in the field of youth education, public health and women's rights. However, it remains to be seen whether this policy shift will indeed put the construction of individual paths in the forefront and make the future biopolitics of teenage reproductive behaviour not merely 'effective', but also more 'affective'.

Notes

[1] Although the *loi Neuwirth* was voted in 1967, it only came fully into force in 1974.

[2] The female-led 'second contraceptive revolution' is opposed to the 'first contraceptive revolution' in which birth control rested upon 'natural' methods (Ogino method, *coïtus interruptus*), which disempowered women (see Bozon, 2002). A well-known feminist battle that led to this second revolution was that of the infamously named '343 bitches' who publicly admitted to having undergone an abortion, a group of feminists which included celebrities such as Simone de Beauvoir, Françoise Sagan and Catherine Deneuve.

[3] The data from the INSEE is for 15- to 19-year-olds. The reproduction rate corresponds to the average number of live daughters that would be born to a hypothetical female birth cohort, which would be subjected to current age-specific fertility and

mortality rates. When adding the overseas departments and territories (known as the 'DOM-TOM'), in 2004, the reproduction rate was slightly higher at 4.43.

[4] This data must be set against the fact that the total population for England is currently 50 million against 59 million for France; in both instances, the population aged below 20 represents 19% of the total. France therefore has a higher population of girls aged below 16 than England.

[5] Interview with officials of the French Ministry of Health and Social Protection, 7 March 2005.

[6] The concept of '*insertion*' is used in French in the similar sense as that of '*inclusion*' in the Anglophone terminology, that is, as the opposite of '*exclusion*'. Hence, 'social inclusion' is translated in French using the expression '*insertion sociale*'.

[7] There is, however, no national dataset on ethnicity as this information is only recorded by individual hospitals.

[8] In March 2006, the official unemployment rate for those under the age of 25 was 22.1% against 9.5% for the whole population. It was 20.8% for males under the age of 25 and 23.9% for females under the age of 25 (source: INSEE, www.insee.fr).

[9] When created in 1956, it was first known as the *Mouvement pour la maternité heureuse* (the Movement for a Happy Motherhood) and became the MFPF in 1960. Today, the MFPF is still active in campaigns against all forms of sexist violence and harassment inflicted upon women.

[10] The *Conseil d'Etat* is one of the most traditional institutions of the French administration. It is the supreme court of administrative law and has a consultative function verifying the legality of Bills and Green Papers to be submitted to the Council of Ministers.

[11] Interview with a representative of the Directorate General of Social Affairs, 17 February 2005.

[12] The term *laïcité* refers to the idea that citizenship must explicitly rest upon a separation between the powers of the nation-state and

those held by the Church. In France, this principle is enshrined by law, notably in the Law on the separation between the State and Church of 9 December 1905 and in Article No 1 of the Constitution of the Fifth Republic (1958).

[13] There are eight different types of minimum income.

[14] Interview with the director of *Le Mardanson* (centre for teenage mothers), 8 March 2005.

[15] Interview with the director of services for single-parent families (*Pôle mère-enfant*), County Council of the Seine-Saint-Denis, 26 April 2005.

References

Aït El Cadi, H. (2003) 'Au féminin', in D. Le Breton (ed) *L'adolescence à risque*, Paris: Hachette Littératures, pp 200-15.

Amara, F. (2003) *Ni putes ni soumises*, Paris: La Découverte.

Arai, L. (2003) 'British Policy on Teenage Pregnancy and Childbearing: The Limitations of Comparisons with other European Countries', *Critical Social Policy*, vol 23, no 1, pp 89-102.

Bajos, N., Moreau, C., Leridon, H. and Ferrand, M. (2004) 'Pourquoi le nombre d'avortements n'a-t-il pas baissé en France depuis 30 ans?', *Populations & Sociétés*, no 407, Newsletter of the Institut National des Études Démographiques.

Barbier, J.C. and Théret, B. (2004) *Le nouveau système de protection sociale*, Paris: La Découverte.

Bellil, S. (2002) *Dans l'enfer des tournantes*, Paris: Denoël.

Boltanski, L. (2004) *La condition fœtale*, Paris: Gallimard.

Bonoli, G. (2005) 'The Politics of the New Social Policies: Providing Coverage against New Social Risks in Mature Welfare States', *Policy & Politics*, vol 3, no 3, pp 431-49.

Bozon, M. (2002) *Sociologie de la sexualité*, Paris: Nathan.

Brin, H. (2001) *Familles et insertion économique et sociale des adultes de 18 à 25 ans*, Paris: Conseil économique et social, Section des affaires sociales.

Carpentier, N. (2003) *Adosmamans: Le tiers et le lien*, Paris: Téraèdre.

Charbonneau, J. (2003) *Adolescentes et mères*, Laval: Presses de l'Université Laval.

Chaupin-Guillot, S. and Guillot, O. (2004) 'Le devenir des mineures bénéficiaires de l'allocation de parent isolé', *Recherches & Prévisions*, no 78, pp 67-75.

Chauvel, L. (1998) *Le destin des générations: Structure sociale et cohortes en France au vingtième siècle*, Paris: Presses Universitaires de France.

Cichelli, V. and Martin, C. (2004) 'Young Adults in France: Becoming Adult in the Context of an Increased Autonomy and Dependency', *Journal of Comparative Family Studies*, vol 35, no 4, pp 615-26.

Commaille, J., Strobel, P. and Villac, M. (2002) *La politique de la famille*, Paris: La Découverte.

Daguerre, A. (2000) 'Policy Networks in England and France: The Case of Child Care Policy', *Journal of European Public Policy*, vol 7, no 2, pp 244-60.

Daguet, F. (1999) 'Mamans après 40 ans', in Institut National de la Statistique et des Études Économiques (ed) *Données Sociales*, Paris: INSEE, pp 21-7.

Darroch, J., Frost, J. and Singh, S. (2001) *Teenage Sexual and Reproductive Behaviour in Developed Countries*, Occasional Report No. 3, New York, NY: The Allan Guttmacher Institute.

Dubet, C. (1987) *Jeunes en galère*, Paris: Fayard.

Duret, P. (1999) *Les jeunes et l'identité masculine*, Paris: Presses Universitaires de France.

Esping-Andersen, G. (1990) *The Three Worlds of Welfare Capitalism*, Oxford: Polity Press.

Fassin, D. and Memmi, D. (2004) *Le gouvernement des corps*, Paris: Editions de l'Ecole des Hautes Etudes en Sciences Sociales.

Fassin, E. (2001) 'Same Sex, Different Politics: Comparing and Contrasting Gay Marriages in France and the United States', *Public Culture*, vol 13, no 2, pp 215-32.

Faucher, P., Dappe, S. and Madelenat, P. (2002) 'Maternity in Adolescence: Obstetrical Analysis and Review of the Influence of Cultural, Socioeconomic and Psychological Factors in a Retrospective Study of 62 cases', *Gynécologie obstetrique et fertilité*, vol 30, no 12, pp 944-52.

Foucault, M. (2001) 'La naissance de la médecine sociale', in M. Foucault (ed) *Dits et écrits*, vol 2, Paris: Gallimard, pp 207-28.

Galland, O. (1997) *Sociologie de la jeunesse*, Paris: Armand Colin.

Galland, O. and Lambert, Y. (1993) *Les jeunes ruraux*, Paris: L'Harmattan.

Gauthier, X. (2002) *Naissance d'une liberté: Contraception, avortement, le grand combat des femmes au vingtième siècle*, Paris: Robert Laffont.

Giddens, A. (1992) *The Transformation of Intimacy: Sexuality, Love and Eroticism in Modern Society*, Cambridge: Cambridge Polity Press.

Harris, N. and Meredith, P. (eds) (2005) *Children, Education and Health: International Perspectives on Law and Policy*, Aldershot: Ashgate.

Iacub, M. (2004) *L'empire du ventre: Pour une autre histoire de la maternité*, Paris: Fayard.

Jaspard, M. (2005) *Sociologie des comportements sexuels* (2nd edition), Paris: La Découverte.

Kafé, H. and Brouard, N. (2000) 'Comment ont évolué les grossesses chez les adolescentes depuis vingt ans?', *Populations & Sociétés*, no 361, newsletter of the Institut National des Études Démographiques.

Knibiehler, Y. (1997) *La révolution maternelle. Femmes, maternité, citoyenneté de 1945 à nos jours*, Paris: Perrin.

Lacoste-Dujardin, C. (1992) *Yasmina et les autres de Nanterre et d'ailleurs: Filles de parents maghrébins en France*, Paris: La Découverte.

Lafore, R. (2004) 'La décentralisation de l'action sociale: l'irrésistible ascension du «département providence»', *Revue française des affaires sociales*, vol 58, no 4, pp 19-34.

Lagrange, H. (1999) *Les adolescents, le sexe et l'amour*, Paris: Syros.

Lagrange, H. and Lhomond, B. (eds) (1997) *L'entrée des jeunes dans la sexualité: Le comportement des jeunes dans le contexte du sida*, Paris: La Découverte.

Leridon, H. (1995) *Les enfants du désir*, Paris: Pluriel.

Le Van, C. (1998) *Les grossesses à l'adolescence*, Paris: L'Harmattan.

Lewis, J. and Knijn, T. (2002) 'The Politics of Sex Education Policy in England and Wales and in the Netherlands since the 1980s', *Journal of Social Policy*, vol 31, no 4, pp 669-94.

Maia, M. (2004) 'Relations amoureuses des jeunes de banlieue', *Agora*, no 35, pp 22-31.

Maillochon, F. (2001) 'Entrer en couple ou 'sortir ensemble', topographie intime des premières relations amoureuses', *Agora*, no 23, pp 35-50.

Marcault, G. and Pierre, F. (2001) 'Grossesse chez l'adolescente', *Revadosanté*, no 3, available at: www.revadosante.net/Article.php?M_ID=3018

Mathieu, L. (2000) *Prostitution et sida: Sociologie d'une épidémie et de sa prévention*, Paris: L'Harmattan.

Memmi, D. (2003) 'Qui contrôle la sexualité de nos enfants?', in M. Lacub and P. Maniglier (eds) *Famille en scènes*, Paris: Autrement, pp 40-7.

Minkenberg, M. (2003) 'The Policy Impact of Church-State Relations: Family Policy and Abortion in Britain, France and Germany', *West European Politics*, vol 26, no 1, pp 195-217.

Mossuz-Lavau, J. (2002) *Les lois de l'amour: Les politiques de la sexualité en France de 1950 à nos jours*, Paris: Payot.

Musick, J.S. (1993) *Young, Poor and Pregnant: The Psychology of Teenage Motherhood*, New Haven, CT: Yale University Press.

Pfau-Effinger, B. (2005) 'Culture and Welfare State Policies: Reflections on a Complex Interrelation', *Journal of European Social Policy*, vol 34, no 1, pp 3-20.

Prioux, F. (2004) 'L'évolution démographique récente en France', *Population*, no 5, pp 683-724.

Rey, C. (ed) (2000) *Les adolescents face à la violence*, Paris: Syros.

Rubi, S. (2005) *Les crapuleuses: Ces adolescentes déviantes*, Paris: Presses Universitaires de France.

TNS-SOFRES (2005) *Consultation des jeunes Ile-de-France* (Youth survey conducted on behalf of the Ile de France regional authorities), Montrouge, France. Technical summary available at: www.tns-sofres.com/etudes/pol/180405_jeunes_r.htm

UNICEF (United Nations Children's Fund) (2001) *A League Table of Teenage Births in Rich Nations*, Innocenti Report Card, No. 3, Florence: Innocenti Research Centre.

Uzan, M. (1998) *Rapport sur la prévention et la prise en charge des grossesses des adolescentes*, Paris: Ministère des Affaires Sociales.

Vilain, A. (2004) 'Les interruptions volontaires de grossesses en 2002' (Induced abortions in 2002), *Études et Résultats*, Newsletter no 348, Direction de la Recherche, des Études, de l'Évaluation et des Statistiques, Paris: Ministère de l'Emploi, du Travail et des Affaires et Ministère de la Santé et de la Protection Sociale.

SEVEN

Early motherhood in Italy: explaining the 'invisibility' of a social phenomenon

Elisabetta Pernigotti and Elisabetta Ruspini

Introduction

This chapter focuses on the peculiarities of early motherhood in Italy.[1] Italy is undoubtedly an interesting case study as it displays one of the lowest teenage birth rates within the countries of the Organisation of Economic Co-operation and Development (OECD). With a birth rate of 6.6 children per 1,000 women aged 15 to 19, it ranks in sixth position – behind Korea, Japan, Switzerland, the Netherlands and Sweden – in the United Nations Children's Fund's (UNICEF's) league table of teenage births (Singh and Darroch, 2000; UNICEF, 2001). This fact can be explained through the mix of continuity and diversity that characterises Italian society: traditional behavioural patterns and family relationships still exist alongside dramatic socioeconomic changes and rapid modernisation.

Italy has one of the lowest divorce rates in the European Union (EU) although the number of divorces and separations is slowly rising. Despite the growing trend towards the postponement of first marriages and the increase of out-of-wedlock parenthood – also observable in the rest of Europe – marriage continues to represent the prevalent form of union and parenthood is placed almost solely within it. This norm is accompanied by a delayed entry into adult sexual life both compared with Europeans of the same age and with previous generations. Moreover, birth control is still entrusted to relatively traditional methods (De Sandre et al, 1999).

Italy is indeed characterised by a specific arrangement between the family, the labour market and the welfare state in which the family plays a predominant role. Especially in the southern part of the country, the network of social relationships between extended family, kin and neighbourhood – which rests upon personal connections, affective links, networks of exchange and a non-cash economy – still constitutes a safety net against poverty and social exclusion. Even in families with a single breadwinner, young adults (both male and female) tend to reside with their parents until they get married, even when they earn an independent income. This prolonged cohabitation is often seen as the outcome of long study periods, high housing costs and the lack of employment opportunities. However, explanations referring to the lack of jobs as the main reason for this prolonged cohabitation are insufficient and fail to grasp the true nature of the problem, all the more so since this phenomenon is more frequent in Northern Italy, where youth unemployment is less concentrated. Instead, reference must be made to the transformation of relationships within the family; children enjoy more or less total freedom in their families of origin and, in addition, are free from many economic and material responsibilities.

What we are witnessing is a shift in biographical chronologies, with fewer immediate consequences than in the past: entry into the job market and getting married do not necessarily take place at the same time and take a relatively long period of time to come into effect, and this time, in the case of Italy, is spent in the parental home. This phenomenon is known as the '*famiglia lunga*' (long family) (Scabini and Donati, 1988). Within a context of growing uncertainty, fragmentation, diversity and risk, the 'ideal' transition to adulthood seems to be the outcome of a sequence of events that ends with the decision of leaving home 'at the right time', having successfully finished one's studies, started a high-quality and financially rewarding job, found a 'good' partner and, possibly, legalised the union. Young women in Italy are particularly well aware that education will allow them to lead a satisfactory life. They achieve higher educational performance and have higher expectations regarding their professional careers than older generations of women. Various research studies show that, for girls, the lengthening of time spent in education brings much greater professional rewards compared to those that accrue to boys (see, for example, Schizzerotto et al, 1995; Bianco, 1997).

In a context marked by the prolonging of youth and adolescence, young mothers embody significant contradictions, mixing the needs of adult life and those of adolescence. They accelerate and, at the same time, overlap the events that accompany the transition into adult life.

They have brought forward the reproductive function: motherhood precedes the completion of their education, their entry into the labour market and the establishment of an autonomous household. This 'wrong' sequence of events is the cause of their vulnerability. The lives of young mothers seem to summarise an important feature of the transitions to adulthood as they appear today: their growing complexity, which creates both greater spheres of freedom for those involved and greater risks of dispersion of identity (Ruspini, 2005).

As well as providing a discussion of the specificities of early motherhood in Italy, this chapter has two further aims. First, to provide a detailed and critical analysis of the social policies available to young mothers. Second, to explore the effectiveness of welfare provision reserved for young mothers, particularly for young *lone* mothers, in a Mediterranean welfare state. Overall, welfare policies and training strategies targeted at lone mothers are scarce (Ruspini, 2002). This scarcity is linked to the low social visibility of teenage mothers, which consequently delays the implementation of focused intervention strategies. However, if the numerical insignificance somewhat explains the delay in developing a rights-based social policy framework, young lone mothers remain 'invisible' to policymakers because of entrenched cultural obstacles that prevent their needs from being voiced.

Due to the fact that teenage childbearing and motherhood is an uncommon phenomenon in Italy, for the purpose of this chapter, we will extend our discussion of early motherhood to include young mothers under the age of 25.

Early motherhood in Italy

According to Lagrée (1997), the socio-historical construction of youth can help explain the variations between individual biographies across various national transition patterns. Among the European social transition markers, three elements are usually considered: entry into the labour market, the departure from the family home, and the beginning of married life. National transition patterns contribute to establishing a timing schedule according to which certain events are deemed to be either too early or too late.

We find it useful to approach the Italian case through the lens of social transition patterns into adulthood because early motherhood is occurring within a set of social norms that serve to define such lifecourse transition patterns at the national level. Thus, the dynamics that affect the transition from youth to adulthood must be considered.

In addition, young people are undoubtedly influenced by adults when constructing their image of 'adult life'. Since young people are tied to society by adults, through family relationships, neighbourhood communities and other social bonds, understanding the reproductive behaviour of young Italian girls thus requires some understanding of the meaning of womanhood in the Italian context. After all, the 'adult world' participates in the multifaceted construction of young girls' identities, providing models on what womanhood is and is not.

If the low rate of teenage motherhood stands out when compared to other countries of the industrialised world, when viewed in the context of the Italian pattern of transition to adulthood it is congruent with the normative social framework. This chapter focuses on young mothers – as opposed to young parents – in the understanding that when births occur out of wedlock, it is clearly a 'female matter', which involves an extended female role and increased responsibilities. It is striking that fatherhood received scant attention in the context of adolescent parenthood. Nonetheless, we consider this societal norm as culturally embedded in contemporary yet fluctuating gender relations that prioritise and distinguish motherhood from fatherhood. These lead to a devaluation of fatherhood and its obligations, especially in the case of adolescent parents, which is confirmed by sometimes alarmist public attitudes towards low fertility rates. For example, the former President of the Republic, Carlo Azeglio Ciampi, argued in a Women's Day Message of 7 March 2004 that 'the real problem of Italy is the empty cribs.... The destiny of a society with few children and few mothers is to disappear' (*La Repubblica*, 7 March 2004). Women, it seems, should feel guilty for seeking a stable financial situation before giving birth while men's social position is not particularly criticised in relation to fertility,

Table 7.1: Fertility indicators for Italy and the EU15 and EU25 countries

	Mean age of women at childbirth (2001)	Births outside wedlock (2002) (%)	Mean age at first marriage for women (2000)	Mean age at first marriage for men (2000)	Fertility rate (2003) (%)
Italy	30.3	10.8	27.4	30.4	1.29
EU15	29.4	30.6	27.5	29.9	1.52
EU25	29.1	29.2	27.0	29.3	1.48

Source: Eurostat demographic indicators (2005)

this despite males being on average two years older than females when entering marriage and parenthood (see Table 7.1).

Moreover, differences in a couple's status (partnered or married) and age (teenage parents or older) largely account for the relative weight given to motherhood and fatherhood responsibilities, including the acceptance of a father's absenteeism in the case of young fathering, and a 'female intergenerational share' of mothering. Arguably, men's responsibilities for fatherhood are linked to their marital status and not to their offspring, which is symptomatic of the social differentiation made between what is regarded as legitimate and illegitimate parenthood. Gendered adolescent parenting practices, then, provide a clear indication of the social construction of fatherhood as much as for motherhood.

Sexual and family behaviour in the light of religious morality

Religion is often used to identify the Mediterranean welfare state (Trifiletti, 1999; Ferrera, 2005). Indeed, Italy retains a close connection with the Catholic culture, if not just for the unavoidable geographical proximity of the Vatican. In compliance with Catholic principles, marriage continues to provide the basis for family formation, which in turn determines women's social status (Trifiletti, 1999). Only 10.8% of births occur outside wedlock in Italy compared to 30.6% in the EU (see Table 7.1).

Moreover, a national survey of children and adolescents revealed that 54.9% are in favour of divorce and 49% are opposed to abortion (Telefono Azzurro – Eurispes, 2004).[2] Within the context of traditional marriage laws, it can be a stigma for a girl or young woman to have a child because it puts her at a disadvantage in terms of accessing a 'good' husband.

As already mentioned in the introduction to this chapter, the Italian familial relationship between children and parents involves strong emotional bonds characterised by 'intensity' and 'localism' (see, for example, Naldini, 2003). According to a qualitative study of intergenerational conflicts throughout adolescence carried out in Paris, Rome and Montreal, Italy has more frequent conflicts compared to France and Canada (Claes et al, 2003). This is because, following traditional patriarchal rules, Italian girls are placed under stricter control than boys. The role of confidante is commonly ascribed to the mother. According to a national survey on adolescents' sexual knowledge conducted by the *Istituto Superiore di Sanità* (National Institute of

Table 7.2: Sexual knowledge and the role of confidante in Italy (multiple choice questions) (%)

	Question 1 - What sources did they use to obtain information about sexual matters?			Question 2 - Who did they last approach to speak to about their body's sexual transformations?		
	Boys	Girls	Total	Boys	Girls	Total
Mother	23.5	55.2	38.5	32.6	76.5	53.5
Father	33.4	7.6	21.1	34.0	10.6	22.8
Friends	49.5	49.6	49.5	58.5	50.3	54.6
Television	7.4	3.6	5.6	30.2	19.2	25.0
Doctor	24.5	31.0	27.6	10.4	7.9	9.2
School	12.3	10.6	11.5	32.0	33.2	32.6
Brother/ sister	12.2	14.8	13.5	9.0	12.9	10.8
Books/ magazine	20.0	24.2	22.0	23.9	31.3	27.4
Magazine for adults	13.6	4.4	9.2	20.3	3.8	12.4
Other	2.4	3.5	2.9	2.6	2.7	2.6

Source: Donati et al (2000)

Health) (Donati et al, 2000), the mother is by far the most common first reference point for sexual matters for girls (see Table 7.2).

The survey also shows that girls' sexuality is represented in association with risk and fear, not pleasure and happiness. Adolescents' vision of sexuality is coupled with the danger of pregnancy, sexually transmitted diseases and paedophilia. This vision is further amplified by relatively scarce, if not negative, information on sexual matters provided by schools. Statistics on Italian youngsters' sexual activity validate this hypothesis. The age gap between girls and boys at the time of first sexual intercourse has narrowed. However, gender differences in moral rules are significant along the Italian peninsula, being stricter in the South, lenient in the centre, and liberal in the North (Donati et al, 2000).[3]

Unsafe and illegal sex practices

Sex education is strikingly absent from the school curriculum and abortion rates are very low. Since 1977, the family planning centres known as '*consultori*' have been offering free medical consultation on matters of reproductive health. In 1978, the reform on family law legalised abortion and contraception, although it only came into effect in 1981. Since 1982 (234,801 cases for all ages), abortion has been decreasing. This is surprising when viewed in light of youngsters' sexual practices: in 2003, 60% of young people under the age of 18 admitted to having unprotected sex (Donati et al, 2000).

In 2003, Italy recorded 132,795 abortion cases (9.5 per 1,000 women aged 15 to 49). Even so, the abortion cases were concentrated among the youngest: among those under the age of 20, the rate rose by 5 cases per 1,000. More alarmingly, the abortion rate of the growing immigrant female population was 3.5 times higher than that of Italian women (Donati et al, 2000).

Tracing the linkages between fertility and the labour market

Since the 1960s, young motherhood has decreased in unison with the overall Italian fertility rate. Comparing Italian fertility data with that of the EU clarifies the gendered dynamics of living in a risk society, and in particular the growing delay in giving birth. Italy has continuously displayed very low fertility rates since the mid-1980s (Saraceno, 2003).

Italy is far from being an exception in Europe with regard to low fertility. The 'birth-rate blues' is shared with other Southern European countries, with the German-speaking countries as well as with some new EU member states. However, Italy (together with Spain) *is* exceptional in having a strong pattern of protracted reliance ('economic housing') on the family of origin: around 85% of young people aged under 25 still reside with their parents (Sabbadini, 1999). According to Eurostat (2004a), in 1996, both in Italy and Spain, three quarters of young people living independently were also young parents. This fact is not surprising given that housing benefits for young people are non-existent. Hence, young parents could in principle choose single living as a rational choice in order to draw the single parent allowance, although as will be argued later, its provision varies significantly across the Italian territory.

The rapid pace of economic growth following World War Two led to a decline in fertility (Saraceno, 1984). After centuries of rural poverty, Italian families enjoyed a new quality of life. New patterns of womanhood appeared. The large family unit that used to prevail started to disappear as a symbol of the Italian family.

The postponement of childbearing is undoubtedly one of the major dimensions of demographic change largely driven by high female unemployment rates and a fragmented welfare state. So far, women's limited involvement in active labour market policies has not helped lower one of the highest EU female unemployment rates. Unemployment is higher in the South, where the female unemployment rate for 2002 reached 26.4% in contrast to 14.1% for males, this in spite of a lower female activity rate in the South (29.2%) compared to the Northern female activity rate of 41.9%. This situation is all the more worrying as Italian unemployment is coupled with the highest female inactivity rate in the EU. The gender gap is even more striking when compared to male activity rates of 60.3% for Southern and 63.1% for Northern male workers (Bank of Italy, 2004). Additionally, women are nearly twice more likely as men to become long-term unemployed. According to Eurostat (2005), in 2001, women's long-term unemployment was 8% and men's was 4.5%.

Youth unemployment is characterised by similar gender divisions with 32.2% of females under the age of 25 officially unemployed in 2001 as opposed to 23.2% of males. This represents a gap of almost 10%. There is no doubt that the risk of unemployment is affecting Italian females' transition into adulthood. Young women's search for autonomy therefore consists of combating its opposite, namely the risk of dependency arising from unemployment. Confirming this hypothesis, young Italian women are increasingly involved in education at higher levels, performing better than men, clearly displaying a strategy to prevent the risk of unemployment (OECD, 2005).

Motherhood without economic security and without higher education is not considered a distinctive marker of adulthood in Italy. It is thus clear that the Italian transition pattern to adulthood takes a relatively longer time to be effected when compared to other Western countries.

The Italian welfare state

Italy is seen by Esping-Andersen as an 'underdeveloped' model of welfare state or capitalist form (Esping-Andersen, 1990). Implicitly rejecting this hierarchical assessment of Italy, several authors (among others, Ferrera, 1993, 2005; Leibfried, 1993; Trifiletti, 1999; Naldini, 2003) have underlined the idiosyncracies of the Italian welfare state within the Southern welfare model. According to Leibfried (1993), 'Latin Rim' countries have in common the absence of a minimum social income and an absence of the right to welfare. Thus, the family has a welfare function.

The Italian welfare state supports the familial structure of society and is based upon occupational status (Trifiletti, 1999). In fact, the labour market and social protection systems favour the protection of those in the labour market at the expense of those outside the labour market. Moreover, at 0.3%, Italy's expenditure on housing and family policies is the lowest of the EU15 member states, the average EU expenditure standing at 3.6% (Eurostat, 2004a). This lack of public provision is consistent with the extended cohabitation practice described earlier, which places the responsibilities for looking after children within the confines of kin relationships. Parents are bound by law to support their children according to Article 147 of the Civil Code, which refers to the obligation of maintenance, upbringing and education of children. Yet not only parents, but also sisters, brothers and relatives are legally responsible for the maintenance of the child, beyond the residential boundary of the household (Articles 433, 439, Civil Code) (Naldini, 2003). If parents do not have enough resources to meet their obligations, relatives are under the obligation to provide substitute parental means for the children (Article 148, Civil Code). This form of solidarity between family and children is 'socially translated' for men into a breadwinning responsibility and for women, into a caregiving responsibility (Naldini, 2003). In 2003, 37% of women of working age were officially declared inactive because of their involvement in the care for another person on a full-time basis (Bettio and Plantanega, 2004). Despite many references to the 'family', the fact is plain that most of the welfare duties are performed by women.

The high proportion of public spending on old-age pensions and unemployment insurance compared to family and social inclusion policies shows that state intervention is mainly designed to respond to breadwinners' needs, hence to men (Naldini, 2003). Trifiletti (1999) sheds light on how the Mediterranean welfare state, by precluding motherhood-friendly policies, contributes to maintaining high activity rates among lone mothers. Moreover, delayed childbearing is clearly related to the lack of part-time employment opportunities. In 2003, 9.9% of the Italian working population was in part-time employment, which compares to an EU average of 12.8% (Eurostat, 2004a). Thus, Italy, as all Mediterranean countries, has an important gendered feature in determining women's social position: women need to be both married housewives and workers – in the labour market and in the marriage market (Trifiletti, 1999).

Additionally, the lack of universal cash benefits means that the cost of raising a child is often associated with child poverty. Child poverty is four times higher in the South than in the North, which is not surprising as unemployment is also higher in the South

(Telefono Azzurro – Eurispes, 2004). Since child care provision is under the responsibility of municipalities, it remains limited: in 2001, it only covered 6% of the child population aged under three (Eurostat, 2004b). With this in mind, it is difficult to understand why the fertility decline is mostly attributed to women's behavioural patterns. Teenage pregnancy would strongly undermine the opportunity for the adolescent mother to gain autonomy since she would have no other choice than to permanently rely on the family for her and her child's welfare. An unwanted consequence of early motherhood, then, would be the extension of family control to the detriment of individual freedom of choice.

Another specific feature of the Italian welfare state is its territorial fragmentation. This uneven geography has important consequences for young mothers since welfare provision for children and single mothers occurs through the provinces (Ruspini, 2000). In 2004, 22.4% of single parents were living in poverty in the South compared to 5.9% in the North (Istat, 2004).

Young lone mothers and social policies

The purpose of this section is to reflect upon the policy discourse and the main options regarding lone mothers – and particularly young lone mothers – in the Italian context. Lone-parent families have only been the subject of study since the mid-1980s (Golini et al, 1987; Menniti and Palomba, 1988). Lone mothers remain an invisible, suppressed group (Bimbi, 2000). Due to the crucial role played by the family in the process of social reproduction, the Italian welfare system has no particular reasons to protect them.

In Italy, there is no national specific policy of support for lone parents, even if they may receive preferential treatment under more general provisions, such as nursery and child care places. Lone mothers may also benefit from family and maternity allowances, from partial or total exemption from medical care costs and, until recently, from the *Reddito Minimo di Inserimento* (Minimum Income Support) – introduced experimentally in 1998 and abolished by the Berlusconi government in 2003, a point that we will return to later.

As argued earlier, Italian social policy is oriented towards the continued existence of the 'traditional family', which is based on the assumption that women still offer their services as caregivers. It also involves the 'dramatisation' of personal resources invested by women and a widespread support network provided by the extended family (Saraceno, 1994; Mingione, 2001). While it is true that Italian lone mothers are more likely to work full time than married mothers, their presence in the labour market is heavily dependent on reallocating their caregiving work to older women: mothers or mothers-in-law who assist them with care activities such as the raising of children. The mother's greater responsibility in child care is also confirmed in legal practice, when deciding on the custody of children in divorce or separation proceedings:[4] in 2003, in 86% of cases of both divorce and separation, children under the age of 18 are entrusted to their mother. In both cases percentages are over 89% when the children are less than six years old. Fathers are given exclusive custody in 6.6% of cases, but this percentage rises if the child is older (Istat, 2003).

The absence of both political debate on the subject of lone mothers and welfare policies concerning them should be placed within the framework of the general lack of family policies, which is a persistent feature of the post-war period (De Grazia, 1992; Bimbi, 1997; Bimbi and Della Sala, 1998; Saraceno, 1998). The reasons for this lack are manifold. We have already argued that the legislation on caring obligations was accompanied by the state's residual responsibility for family welfare. In addition, we must recall that, for the first and only time in Italian history, Fascism had produced policies explicitly encouraging births, centred on lone mothers. Post-war governments may have attempted to disassociate themselves from Fascist policies by neglecting this area. Moreover, for a long time, Italy has thought of itself as too fertile. Therefore, any measure that may be suspected as being pro-natalist (for example universal child allowances) is denounced not only as Fascist, but as encouraging births that are not needed at all, especially within the poorest groups. Finally, we must recall the conflicting values which founded the political division of a country which, up to the fall of the Berlin Wall in 1989, had both the largest Catholic Party (in addition to hosting the Vatican) and the largest Communist Party in the Western world.

From Fascist legislation to the welfare services provided by the provinces

The Fascist period saw the first and only systematic attempt, in the history of Italy, of explicit categorical and pro-natalist family policies aimed at mothers, and at lone mothers in particular (De Grazia, 1992; Saraceno, 1998; Bimbi, 2000). Between 1923 and 1934, important regulations were introduced on the subject of assistance to the poor. As a result of these laws, the Province became, and still is, the sole institution expressly entrusted with competence on the subject of lone mothers, as it is required to guarantee, directly or indirectly, interventions aimed at the 'illegitimate and exposed; mothers and children who need assistance, who are abandoned or face the risk of being abandoned'. These innovations contributed to create some sort of safeguard of minors and lone mothers, even if clearly aimed at social control and at raising the birth rate (Bordin and Ruspini, 2000, pp 135-9).

More specifically, Regio Decreto Legislativo (legislative decree) no 798 of 8 May 1927 provided regulations for assistance to illegitimate children who had been abandoned or who risked being abandoned. The institution in charge of these duties was the Province, and for this purpose a considerable number of laws was issued, the greater part of which still produce their effects today. According to Article 1of the Decree, the assistance service was entrusted, under the direction and supervision of *Opera Nazionale per la Protezione della Maternità e dell'Infanzia* (ONMI) (National Maternity and Child Welfare Organisation),[5] to the provincial administration:

> which will provide, either by granting adequate benefits
> to mothers who are nursing or raising children, or by
> providing accommodation and support of the children
> in foundling hospitals ... ensuring to recover them,
> whenever possible, along with the mothers when they
> are nursing, or provide for placing them in foster homes
> or external nursing.

The following categories were entitled to assistance: abandoned children; the children of unknown persons found in the territory of the Province; children born in the municipalities of the Province from illegitimate alliances and reported to the registry as the children of unknown persons; every child born from illegitimate alliances and only recognised by the mother, if she could prove her poverty and moreover provide for nursing and raising her child herself (Article 4).

After the fall of Fascism, the management of the assistance granted to unmarried mothers appeared uncertain in terms of regulations, stratified and fragmented. As to initiatives in favour of illegitimate minors and lone mothers, the Provinces[6] have for all intents and purposes, essentially all over the country, remained in charge of such services and their direct management. The current legislation identifies the following categories as addressees of provincial services: abandoned minors; children under 18 of unknown parents; minors born outside wedlock and recognised only by the mother when the latter is in need; minors aged 18 belonging to needy families; needy expectant mothers without family support; mothers (with children aged up to five) in need and without family support. The assistance supplied by the Province demands as *condition sine qua non* the existence of a condition of need generically defined as 'absence of sufficient resources', 'belonging to needy families', 'state of poverty'. Lone mothers therefore receive relief only on the basis of an evaluation of their economic situation and income, and not on the basis of a fuller consideration of their specific needs.

Minimum Income Support

Italy is still far from having a universalistic type of system of safeguard and assistance. The introduction of the *Reddito minimo di inserimento* (RMI) (Minimum Income Support) by legislative decree no 237 in 1998 signalled some positive steps in this direction. However, the Berlusconi government abolished the RMI in 2003 while it was still in the process of being piloted and contemplated the idea of replacing it with an alternative measure, the *Reddito di ultima istanza*.[7] It was argued that individual eligibility cannot be identified through central social security systems and that local and regional agencies, and not central government, should be entrusted with the task of allocating the minimum income to individuals since they are better informed of individual and local labour market circumstances (Italian Government, 2003). Thus, even today, in spite of the programmed experimentation of the RMI, social assistance in Italy remains categorical and a responsibility of the municipalities not only in terms of implementation, but in the very large margins of autonomy in relation to the magnitude of the expense and the entitlements recognised on a local level.

The RMI is aimed at fighting poverty and social exclusion 'through the support of the economic and social conditions of persons exposed to the risk of social exclusion and in the meantime not able to provide, due to psychological, physical and social circumstances, for the support of themselves and their children (Article 1 of legislative decree no 237). As the second paragraph of Article 1 puts it, 'the Minimum Income Support consists of initiatives aimed at pursuing the social integration and economic independence of the persons and families benefiting from it, through customised programmes and money transfers aimed at supplementing the income'.

In particular, the RMI is guaranteed to individuals who do not have any income or whose income is below the poverty threshold (established for 1998 as Itl. 500,000 – around €250 per month for a person living alone and determined on the basis of the equivalency scale enclosed with the legislative decree for family units of different sizes). The RMI is principally intended for persons who support minor children (or disabled children). However, no explicit reference is made to lone mothers as persons entitled to the benefit.

The income in question is the sum of the amounts earned by the family unit comprising the applicant, the persons living together with the latter and those considered as supported by the applicant (Article 6). Persons entitled to the RMI are moreover required not to own any assets, either movable assets, such as cars, or real estate properties. These prerequisites must be verified year by year. Persons who take care of children under three years of age (or disabled persons) or participate in retraining or professional training courses are exempted from the obligatory registration with the employment office, which documents their availability for work, something which on the contrary applies to all other persons of working age, if unemployed and able to work (Article 7). Particular importance is attributed, along with payments in cash, to social integration measures aimed at overcoming the exclusion of the individuals and the families through the promotion of individual abilities and the economic independence of persons (Article 9).

Allowances for the family unit and for maternity

No measure analogous to the allowance for children paid in other countries exists in Italy. Rather, first, an allowance is paid to the family unit (*Assegno per il nucleo familiare*), which represents a contribution intended for employees and equivalent categories on low incomes (working employees, unemployed people entitled to benefits, former workers receiving unemployment benefits, workers who have been laid off or are employed in socially useful projects, pensioners and former employees), which rather represents a measure similar to the English *family credit* or the US *earned income tax credit*: it supplements a modest income on the basis of a triple criterion: status of worker (employee), income threshold and family size. About half of those who receive this benefit are pensioners. As of 1 January 1999, the allowance is also payable to the separate administration of self-employed workers, which includes temporary workers, door-to-door salespeople and freelance professionals.

The amount is determined on the basis of the composition of the family unit and its income. At the time of writing, it may vary from €10.33 – in the case of family units without children and without disabled members, with an annual family income not exceeding €20,325.10 – to €965.26 in the case of family units comprising seven persons *with a single parent*, at least one minor child, at least one disabled member and a family income per year not exceeding €23,841.18. It is only due if the sum of the income obtained by the family unit from employment, pensions or social security contributions amounts to at least 70% of the total income of the family.

Second, a maternity allowance (*Assegno di maternità*) of €283.92 per month can be granted for a maximum period of five months . It is paid to mothers who are resident Italian citizens (or who have a work permit), who are not entitled to the maternity allowance paid by the social security institution and whose annual income is below €29,596.45 per family unit with three members. The maternity allowance is granted by the municipalities and paid by the Istituto Nazionale Previdenza Sociale (INPS) (National Institute for Social Security), as of the date of childbirth. Municipalities are obliged to inform those who are eligible, inviting them to certify or declare possession of the prerequisites at the moment the child is entered in the municipal registry.

Early childhood policies

The policies aimed at children are closely linked to the well-being of lone mothers, as they may to a greater or lesser extent facilitate the conciliation between reproductive and productive tasks.

The vulnerability to situations of economic deprivation and social exclusion characterising lone mothers (as compared to other categories of women such as 'non-mothers' or 'non-lone mothers') is mainly due to the phenomenon known as '*doppia presenza*' ('double presence'), that is, the simultaneous assumption of the two roles of *caregiver* and *breadwinner*. Only if care services are diffused in the territory and also economically accessible does it become possible for the mother to look for, find and keep a job. On the other hand, a mother may stay at home and take care of the child only if she can benefit from some sort of public aid that will guarantee a dignified standard of living to her family.

In Italy, care services are distinguished on the basis of two variables: availability and costs. While government-run nursery schools, as outlined by law 444/68, guarantee universal access (in fact, this service is only partially paid for by the families; it is available all over the country and to almost 90% of children from three to six years of age), the crèches, created some years later (law 1044/71), are services available on individual request and thus paid for by the families on the basis of the family income (Simoni, 2000, pp 92-3). Pursuant to the law the municipality may charge the user with part of the cost (30%), but it is important to underline that some categories of users may obtain exemptions according to a series of cases that vary from municipality to municipality.

A brief analysis confirms that there are no particular difficulties for lone mothers with children in the three to six age bracket. In fact, enrolment and attendance at the nursery school is free, while canteen service is guaranteed with a contribution from the families (the provincial council determines the extent of the contribution and any criteria for total or partial exemption from its payment). If the school should be temporarily unable to accept all children applying for enrolment, certain priorities are respected. In the Autonomous Province of Trento, for instance, priority is granted to children whose attendance at the school is necessary due to the work activities or impediments of the parents, or due to specific socio-educational motives; in the Municipality of Florence, disabled children, and children for whom the relevant welfare services have forwarded documentation to the kindergarten proving their difficult circumstances or socio-cultural risk, are prioritised. Apparently, even if the category of lone mothers is never (or almost never) explicitly mentioned, these conditions should guarantee their priority if the available places are insufficient.[8]

In contrast, the situation is more complicated for children under three years of age. In fact, crèches have not been created with the intention of guaranteeing a generalised service; it therefore becomes crucial to ascertain whether lone mothers can or cannot count on a privileged position in the classification lists for assignation of places.

A review conducted by the authors of internet sites concerning regulations for crèches in different municipalities in Italy has revealed that, in most cases, no channels are reserved for the children of lone mothers: the lists are prepared on the basis of different factors such as registration as residents in the municipality, age of the child, and the composition and income of the family. The financial contribution charged to the families is differentiated according to their socioeconomic circumstances, and features benefits or exceptions. As a rule, the assignment of points in the classification list also takes place on the basis of employment circumstances,[9] the workplace and working hours of each parent, the number and age of the children they support. However, if the parents are separated and/or divorced, the points are, as a rule, doubled.

Only in a very few cases are specific references made to the category of 'lone mothers'. For instance, the Municipality of Pisa establishes priority for those who prove, by presenting certification issued by the local health services, the existence of serious problems of a medical or psychological kind on the part of the child and/or the family unit, and secondarily, of lone parents (lone mother, lone father, widow/ widower) who actually live alone with their son/daughter. Generally speaking, the certification issued by the social assistant serves to obtain priority for purposes of enrolment (regardless of the employment situation of the mother/parent), provided one proves it is necessary for the 'best interests of the child'. Access to crèches is thus guaranteed for the children of working mothers, for children belonging to needy families, and sometimes also to those of lone mothers (divorced or unmarried) (Simoni, 2000, pp 92-3).

Training policies

Previous research (Trivellato, 2002) revealed a lack of training strategies specifically designed for lone mothers, young or otherwise.[10] The main empirical evidence comes from a small survey whose aim was to ascertain if and where lone mothers were present among the actual or potential beneficiaries of professional training courses organised directly or indirectly by Italian regions.[11] It clearly emerged that the scarcity of strategies specifically oriented towards the training and placement of young lone mothers is associated with the poor social visibility of the phenomenon, which consequently hinders the implementation of focused intervention strategies.

Concluding comments

Teenage mothers – like lone mothers – are not the subject of any explicit policy discourse in Italy. As a social group, they represent an unexplored issue in sociological analysis. Indeed, today, both teenage and lone motherhood remain of little interest for political debate and invisible subjects in Italian social policies.

In the current Italian welfare scenario, almost no specific measures focus on young mothers, a category that is included in the regulations only as part of larger and more general categories, as for instance 'the poor', 'needy persons', and so on. The prerequisite for any social intervention is never, therefore, the recognition of a right, but rather the existence of a condition of need. Moreover, access to benefits is concealed behind the rights of the child, even if childhood protection depends on the legal and social status of the mother. Finally, support measures specifically oriented towards lone parents are almost always means-tested.

In cases of youth maternity, the Italian welfare system forces dependency onto the young mother, keeping her in the social position of a youth much longer than would otherwise have been the case. This notwithstanding the fact that social policies may only be effective when linked intrinsically to a more comprehensive supply of care, guiding young mothers towards adulthood and enabling them to organise a 'plan for living'. For example, the growing experience of lone parenthood among migrant women demands decisive change in intervention models. The prevention of the dependency risk must necessarily combine active re-inclusion: educational/training activities, assistance, the development of self-esteem, guidance towards autonomy, preparation for motherhood and adulthood, and the recovery, activation and enhancement of support networks.

Notes
[1] While this chapter is the outcome of shared reflections, Elisabetta Pernigotti wrote the second and third sections; Elisabetta Ruspini wrote the introduction, fourth section and conclusion.

[2] National survey on childhood and adolescence in Italy, conducted among a sample of 6,276 youngsters aged between seven and 19 across Italy.

[3] Random survey conducted among 6,532 pupils aged 13 to 15 in 11 Italian regions (see Donati et al, 2000).

[4] For more details on legal arrangements for the custody of children, see Andreotti et al (2002).

[5] ONMI was created in 1925 and abolished in 1975. It was divided into provincial federations and municipal institutions and had various tasks. The most important were those concerning the safeguard of the maternity of working women (Rdl 22-3-34 n. 654), the assistance and safeguard of abandoned illegitimate children (Rdl 8-5-27 n. 798; Rdl 29-12-27 n. 2822), school assistance (law n. 17 of 3-1-29) and the safeguard of work and of the child (law n. 653 of 26-4-34).

[6] Today, the Province plays two roles: first, it is a decentralised arm for the delivery of government services and houses, in some instances certain peripheral government bodies. Second, it is a public territorial body entrusted with general functions of territorial coordination and planning.

[7] In 2003, 42,000 families and 185,000 persons in 306 Italian Communes benefited from the RMI. The general election of April 2006, which saw Silvio Berlusconi lose his seat of Prime Minister to Romano Prodi, the centre-left leader, is likely to impact upon the legislation over the minimum income support and, more generally, over welfare provision.

[8] See www.provincia.trento.it/materna/SCUOLA.htm

[9] A delicate issue is raised at this point: the tendency to prioritise working mothers (or more generally speaking, working parents), presuming that those who are unemployed have chosen this state and are thus able to and have the time to care for their child, actually tends to worsen the disadvantage faced by lone mothers who are unemployed/looking for their first job.

[10] This issue was analysed within the EU-funded research programme 'Education and Training for Teenage Mothers in Europe', which was carried out with the support of the Commission of the European Communities under the Leonardo da Vinci Programme. The countries surveyed included the UK, Italy, Ireland, Norway and Poland.

[11] Officers in charge of managing the professional training area in the 20 Italian regions were asked to complete a questionnaire and telephone interviews were conducted with a smaller sample.

References

Andreotti, A., Gori C., Mingione, E., Ruspini, E., Sabatinelli, S. and Tognetti, M. (2002) *Changing Family Structures and Social Policy: Child Care Services in Europe and Social Cohesion, National Report Italy*, Milan: Università degli Studi di Milano-Bicocca, available at: www.emes.net/fileadmin/emes/PDF_files/Child_care/National_Reports/Child_care_NRI.pdf

Bank of Italy (2004) *Statistiche*, www.bancaditalia.it/statistiche

Bettio, F. and Plantanega, J. (2004) 'Comparing Care Regimes in Europe', *Feminist Economics*, vol 10, no 1, pp 85-113.

Bianco, M.L. (1997) *Donne al lavoro: Cinque itinerari fra le diseguaglianze di genere*, Torino: Scriptorium.

Bimbi, F. (1997) 'Lone Mothers in Italy: A Hidden and Embarrassing Issue in a Familist Welfare Regime', in J. Lewis (ed) *Lone Mothers in European Welfare Regimes: Shifting Policy Logics*, London and Philadelphia, PA: Jessica Kingsley Publishers, pp 171-202.

Bimbi, F. (2000) 'Un soggetto tacitato in un regime di welfare familistico', in F. Bimbi (ed) *Madri sole: Metafore della famiglia ed esclusione sociale*, Roma: Carocci, pp 101-34.

Bimbi, F. and Della Sala, V. (1998) 'L'Italie: concertation sans représentation', in J. Jenson and M. Sineau (eds) *Qui doit garder le jeune enfant? Modes d'accueil et travail des mères dans l'Europe en crise*, Paris: Librairie Générale de Droit et de Jurisprudence, pp 173-202.

Bordin, M. and Ruspini, E. (2000) 'Continuità delle politiche categoriali e frammentazione del sistema di welfare: le province', in F. Bimbi (ed) *Madri sole: Metafore della famiglia ed esclusione sociale*, Roma: Carocci, pp 135-64.

Claes, M., Lacourse, E., Bouchard, C. and Perucchini, P. (2003) 'Parental Practices in Late Adolescence: A Comparison of Three Countries: Canada, France and Italy', *Journal of Adolescence*, vol 26, no 4, pp 387-99.

De Grazia, V. (1992) *Le donne nel regime fascista*, Venice: Marsilio.

De Sandre, P., Pinnelli, A. and Santini, A. (1999) (eds) *Nuzialità e fecondità in trasformazione: Percorsi e fattori del cambiamento*, Bologna: Il Mulino.

Donati, S., Andreozzi, S., Medda, E. and Grandolfo, M.E. (2000) *Reproductive Health among Adolescents: Knowledge, Attitude and Behaviour*, Rome: Istituto Superiore della Sanità.

Esping-Andersen, G. (1990) *The Three Worlds of Welfare Capitalism*, Oxford: Polity Press.

Eurostat (2004a) *Social Protection in Europe*, Luxembourg: Office for Official Publications of the European Communities.

Eurostat (2004b) *European Labour Force Survey*, Luxembourg: Office for Official Publications of the European Communities.

Eurostat (2005) *Demographic Statistics*, Luxemburg: Office for Official Publications of the European Communities.

Ferrera M. (1993) *Modelli di solidarietà: Politica e riforme sociali nelle democrazie*, Bologna: Il Mulino.

Ferrera, M. (2005) (ed) *Welfare State Reform in Southern Europe: Fighting Poverty and Social Exclusion in Greece, Italy, Spain and Portugal*, London: Routledge.

Golini, A., Menniti, A. and Palomba, R. (1987) 'Social Needs and Use of Services Made by One-parent Families', in L. Shamgar-Handelman and R. Palomba (eds) *Alternative Patterns of Family Life in Modern Societies*, Rome: Istituto di Ricerche sulla Popolazione –Consiglio della Ricerche.

Istat (2003) 'Affido congiunto all'8% dei casi, Divorzio', Online News, available at: www.divorzionline.it/news/dettaglionews.php?uid=61

Istat (2004) *Annuario Statistico Italiano*, Rome: Istat.

Italian Government – Presidency of the Council of Ministers (2003) 'Libro bianco sul welfare', Rome, available at: www.governo.it/GovernoInforma/Dossier/librobianco_welfare/agenda.html

Lagrée, J.-C. (1997) 'Cultural Patterns of Transition of European Youth', *Berkeley Journal of Sociology*, vol 41, pp 67-101.

Leibfried, S. (1993) 'Towards a European Welfare State?', in C. Jones (ed) *New Perspectives on the Welfare State in Europe*, London: Routledge, pp 133-50.

Menniti, A. and Palomba, R. (1988) *Le famiglie con un solo genitore in Italia*, Rome: Istituto di Ricerche sulla Popolazione – Consiglio della Ricerche.

Mingione, E. (2001) 'Il lato oscuro del welfare: trasformazioni delle biografie, strategie familiari e sistemi di garanzia', Conference Proceedings Convegni Lincei, no 172, Convegno CNR-Accademia Nazionale dei Lincei 'Tecnologia e Società', 5-6 April, Rome, pp 147-69.

Naldini, M. (2003) *The Family in the Mediterranean Welfare States*, London: Frank Cass.

OECD (Organisation for Economic Co-operation and Development) (2005) *Education at a Glance*, Paris: OECD Publications.

Ruspini, E. (2000) 'Madri sole e povertà nel contesto delle politiche familiari europee', in F. Bimbi (ed) *Madri sole: Metafore della famiglia ed esclusione sociale*, Rome: Carocci, pp 25-50.

Ruspini, E. (2002) 'Le giovani madri sole nel labirinto delle politiche', in P. Trivellato (ed) *Giovani madri sole: Percorsi formativi e politiche di welfare per l'autonomia*, Rome: Carocci, pp 57-82.

Ruspini, E. (2005) 'Going against the Tide: Young Lone Mothers in Italy', in C. Leccardi and E. Ruspini (eds) *A New Youth? Young People, Generations and Family Life*, Aldershot: Ashgate, pp 253-75.

Sabbadini, L.L. (1999) 'La permanenza dei giovani nella famiglia di origine: modelli di formazione e organizzazione della famiglia', Paper presented at the conference *Le famiglie interrogano le politiche sociali*, Bologna, 29-31 March.

Saraceno, C. (1984) 'Shift in Public and Private Boundaries: Women as Mothers and Service Workers in Italian Daycare', *Feminist Studies*, vol 10, no 1, pp 7-29.

Saraceno, C. (1994) 'The Ambivalent Familism of the Italian Welfare State', *Social Politics*, vol 1, no 1, pp 60-82.

Saraceno, C. (1998) *Mutamenti della famiglia e politiche sociali in Italia*, Bologna: Il Mulino.

Saraceno, C. (2003) *Mutamenti della famiglia e politiche sociali in Italia*, Bologna: Il Mulino.

Scabini, E. and Donati, P (1988) (eds) *La famiglia 'lunga' del giovane adulto: Verso nuovi compiti evolutivi*, Milano: Vita e Pensiero.

Schizzerotto, A., Bison, I. and Zoppè, A. (1995) 'Disparità di genere nella partecipazione al mondo del lavoro e nella durata delle carriere', *Polis*, vol 9, no 1, pp 91-112.

Simoni, S. (2000) 'La costruzione di un'assenza nella storia del sistema italiano di welfare', in F. Bimbi (ed) *Madri sole: Metafore della famiglia ed esclusione sociale*, Rome: Carocci, pp 85-100.

Singh, S. and Darroch, J.E. (2000) 'Adolescent Pregnancy and Childbearing: Levels and Trends in Developed Countries', *Family Planning Perspectives*, vol 32, no 1, pp 14-23.

Telefono Azzurro – Eurispes (2004) *Quinto rapporto sulla situazione dell'infanzia e dell'adolescenza in Italia*, Rome: Eurispes.

Trifiletti, R. (1999) 'Southern Welfare Regimes and the Worsening Position of Women', *Journal of European Social Policy*, vol 9, no 1, pp 49-64.

Trivellato, P. (2002) (ed) *Giovani madri sole: Percorsi formativi e politiche di welfare per l'autonomia*, Rome: Carocci.

UNICEF (2001) *A League Table of Teenage Births in Rich Nations*, Innocenti Report Card No 3, Florence: Innocenti Research Centre.

EIGHT

Teenage reproductive behaviour in Denmark and Norway: lessons from the Nordic welfare state

Lisbeth B. Knudsen and Ann-Karin Valle

Introduction: the Nordic setting

The populations in the Nordic countries – Denmark, Finland, Iceland, Norway and Sweden – are well known for being open about sexual topics, for the widespread use of contraceptives and for a somewhat pragmatic attitude in this respect. Non-marital sexual activity is generally accepted, and cohabitation is a more common family form for young people than marriage. In recent years, more than half of first-born babies in Denmark were born into a cohabiting family.

The acceptance of both non- and pre-marital sexual activity is concomitant to the acceptance of adolescent sexuality – at least above the age of sexual consent which is 15 in Denmark and 16 in Norway. Young people are expected to act like responsible adults with regard to their sexual and reproductive behaviour. In other words, they are expected to use contraceptives and delay pregnancy until they are ready for parenthood, that is when the conditions of educational attainment, economic independence and personal maturity are met.

Sex education is part of the school syllabus and includes information on how to use contraceptives (David et al, 1990). Condoms are easily available from chemists and supermarkets while oral contraceptives require a medical prescription. In Norway, condoms have been provided free of charge to young people under the age of 20 since 1999 as part of the governmental action plan to reduce unwanted pregnancies and the need for abortion and the strategy to prevent HIV and sexually transmitted infections. Oral contraceptives have been free of charge for women between 16 and 20 years of age since 2002 and Norway was also among one of the first countries worldwide to allow the morning-after pill over the counter in 2002 (Austveg and Sundby, 2005). For both girls and boys, the mean age at first sexual intercourse is around 17 years in both Denmark and Norway, although slightly higher for boys in Norway (Knudsen et al, 2003). The mean age at first birth has progressively increased since the late 1960s, when women had their first child in their early 20s compared with an average of 30 years in 2005. Delayed family formation is often interpreted as a consequence of young people's wish to complete their education and establish themselves in the labour market before having children.

In the 1960s and early 1970s, preventive activities were focused on the use of contraceptives with the purpose of avoiding unintended and unwanted births so as to improve the possibility of timing and spacing childbirths. Today, unintended pregnancies are closely linked to induced abortions (Knudsen, 2002). Two thirds of pregnant teenagers (aged 15-19) choose to interrupt their pregnancy (Nordic Statistics on induced abortions, 2004). In both Denmark and Norway the national health authorities have issued a number of so-called 'action plans' directed towards the national and local prevention of unintended pregnancy and abortion.

Before going into a more detailed discussion of teenage pregnancy and relevant policies in Denmark and Norway, some of the key characteristics of the Scandinavian welfare state must be sketched as they provide the setting for contemporary reproductive behaviour and policies. In this respect, it is important to bear in mind that the Scandinavian welfare regime is based on principles of equal rights for men and women as individuals. In both countries, this development dates back to over a century: in Denmark, laws passed in the 1880s gave women a more independent status as regards financial self-determination. Mutual rights in marriage and in cases of divorce were obtained from the 1920s when women acquired the right to keep the custody of their children (Knudsen, 2004).

Today, more females than males opt for longer formal education. Female labour force participation is high and about 70 to 80% of the women participate in the labour market while having young children at home. Most women are capable of providing for themselves and their children without the presence of a male breadwinner; and if not, the welfare state supports the family if needed (Borchorst, 1993; Knudsen, 2003). These equal rights are accompanied by equal responsibilities in relation to providing for the spouse and the children. High levels of taxation are legitimised as a common responsibility to finance all or part of the common goods provided by the welfare state, such as day care institutions for children, schools, hospitals, nursery homes for elderly people, and so on.

Teenagers are growing up in countries where an easy access to contraceptives and induced abortion on demand enables them to live a sexually active life without establishing a family until they choose to (Lappegård, 2001; Knudsen et al, 2003). Under these circumstances, family formation, onset of childbearing, timing and spacing of births and the total number of children a mother gives birth to, must be regarded as subject to deliberate decisions made by women and couples (Giddens, 1991).

This background setting means that young people are confronted with both freedom and dependency: they are allowed to live more or less like adults but are still dependent upon their families as long as they are going to school. When entering further or higher education, they are supported by a student's allowance, which enables them to leave the parental home at a considerably earlier age than in the Mediterranean countries.

This chapter examines teenage reproductive behaviour and policies in Denmark and Norway, two countries with striking similarities rooted in similar historical conditions. We focus on 'Nordic similarities', even though the countries display cultural, normative and ideological differences in relation to adolescents' sexual and reproductive behaviour, which is reflected in the patterns of childbearing and induced abortions.

Teenage pregnancy: a social problem?

Teenage *pregnancies* do occur in Denmark and Norway, although the numbers are very small. In 2004, 21 and 24 out of 1,000 15-19 year old women, respectively, either gave birth or had an induced abortion in the two countries. Teenage *childbearing*, however, is even rarer: in 2004, 5.7 out of 1,000 women aged 15 to 19 gave birth in Denmark and 8.2 in Norway, both at a lower level than the average for all Nordic countries. The consequence of an adolescent unwanted pregnancy is most commonly not parenthood, but abortion: at the country level, this is the case for approximately two thirds of pregnant teenagers. A recent survey in Denmark revealed that teenagers aged 15-19 who had become pregnant were almost 40 times as likely to have an abortion as the pregnant women who were 10 years older (that is, aged 25-29 years) (Rasch et al, 2005).

Adolescents are generally expected to control their sexuality and ensure that girls will not become pregnant and have a child. Teenage pregnancy is considered either to be both unintended and unwanted or accidental as very few young girls deliberately choose to become pregnant (Rasch, 2000). Teenage pregnancy and youth sexuality do not raise public concern. It is rather the circumstances of unprotected sex or insufficient use of contraceptives that receive public attention, which points to further needs for sexual and reproductive health promotion and preventative activities.

Becoming a parent as a teenager, is not considered as a desirable situation by public authorities, by the youngsters or by their parents. Nine years of basic schooling (from age 7-16) and an increasing proportion of young people continuing in further or higher education have contributed to prolonging youth as a phase without responsibility and accordingly also without opportunities – economic as well as social – to enter into parenthood in a a manner deemed acceptable by society.

One may argue that the relatively positive picture of teenage pregnancy as a non-existing social problem in the Nordic countries may mask individual issues not necessarily sufficiently acknowledged, understood and dealt with in the late modern reality of cultural and social contexts and within new generations (Knudsen, 2006). When the proportion of young women wanting to give birth is so small, as is the case in these two countries, the group of young mothers will become more and more selective in terms of socioeconomic characteristics. In recent years, the majority of the very young mothers aged below 20 in Denmark were single, neither married nor cohabiting with the father of the child, although a growing proportion of young mothers are married, primarily those of foreign origin (Statistics Denmark, 2004).

Some studies have stressed the positive picture provided by the low frequency of teenage childbearing and dropping fertility rates among these young girls while others have focused their attention on risk-taking behaviour. In the risk perspective, teenage childbearing and teenage parenthood are seen as problematic and analytically related to risk factors during the girls' childhood. What is seen as problematic is less the fact that girls are sexually active but that they have failed to contracept and decided to carry the pregnancy to term. Teenage childbearing is considered to be a negative outcome related to poor socioeconomic background with negative exposures and experiences in childhood, such as family dissolution, parental drug abuse and the girls' mothers being teenage mothers themselves (Nygaard Christoffersen and Soothill, 2003). These studies, covering only small samples, have limited explanatory power regarding the reproductive behaviour of all teenagers.

Hence, if youthful childbearing does indeed occur, the extent to which teenage pregnancy and teenage parenthood live up to the criteria for being constructed as a social problem is highly debatable. Even though there are some concerns about these issues, particularly about the social challenges for the young women who do become mothers, teenage pregnancy is not considered a serious problem by many politicians in the two countries, which will be elaborated on later in the chapter.

Trends since the 1970s

The overwhelming majority of the teenagers who gave birth in recent years in Denmark and Norway were having their first child. This is a significant change compared to the 1950s and 1960s, which were characterised by early marriages and relatively high fertility rates among women under the age of 20. In Denmark, fertility rates in this age group increased from 27.2 per 1,000 in 1940 to 40.2 per 1,000 in 1950 and to a peak in 1966 at 49.6 per 1,000. The decreasing fertility rates among adolescents is concomitant with the 'second demographic transition', which took off in both countries in the late 1960s and which was characterised by delayed marriage and late entry into parenthood. Today, childbirth frequently occurs before marriage (Kuijsten, 1996).

Any discussion of the decrease in teenage childbearing must take into account the rate of induced abortion as this is also an option for young women. The laws on induced abortion in Denmark and Norway provide a right to abortion on demand until the 12th week of pregnancy, with some restricted possibilities for later abortions, which also require a special permit from a local council. Minors (younger than 18 in Denmark and 16 in Norway) need a custodial consent and in Norway, the minors' parents have to be informed. In both countries, however, minors who have reasons not to inform their parents may seek permission from the county medical officer. Abortions are performed in public hospitals within the health insurance scheme and at no cost for the women (Knudsen et al, 2003). It is generally assumed that virtually no illegally performed abortions occur.

The laws on induced abortion were liberalised in the 1970s. In Denmark, the first piece of legislation removing abortions from the penal code was passed in 1939. The law was revised in 1956 and 1970 and since 1973, any woman resident in Denmark aged 18 and over has the right to have her pregnancy terminated on demand (Act no. 350, 1973). Wielandt (2005) notes that being a 'very young woman' was stated as a reason for interruption in the 1956 Act and thus made being under age an explicit risk factor. This clause could be interpreted as the premise of the construction of teenage pregnancy as a social problem as defined by Hacking (2003). One of the reasons for a late abortion stated in the Act is that the woman is unable to take care of the child due to her young age, immaturity or mental illness, which are all considered risk factors.

In Norway, induced abortion was legal only on medical, eugenic and humanitarian grounds until 1975 when it was removed from the penal code, and a new Act passed in 1978 guaranteed women the right to apply for an abortion also for social reasons. Like in Denmark, the abortion services are performed in public hospitals free of charge. After the 12th week of pregnancy, the right to abortion is only granted upon the approval of a local committee, although there is no explicit reference to being under age.

Overall trends

In 2003, 26.3 out of 1,000 women aged 15-19 in the Nordic countries became pregnant, and a little more than one third (7.7 per 1,000) gave birth, while slightly under two thirds (18.6 per 1,000) had an abortion (Nordic Statistics on induced abortions, 2004 ff). A recent analysis of the trends in legally induced abortion among women aged under 30 in the Nordic countries from the early 1970s to the late 1990s, predicted that Denmark had achieved the lowest rate of teenage abortion among the Nordic countries in 2000 (Knudsen et al, 2003).

Figure 8.1: Rate of live births per 1,000 women aged 15-19 years old in the Nordic countries (1974-2004)

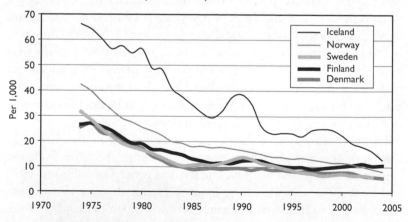

Source: Nordic Statistics on induced abortions (2004 ff)

Figure 8.1 shows the trends in live births for 15- to 19-year-old women in each of the Nordic countries since 1974. The overall picture is a strong decrease in each country; strongest in Sweden, Iceland, Norway and Denmark (78-82% decrease) and lowest in Finland (60%). Furthermore, live births accounted for a larger proportion of all teenage pregnancies in the early 1970s than did induced abortions. Throughout the 1980s, this pattern changed as a still-increasing proportion of pregnancies were terminated by inducing abortions, primarily due to the strong and continued decrease in birth rates. Another noteworthy element is that the rates of births and abortions have decreased during the same period, a fact that is often attributed to a widespread use of contraceptives, as the age of first sexual intercourse has not changed considerably in the period under study, while the average age at first child birth has increased by several years (Knudsen et al, 2003).

If we turn more specifically to Denmark and Norway, Figure 8.2 illustrates the parallel decrease in these countries. Moreover, it shows that birth rates in Norway became much closer to the Danish level at the end of the period. Also worth mentioning is the fact that very few girls younger than 15 give birth: since 1993, the annual number in Denmark has been between zero and seven out of a total number of

Figure 8.2: Rate of live births, induced abortions and pregnancies per 1,000 women aged 15-19, Denmark and Norway (1974-2004)

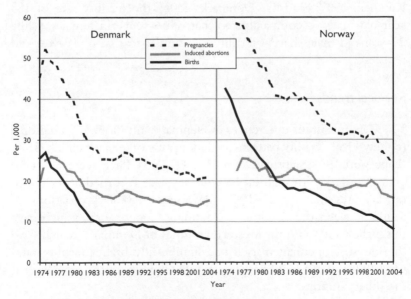

Source: Nordic Statistics on induced abortions (2004 ff)

live births of 64,000-70,000. In Norway, each year between 30 and 50 girls of this young age give birth out of an annual number of births of 57,000 (2004). Thus, both the pregnancy rate and the birth rate are somewhat higher in Norway than in Denmark, although in both countries they are still considerably below those displayed in the UK and the US. Since the early 2000s, the teenage birth rate in Norway has decreased and is now lower than, for instance, in Sweden (births and abortions combined) but still higher than in Denmark. The strong decrease in the birth rate in both countries up to the 1980s must be seen as part of the general decline in the birth rate in both countries and for teenagers, especially, this period up to the 1980s was characterised by an increasing proportion undergoing vocational education. In Denmark, compulsory sex education was introduced in schools in the 1960s, a fact which explains the now widespread use of contraceptives and the fall in unwanted pregnancies (David et al, 1990). There seems to have been a more systematic focus on sex education from an earlier age in Denmark than in Norway where there is very little space for sex education in the school curriculum, with the exception of very basic sex education in 5th grade (11-12 years). Moreover, practices tend to vary between schools with regard to the content of educational material and the age at which it is introduced to pupils.

Finally, the available statistics show that men tend to be a few years older than the women with whom they have children (Wielandt and Knudsen, 1997; Statistics Denmark, 2004): the fertility rate of 18-year-old males is comparable to that of 16-year-old females, while 21-year-old males have a fertility rate similar to that of 19-year-old females .

Regional trends

There are persistent differences in Denmark and Norway in regional (county-level) fertility patterns, including rates of teenage childbearing (Lappegård, 1999; Statistics Denmark, 1997, 2004; Thygesen et al, 2005).

In Denmark, although its 16 counties have recorded a decline in fertility rates since the late 1960s (Pedersen, 1988), stark variations are found between the counties surrounding Copenhagen, which have the highest rates and the western counties of Denmark, which have the lowest. Copenhagen itself had significantly higher fertility rates until 1998 when a rapid decrease brought it down to the same level as the other counties.

Sub-national differences are visible with regard to both teenage fertility rates and age at first child. In Denmark and Norway, the lowest maternal age at the birth of the first child is found in remote regions (Statistics Denmark, 1997; Lappegård, 1999). In 2003, the mean maternal age at first birth in Denmark showed the lowest value of 25.1 years in one of the rural counties, compared to 28.2 years in Copenhagen (Personal communication, 2005).

The regional variations in fertility rates have been larger in Norway than in Denmark throughout the period considered in Table 8.1. The table also shows that in Norway, the relative difference between the lowest and highest region was smaller in 2003 than in 1983, while in Denmark, this relative difference remained stable. Additionally, in contrast to Denmark, Norway has the highest rate of teenage pregnancy in a sparsely populated region (Finnmark) far from the metropolitan area, which historically has had a high rate of young unmarried mothers. These findings could possibly be linked to overall social and material inequalities but also to local cultural factors. However, the issues are not sufficiently understood or dealt with so far in Norway.

Socioeconomic characteristics

In the early 1970s, the majority of the youngest mothers gave birth within one year of getting married. The availability of housing was limited, with very few possibilities to buy a dwelling. Married couples and those expecting a child were given priority on housing waiting lists. In 1975, 1,106 of 1,457 Danish mothers (75%) aged under 20

Table 8.1: Regional differences in fertility rates per 1,000 women aged 15-19, Denmark and Norway, selected counties

	Denmark			**Norway**			
		Municipality of Copen-				Municipality	
	All of	hagen	Ringkøbing		All of	Finnmark	of	
	Denmark	(highest)	county	Lowest[a]	Norway	(highest)	Oslo	Lowest[b]
1973	26.1	40.2	24.8	20.1	44.0[c]	79.9	26.9	26.9
1983	10.6	19.8	7.9	7.2	20.0	28.5	13.8	10.0
1993	8.8	18.0	7.4	6.2	14.0	27.6	12.3	6.5
2003	6.2	9.2	3.8	3.4	9.1	14.6	5.1	3.1

Notes:

[a] Storstrøm county in 1973, Roskilde county in 1983, Viborg county in 1993 and Roskilde county in 2003.

[b] Oslo municipality in 1973, Akershus municipality in 1983, 1993 and 2003.

[c] Average for 1971-75.

had been married for less than a year when they gave birth. Today, the majority of the very young mothers aged under 20 in Denmark, who are relatively few in number, are single, neither married nor cohabiting with the father of the child. Around 60% of first-born children in Denmark are born outside wedlock although the majority are born to partnered couples. The proportion of children born to unwed mothers is 78% among teenagers giving birth (Statistics Denmark, 2004). As of January 2004, none of the 86 teenagers who were 15 to 17 years old and had a child younger than one year old was married; 62% were single, while 28% were living with the father of the child (Statistics Denmark, 2005).

The general pattern for young people leaving their parental home in both countries is to choose single living and wait until later to establish a family of their own with a co-resident partner (Carneiro, 2003). In 2003, only 3.1% of 15- to 19-year-old females and 1.6% of males of the same age were married in Denmark (Statistics Denmark, 2004).

In both countries, regional variations in higher education overlap with regional differences in teenage pregnancy. Of course, family and fertility patterns are correlated with educational attainment: women who spend a shorter time in education tend to have their first child earlier than their highly educated counterparts.

Various studies have shown that the proportion of young mothers who obtain a college or university degree is lower than those without children. An analysis based on 1994 register data in Denmark showed that while 18.4% of the women born in 1944/48 had given birth as teenagers, the corresponding figure was only 4.8% for women born 20 years later (1964/68). Moreover, the proportion of teenage mothers holding a degree was very low (3.8% in first cohort and 0.3% in the second cohort) (Carneiro and Knudsen, 2001). Similar trends were observed in Norway (Noack and Østby, 1996). A Norwegian study argues that education should not be regarded as a fertility-inhibiting factor since part of the explanation may be that women choose their education and subsequent occupation in accordance with their preferences regarding family size (Lappegård, 2001).

In order to study why some adolescents choose childbearing in Denmark, Nygaard Christoffersen (2000) showed that teenagers whose parents possess low levels of education and prolonged experiences of unemployment are at risk of becoming pregnant. Another register-based study shows that there are still intergenerational similarities regarding early childbearing in Denmark – girls in particular have the propensity to begin childbearing early if their mothers did (Murphy and Knudsen, 2002).

On average, young women in Denmark belonging to minority ethnic groups have higher birth rates than their Danish counterparts: from 1999 to 2003, 6.0 per 1,000 Danish teenagers gave birth, compared to 32.7 and 10.2 per 1,000 immigrant and descendant women (as defined in the official statistics), respectively. The highest rates are seen among women from Syria (102.6), Lebanon (74.1) and Turkey (60.5) (Statistics Denmark, 2004). In 2005, immigrants and descendants constituted 11% of all female teenagers in Denmark, compared to 5.5% in 1995. Public concerns in relation to immigrant women are not focused on early childbearing but on whether they have achieved some education and become integrated into Danish society.

Furthermore, almost all of the women who leave the parental home in Denmark and move straight into a married household are immigrants or descendants (Knudsen and Carneiro, 2006). In 2001, 7% of the female teenage immigrants were married compared to 0.6% of all female teenagers in Denmark. Among teenagers from non-Western immigrant families, the corresponding figure was 27% (Rasch et al, 2005).

In Norway, pregnancy among minority ethnic teenagers has not been studied in detail, but trends similar to the ones described for Denmark have been noted, particularly in the urban areas where minority ethnic groups tend to live in close-knit communities. 18% of the teenagers in Oslo belong to minority ethnic groups. A study conducted in 1999 revealed that teenagers aged under 19 from these backgrounds who gave birth at one large hospital in Oslo represented twice as many as expected from their representation in the population. In total, they accounted for half of the births to women younger than 25 years of age (Eskild et al, 2002).

Attitudes to teenage pregnancy

As argued earlier, teenage sexual activity is relatively accepted or at least tolerated in Denmark and Norway, although this does not hold for teenage pregnancy and motherhood. In other words, teenagers are allowed to have sex, but not to have children. Public authorities, although concerned with teenage parenthood, are more concerned with the prevention of unsafe sex and unintended pregnancies leading to induced abortions.

The costs to the welfare state resulting from teenage parenthood do not represent an issue in current debates about welfare reform. For example, while welfare reform is currently advocated by the Liberal/Conservative government of Denmark, it is chiefly focused on the rising costs resulting from an ageing population and late entry into the labour market among cohorts born in the 1980s, but not on young parents. The Nordic welfare state regime is often described as one that incorporates several features such as equality, full employment, universal rights and generous benefits (Esping-Andersen and Korpi, 1987). While it is often argued that this model represents an 'ideal-type' (Kvist, 1999), many of these features are applicable when it comes to the support available to young mothers. The regime is non-discriminatory and young mothers are entitled to the same benefits as other mothers, that is, to a flat monthly allowance per child, and a top-up if there is no father in the household. Recently, the student allowance was doubled for single mothers in Denmark to give them the chance to improve their economic conditions while they are studying. Parents enrolled on an educational course receive the student allowance for a longer period than students without children. While most of these new initiatives are not relevant for teenage parents who are still at school, they do, however, provide some indication that young people, whether single or parents, are provided with the means to study.

In both Denmark and Norway, several private and semi-public organisations have established courses and support groups to provide help and advice to teenage mothers on how to manage their situation, including how to take care of their child. In Norway, some schools have introduced baby-doll programmes similar to those found in the US. These dolls require constant care – just like a real toddler – and are used as a preventive means to raise awareness as to the consequences of unprotected sex.

Public health concerns are predominantly focused on sexually transmitted diseases, especially chlamydia, which has recently increased in Denmark and at present is increasing among young people in Norway. The growing failure of young people to use condoms with new partners featured in recent public debates as a major explanation for the rise in chlamydia infections. These debates were probably influenced by the knowledge of the existence of improved medical treatments for AIDS.

Whether teenagers or adults, unmarried women giving birth are not stigmatised in Denmark and Norway. More than 40% of all births in Denmark and even more among first births are by unwed mothers, of whom the vast majority live in a consensual union with the father of the child. Both the unmarried mother and the child have equal rights to married mothers and children born in wedlock in both countries.

The general acceptance of teenagers being sexually active is linked to a concern that they should not 'be forced into' having intercourse before they want it themselves. In Denmark, the legal age of consent for sexual activity is 15. In Norway, the health authorities issued campaigns in the 1990s with the slogan: 'Draw your own limits!', which clearly sought to encourage teenagers to decide for themselves when and with whom to have intercourse (Knudsen and Wielandt, 1995; Norwegian Ministry of Health and Social Welfare, 1999).

The age of sexual consent was under public debate in the late 1990s in Norway but did not result in any changes. There are some paradoxes in both theory and practice. Arguably, the law could be seen as outdated as it leaves the child with no sexual agency of its own. This legal framework would therefore gain from being updated if sexual agency among young people is to be granted increased recognition. At the same time, the issue of childhood protection is of no less importance today than in the past.

In Denmark, sex education is systematically introduced in the school curriculum from grade 7 (13-14 years), while in Norway, aside from a short introductory class for 5th-grade pupils (11-12 years), it starts later (in grade 10 [16-17 years]) and is more haphazard. The dilemmas and tensions between empowerment, sexual autonomy and agency on the one hand, and the protective traditions linked to 'judgementality' on the other hand are perhaps more acute in Norway than in Denmark.

While formally, sexual and reproductive rights are recognised in theory among health and educational policymakers, interventions and practice differ greatly within and between countries of the Nordic welfare regime.

Social protection, prevention and empowerment

As discussed above, teenage parenthood is very uncommon in Denmark and Norway and the rare cases are considered to be very peculiar and very specific. We also showed that in relation to induced abortions, teenagers are legally considered to be too young for motherhood, which by current social standards is linked to the fact that they are still undergoing some formal education and therefore not able to provide for themselves. Young people are seen as socially immature until they have completed their education and acquired the skills that are needed to join the adult workforce. Furthermore, the discourse on individual responsibility implies the expectation that once 'equipped' with contraceptive means and knowledge of reproductive matters, teenage girls can be trusted to take care of their sexuality and will not get pregnant.

In addition, minors have certain legal rights although they cannot sign any document that carries legal consequences; they have a custodian adult. Expecting and parenting teenagers have therefore the same rights as older women. In Denmark, the social support services for young parents are under the auspices of the Ministry of Social Affairs and the newly established Ministry for Family and Consumption. Preventive matters, contraceptive advice and hospitals are under the responsibility of the Interior Ministry (previously the Health Ministry).

The first family planning institution was established in 1939 with the aim to help and support pregnant and childrearing women in Denmark. The institution was known as 'Mother's Assistance' and, according to the Act on Pregnancy Interruption (1939), a doctor from this institution had to support the women's application for induced abortion before they went to hospital. The institution was closed in 1976 and the responsibility for contraceptive counselling and advice was placed in the hands of the counties. Seven years later, a group of women established a new 'Mother's Assistance of 1983' because they considered the services provided by the counties to be too limited. This institution, which is still active in several cities, is partly based on non-paid voluntary work from female doctors, social workers, and so on. Next to traditional counselling services to young women, it also has significant outreach activities. An important task is to inform young girls about their rights, both in the case of induced abortion and in the case of childbearing.

A recent circular by Danish authorities gave women the right to receive confidential advice in relation to their decision of whether to choose abortion or to carry their pregnancy to term (Civilretsdirektoratet, 2000). These initiatives underline a gender-sensitive approach that recognises the needs that women, especially young women, have to discuss their pregnancy with a professional and to be informed about the possibilities for support if they become a mother.

The Danish Family Planning Association is actively involved in informative and educational activities both in relation to contraceptives, births, induced abortion and sexually transmitted diseases. The organisation is partly funded by the state and receives further funding for specific activities. Some of these are initiated in relation to the various governmental 'action plans' to reduce the number of unwanted pregnancies and induced abortions. One of the more recent activities is the creation of a website with information directed primarily to health and social policy practitioners but also to ordinary citizens (www.abortnet.dk).

In both countries, anti-abortion organisations exist. The 'Alternative to Abortion' (known as 'Amathea') in Norway is more visible and receives more public support than the 'Right to Life' in Denmark, although both organisations have received public funding for some of their activities. In Norway, the organisation is widespread and more actively involved in counselling young girls in the course of their decision regarding whether they should opt for an abortion. Public concern is raised annually in Norway when the state budget is debated in Parliament.

In Denmark, we have seen that the focus has been directed towards the prevention of unintended pregnancies. In contrast, an examination of current public funding priorities for sexual and reproductive health in Norway reveals that the prevention of abortions among young pregnant women has received as much attention as the prevention of teenage pregnancy. Indeed, since 2001, public funding towards Amathea has risen consistently. The annual state budget allocated to this organisation has risen from 12,100,000 NOK in 2001/02 to 14,507,000 NOK in 2005/06. In the same period, the funding allocated to the prevention of unintended pregnancies increased from 19,200,000 NOK to 24,079,000 NOK (Myrberg and Ollendorf, 2006).

Since the beginning of the 1990s, the Norwegian government has financed and carried out three national strategic programmes with the objective, first, to ensure sexual and reproductive health and rights for the whole population, and second, to reduce the rates of induced abortions, especially among teenagers and young adults. The main strategies of prevention include an open and ongoing dialogue with young people on issues of sexuality. They further include a contribution to the education of boys and girls so that they obtain the confidence to make their own informed decisions, and ensuring low barriers to the education of safe contraception practices and easily accessible contraception services that are age, gender and culturally sensitive.

The policy development since the 1990s ensured free contraceptives to teenagers between the ages of 16 and 20, and hormonal prescriptions available from public health nurses and midwives. It has been remarked that overall, the policies and programmes geared towards preventing unwanted pregnancies among adolescents have been a success (Austveg and Sundby, 2005).

While policy debates in Norway occasionally include political statements condemning abortion on demand, such statements are no longer made in Denmark. Neither young people nor adults easily 'go public' with the fact that they have had an abortion. Public spending priorities are indicative of policymakers' preferences: it is somewhat paradoxical that large amounts of state funding are channelled towards organisations that focus on anti-abortion among the already pregnant, while general youth services and non-governmental organisations that offer preventive sexual health services experience chronic financial difficulties because of limited public funding.

The Norwegian example suggests that some of the 'ideal-typical' features of the Nordic welfare model do require constant awareness-raising, debate and 'struggle' in order to argue for funding in line with official policies. In fact, Norway prefers to follow the OECD definition of poverty, which records 100,000 poor citizens, as opposed to the EU figure of 300,000 (out of a population of 4.6 million). Although Norwegian citizens enjoy many advantages and privileges compared to the global population, those who fall between the cracks have a higher probability of experiencing social exclusion. It may be ill-advised to associate early motherhood with such stigma as that of poverty and social exclusion because the individual profile of young mothers may vary greatly. If in some Norwegian localities, early motherhood is more common than elsewhere (as demonstrated earlier in the chapter), teenage motherhood may not be a marker of social exclusion, contrary to popular belief. In small communities, it may even be a criterion of social inclusion as suggested in the case of the UK (Tabberer et al, 2000; Bonell et al, 2003). The links between social inequality and reproductive health may not be sufficiently understood and addressed in Norway, and perhaps so in other countries. Vulnerable age periods and vulnerable stages in individual lives may need increased policy attention as the dilemmas faced by young people are difficult to detect and gauge.

Conclusions

This chapter has shown that the politics of teenage pregnancy in Denmark and Norway are oriented towards the prevention of unwanted pregnancy, induced abortion and securing the right to reproductive health.

What appears to work in the 'Nordic' setting are attempts to develop systematic, early, appropriate and sufficient educational mechanisms and sharing of knowledge about sexual and reproductive health for young people. This approach involves dealing with intimate relationships and promoting responsible, empowered and enjoyable relationship-building as well as ensuring access to youth health services, appropriate counselling, contraceptives and information.

Scandinavian countries have actively participated in the increased global promotion of sexual rights and the reproductive health of young people and more generally sensitive policies towards teenagers. Nonetheless, contradictions still exist within the framework of their own national policies. Prevention of teenage pregnancy and of unsafe sex among youth is a priority, but we have shown that in Norway, the provision of sex education programmes in schools remain uneven and haphazard in contrast to Denmark. Furthermore, public spending allocated to research into youth sexual and reproductive health remains very limited in Norway. Although few young people do choose motherhood, we have insufficient knowledge of the experiences of those that do.

Policymakers therefore need to ensure that the discourse on human rights for women and youth translates into areas of sexual and reproductive health and rights and that funding is channelled accordingly. Our research suggests that more systematic and clearer policies addressing young people are needed, including sex education from an even earlier age than is currently the case. Generally, more research needs to be conducted into matters of teenage sexual attitudes and youth reproductive health based on participatory research methods with youngsters. Finally, the government 'action plans' that we have referred to need to include more systematic evidence-based policy in matters such as access to and quality of youth health, sex education from an early age and counselling services.

Experiences from Finland show that the rates of both pregnancy and abortion among teenagers increased shortly after budgetary cuts in sex education in schools and the removal of a fixed syllabus (Knudsen and Gissler, 2003). However, research and policy efforts should not be allowed to recede simply because in statistical terms, teenage childbearing remains, as we have shown, relatively uncommon in the Nordic countries.

References

Austveg, B. and Sundby, J. (2005) 'Norway at ICPD+10: International Assistance for Reproductive Health does not Reflect Domestic Policies', *Reproductive Health Matters*, vol 13, no 25, pp 23-33.

Bonell, C., Strange, V., Stephenson, J., Oakley, A., Copas, A., Forrest, S., Johnson, A. and Black, S. (2003) 'Effect of Social Exclusion on the Risk of Teenage Pregnancy: Development of Hypotheses using Baseline Data from a Randomised Trial of Sex Education', *Journal of Epidemiology and Community Health*, vol 57, no 11, pp 871-6.

Borchorst, A. (1993) 'Working Life and Family Life in Western Europe', in S. Carlsen and J. Elm Larsen (eds) *The Equality Dilemma: Reconciling Working Life and Family Life, Viewed in a European Perspective – the Danish Example*, Copenhagen: The Danish Equal Status Council, pp 167-81.

Carneiro, I.G. (2003) 'A home of their own: leaving the parental home in Denmark and Brazil', Unpublished PhD thesis, University of Southern Denmark, Odense.

Carneiro, I.G. and Knudsen, L.B. (2001) *Fertility and Family Surveys in Countries of the ECE Region: Country Report – Denmark*, Geneva: United Nations.

Civilretsdirektoratet (2000) *Cirkulæreskrivelse pr. 21. april 2000 til samtlige amtskommuner, Københavns og Frederiksberg kommuner, Hovedstadens Sygehusfællesskab og Amtsrådsforeningen om støttesamtaler før og efter svangerskabsafbrydelse* (Circular as of 21 April 2000 to all counties, Copenhagen and Frederiksberg municipality, HS and the Association of counties on supporting conversation before and after interruption of pregnancy), Copenhagen.

David, H.P., Morgall, J.M., Osler, M., Rasmussen, N.K. and Jensen B. (1990) 'United States and Denmark: Different Approaches to Health Care and Family Planning', *Studies in Family Planning*, vol 21, no 2, pp 1-19.

Eskild, A., Helgadottir, L.B., Jerve, F., Qvigstad, E., Stray-Pedersen, S. and Løset, Å. (2002) 'Provosert abort blant kvinner med fremmedkulturell bakgrunn i Oslo' [Induced abortion among women with foreign background], *Tidskrift for Norsk Lægeforening*, vol 122, no 14, pp 1355-7.

Esping-Andersen, G. and Korpi, W. (1987) 'From Poor Relief to Institutional Welfare States: The Development of Scandinavian Social Policy', in R. Erikson, E.J. Hansen, S. Ringen and H. Uusitalo (eds) *The Scandinavian Model: Welfare States and Welfare Research*, New York, NY: M.E. Sharpe, pp 39-74.

Giddens, A. (1991) *Modernity and Self-Identity: Self and Society in the Late Modern Age*, Cambridge: Polity Press.

Hacking, I. (2003) 'What is Social Construction? The Teenage Pregnancy Example', in G. Delanty and P. Strydom (eds) *Philosophies of Social Science: The Classic and Contemporary Readings*, Philadelphia, PA: Open University Press, pp 421-8.

Knudsen, L.B. (2002) 'Induced Abortion and Family Formation in Europe', in F.-X. Kaufmann, A. Kuijsten, H.-J. Schulze and K.P. Strohmeier (eds) *Family Life and Family Policies in Europe: Volume 2: Problems and Issues in Comparative Perspective*, Oxford: Clarendon Press, pp 217-51.

Knudsen, L.B. (2003) *On the Role of Family Policy in the Nordic Countries*, Sociologisk Arbejdspapir (Working Paper) no 17, Aalborg: Aalborg University.

Knudsen, L.B. (2004) 'Nye familieformer og færre børn' (New Family Forms and Less Children), in N. Ploug, I. Henriksen and N. Kærgård (eds) *Den danske velfærdsstats historie* (The History of the Danish Welfare State), Copenhagen: Socialforskningsinstituttet, pp 224-59.

Knudsen, L.B. and Carneiro, I.G. (2006) Formation of first co-residential unions among Danish and immigrant women in Denmark in the period 1980 – 1994: A register-based study (ongoing analysis).

Knudsen, L.B. and Gissler, M. (2003) 'The Divergent Rates of Induced Abortion among Young Women in Finland and Denmark', *Yearbook of Population Research in Finland 2003*, no 39, pp 227-44.

Knudsen, L.B. and Wielandt, H. (1995) *På vej mod abort* (On the road to induced abortion), Copenhagen: Frydenlund.

Knudsen, L.B., Gissler, M., Bender, S.S., Hedberg, C., Ollendorff, U., Sundström, K., Totlandsdal, K. and Vilhjalmsdottir, S. (2003) 'Induced Abortion in the Nordic Countries: Special Emphasis on Young Women', *Acta Obstetricia et Gynecologica Scandinavia*, vol 82, no 3, pp 257-68.

Knudsen, L.M. (2006) *Reproductive Rights in a Global Context: Women in Seven Countries*, Nashville, TN: Vanderbilt University Press.

Kuijsten, A.C. (1996) 'Changing Family Patterns in Europe: A Case of Divergence?', *European Journal of Population/Revue Européenne de Démographie*, vol 12, no 2, pp 115-43.

Kvist, J. (1999) 'Welfare Reform in the Nordic Countries in the 1990s: Using Fuzzy-set Theory to Assess Conformity to Ideal Types', *European Journal of Social Policy*, vol 9, no 3, pp 231-52.

Lappegård, T. (1999) *Regionale variasjoner i fruktbarheten i Norge* (Regional Fertility Differences in Norway), Oslo: Statistics Norway.

Lappegård, T. (2001) *Tenåringer og graviditet* (Teenagers and Pregnancies), Oslo: Statistics Norway.

Murphy, M. and Knudsen, L.B. (2002) 'The Intergenerational Transmission of Fertility in Contemporary Denmark: The Effects of Number of Siblings (Full and Half), Birth Order, and whether Male or Female', *Population Studies*, vol 56, no 3, pp 235-48.

Myrberg, A. and Ollendorf, U. (2006) Personal communication.

National Board of Health, Copenhagen (2005)Personal communication.

Noack, T. and Østby, L. (1996) *Fertility and Family Surveys in Countries of the ECE Region: Country Report: Norway*, Geneva: United Nations.

Nordic Statistics on induced abortions (2004 ff) *Statistical Summary 32/2004*, Helsinki: Stakes.

Norwegian Ministry of Health and Social Welfare (1999) *Action Plan: Prevention of Unwanted Pregnancy and Abortions 1999-2003*, Oslo: Norwegian Ministry of Health and Social Welfare.

Nygaard Christoffersen, M. (2000) *Why Choose Teenage Childbearing? A Longitudinal Study of 1966 and 1973 Birth Cohorts in Denmark*, Working Paper, Copenhagen: Danish National Institute of Social Research.

Nygaard Christoffersen, M. and Soothill, K. (2003) 'The Long-term Consequences of Parental Alcohol Abuse: A Cohort Study of Children in Denmark', *Journal of Substance Abuse Treatment*, vol 25, no 2, pp 107-16.

Pedersen, L. (1988) *Regional Fertility Differences 1981-1985* (in Danish), Copenhagen: Statistics Denmark.

Rasch, V. (2000) 'Different aspects of women's reproductive choices: results from a study conducted among women with wanted and unwanted pregnancies in Denmark and Tanzania, Unpublished PhD thesis, Faculty of Health Sciences, University of Southern Denmark.

Rasch, V., Knudsen, L.B. and Gammeltoft, T. (2005) *Når der ikke er noget tredje valg: Social sårbarhed og valget af abort* (When there is no Third Choice: On Social Vulnerability and the Choice of Abortion), Copenhagen: National Board of Health.

Statistics Denmark (1997) 'The Fertility Development in Denmark from 1980 to 1993' (in Danish), *Statistiske efterretninger, Befolkning og valg*, no 3, Copenhagen: Statistics Denmark.

Statistics Denmark (2004) *Vital Statistics 2003*, Copenhagen: Statistics Denmark.

Statistics Denmark (2005) Unpublished data from Anna Qvist.

Tabberer, S., Hall, C., Webster, A. and Prendengast, S. (2000) *Teenage Pregnancy and Choice: Abortion of Motherhood: Influence on the Decision*, York: Joseph Rowntree Foundation.

Thygesen, L.C., Knudsen, L.B. and Keiding, N. (2005) 'Modelling Regional Variation of First-time Births in Denmark 1980-1994 by an Age-period-cohort Model', *Demographic Research*, vol 13, no 23, pp 573-96.

Wielandt, H. (2005) 'Prevention in relation to teenage pregnancy: the Danish experience', Unpublished report, Odense.

Wielandt, H. and Knudsen, L.B. (1997) 'Sexual Activity and Pregnancies among Adolescents in Denmark: Trends during the Eighties', *Nordisk Sexologi*, no 15, pp 75-88.

Part Three
Transition states

NINE

Meeting the challenge of new teenage reproductive behaviour in Russia

Elena Ivanova

Introduction

Teenage motherhood as a consequence of early marriage was widespread in Russia during the 20th century. The interest in the phenomenon of adolescent motherhood appeared in the early 1990s, at a time of considerable increase in teenage birth rates. However, by the early 2000s young people's fertility rates dropped to the level observed in the 1970s. How can we interpret these changes? Do they represent a reaction to reforms in the welfare system? Are they the result of the erosion of traditional marriage and family values and rising individualism among the young generation? Indeed, changing family formation patterns reflect new lifestyles and aspirations of young generations. This chapter first analyses statistical trends in young people's reproductive behaviour since 1965. Second, the reasons for these changes in teenage reproductive behaviour are identified. Third, the role of various political actors in the emergence of competing policy discourses in relation to teenage sex and sexual health is analysed. Fourth, the chapter provides an assessment of the various initiatives relating to young people's sexual and reproductive rights. And finally the chapter discusses current and future directions in the politics of teenage reproductive behaviour in Russia.

Statistical trends

For several decades, from the mid-1960s to the early 1990s, Russia experienced a steady increase in adolescent birth rates. The birth rate among 15- to 19-year-old girls more than doubled from 23 births per 1,000 girls in the mid-1960s to 56 births per 1,000 girls in 1990. The teenage birth rates increased significantly between 1980 and the early 1990s (see Table 9.1).

Young mothers' birth rates approached those of 20- to 24-year-old women. By the early 1990s, teenage birth rates began to exceed that of 30- to 34-year-old mothers. Since 1995 adolescent fertility rates have sharply declined. The age-specific fertility rate for 15- to 19-year-old women decreased from 45.6 per 1,000 in 1995 to 28.4 per 1,000 in 2002. The contribution of teenagers to the total fertility rate (TFR) dropped from 16.9% in 1995 to 10.7% in 2002.[1] By contrast, the proportion of older mothers increased. In 2004, lowest fertility rates among teenagers were observed in Moscow (15.6 per 1,000) and Saint Petersburg (15.4 per 1,000). Russia started its second demographic transition at a later stage than Western European countries but increasingly showed strong similarities with reproductive behaviours observed in Western Europe (Ivanova and Zakharov, 1996). In this respect, the sharp increase in out-of-wedlock births is striking, particularly among young women aged 15-19. The percentage of births outside marriage for women aged 15-19 reached 47.2% in 2004 compared to 18.7% in 1980. The increase in out-of-wedlock births was primarily explained by the low use of contraception among young people. However, the popularity of marriage declined among all women of reproductive age. As such, it indicated that traditional family formation patterns became

Table 9.1: Total fertility rates, age-specific fertility rates for women aged 15-19 and their contribution to the total fertility rate (TFR), per 1,000, 1965-2004

Year	Total fertility rate	Age-specific fertility rate for 15-19 age group	Contribution of 15-19 group to the TFR (%)*
1964-65	2.14	22.7	5.3
1969-70	1.97	28.3	6.9
1974-75	1.99	33.9	8.5
1979-80	1.89	42.7	11.6
1985-86	2.11	46.9	11.2
1990	1.89	55.0	14.6
1995	1.34	45.6	16.9
2000	1.21	28.1	11.6
2001	1.25	28.1	11.2
2002	1.29	28.4	11.1
2003	1.32	27.6	10.2
2004	1.34	28.2	10.5

Note: Calculated on basis of the ROSSTAT data.

Source: The Demographic Yearbook of Russia (2005) Rosstat-Moscow, 2005, pp 108, 193.

marginalised even though the change was most pronounced among the youth.

From 1990, marriage rates went through a process of radical transformation, which primarily affected the youngest segment of the population. In 1996 marriage rates were at their lowest in comparison to post-war years: 0.6 marriages for one woman and 0.57 marriages for one man. By the early 2000s the number of marriages rose but still remained extremely low in comparison to preceding decades. Marriage among Russian youth rose between 1980 and 1995, and declined subsequently after 1995, mirroring the fall in teenage pregnancy rates during this period. Therefore the decline in teenage pregnancy rates partially resulted from the constant decrease of early matrimony from 1995 onwards. For instance, early marriage among young women continued to increase until the early 1990s then declined sharply, especially among women born in 1973, 1974 and 1976 (Ivanova, 1996). Russian youth seemed to be diverging from the traditional model of early marriage, which had remained virtually intact since the 19th century, particularly for women. New social norms changed family formation patterns, accentuating the broad social acceptance of cohabitation outside marriage. According to data from a representative public opinion poll conducted in November 1998 (Ivanova, 1998), 88% of people under the age of 20 did not condemn unregistered marriages. However, an important factor counteracting the decline in officially registered marriages among Russian youth was the occurrence of 'shotgun marriages' prompted by a premarital pregnancy. The highest percentage of such marriages (50%) was observed among the youngest age group (aged 15-19). Simultaneously, out-of-wedlock births became more common among very young women (aged 15-19) and older women (over 35).

As in Western Europe, age at first sexual intercourse was constantly decreasing. The results of the Russia Longitudinal Monitoring Survey conducted in 2001 showed that interviewees aged 41-49 lost their virginity at 19.7 years, adults in their thirties lost their virginity at 18.9 years, while young people under the age of 20 lost their virginity at 15.9 years (Vannappagari and Ryder, 2002.) However, teenagers were less sexually active than the rest of the population. Young men were more active (32.7%) than young women (28.1%). Age 15-16 years is the typical mean age at first sexual intercourse (Gavrilova, 1997; Grebesheva, 1998). According to the results of the research conducted by Kon (1997) the mean age was 17.5 for girls and 16.5 for boys.

The decline in teenage births indicated that adolescents were effectively using contraception or other methods of family planning. Usage of hormonal methods among women of reproductive age increased from 2.1% in 1991 to 7.8% in 2001. The proportion of women using an intrauterine device decreased from 18.2 to 15.6 (Vishnevskij, 2002). However, 44% of sexually active teenagers did not use a condom during intercourse (Vannappagari and Ryder, 2002). Lack of sexual competence (belief that contraception would be detrimental to health, resorting to unreliable methods) explained adolescents' failure to use contraception effectively (Sharapova, 1998). In Russia and the former USSR, abortion was used as a family planning method until the mid-1990s. Between 1991 and 2004 the number of abortions among teenagers decreased by more than a half (Table 9.2). According to the results of the poll 'Mother and Infant', the average age of women having an abortion was 27-29 years in the early 2000s (David, 2000). Abortions for social reasons[1] among young women more than tripled between 1991 and 2001.

Explaining changing reproductive behaviours

Broad socioeconomic transformations were one of the main driving factors for change in reproductive behaviours. These transformations created an atmosphere of instability. Russian youth were particularly affected by socioeconomic transformations in terms of health and employment status. But sex education and public health policies remained in their infancy compared to policies implemented in corporatist and social democratic regimes such as France and Scandinavia. Lauwers (2005, p 149) observes that 'the contrast in health, particularly in reproductive health, between the EU countries and the Russian Federation is striking'.

Table 9.2: Number of officially registered abortions for women aged under 15 and aged 15-19, and total number of abortions (per 1,000), 1991-2004

Year	Aged under 15	Aged 15-19	Total
1991	0.3	69	100
1995	0.2	56	73
2000	0.1	36	54
2001	0.1	34	51
2002	0.2	32	49
2003	0.1	31	47
2004	0.1	29	45

Source: The Demographic Yearbook of Russia (2005) Rosstat-Moscow, 2005, p 249.

From the 1990s onwards fundamental changes occurred in social welfare provision.The Soviet state used to consider women as workers. The welfare system was thus relatively supportive of female employment, for instance by providing universal child care such as nurseries for very young children. High levels of female employment were a key characteristic of Russian society during the Soviet period. This changed dramatically after the fall of communism. Married young women are now discriminated against by private firms. Russian women are confined to low-paid jobs in the public sector and few are employed in the private sector. Moreover, the conciliation of paid work and family responsibilities is under threat. Child care and family benefits have been decentralised and are now placed under the responsibility of regional authorities. Poor families have been hit especially hard by the politics of welfare retrenchment in the 1990s and early 2000s. These changes have rendered the conciliation of paid work and motherhood virtually impossible, obliging women to choose between motherhood and professional careers. As a result, young women increasingly tend to postpone marriage and motherhood. Despite rising concerns with the decline in birth rates, the Parliament (the state Duma) has not enacted any family-friendly policies.

Of equal concern to policymakers is the erosion of traditional family values, as mirrored by the decline in marriages and delayed family formation. New social attitudes to sex and marriage have affected all generations, not just the youth. The sexual revolution of the 1970s enabled people to separate sexuality and family life: sexuality outside marriage and without reproductive purposes became relatively common. In the 1990s and 2000s, young generations have pursued this trend, albeit more openly than previous generations (Kon, 2001). However, patriarchal and traditional family values have remained predominant (Botcharova, 1994).

Analysing Russian sex culture, Kon divides Russian history since 1917 into five periods (Kon, 1997). Between 1917 and 1930, in the aftermath of the Soviet revolution and the establishment of a communist regime, the main characteristics were family disintegration and female emancipation. Between 1930 and 1956, the regime promoted traditional family values and condemned sex and eroticism as symbols of bourgeois decadence. This period corresponds to the totalitarian epoch and represents the reign of Stalinism as its peak. After Stalin's death the totalitarian regime softened and became authoritarian, with limited recognition of individual rights. Sexuality was regulated and controlled but no longer banned.The period 1985-90 was characterised by the development of a new sexual revolution and regular outbursts of moral panic concerning sexual freedom. Since then, support for sex education has been growing. As a result, romanticism became increasingly out of fashion and young women started to adopt a utilitarian approach towards sexuality and marriage. A poll conducted in the 1990s showed that 41% of Russian female students were ready to get married without love (Sprecher et al, 1994).

But the youth are not a homogenous category: some sections of the young generation now tend to adopt traditional family values. According to Rotkirch, the transmission of sexual knowledge remains extremely uneven. She notes that:

> ... more than a decade after the end of Communist censorship of sexual and erotic topics, pornography is now sold in the metro stations of the cities, but 13-year-old girls living in the same cities may still be unprepared for their menstruation. The availability and use of modern contraceptives (the pill and IUD [intrauterine device]) is spreading, but abortion remains one of the main ways of birth regulation. Russia lacks a coherent legislation concerning family and reproductive rights. (Rotkirch, 2004, p 93)

These remarks echo the findings of the 2001 UNICEF report on teenage pregnancy. As in other Organisation for Economic Co-operation and Development (OECD) countries, social and cultural changes have occurred in an extremely short time, thus leaving adolescents unprepared to cope with these transformations.

The decision of a young pregnant woman to keep her pregnancy is influenced by a number of factors: family status, level of education, professional occupation, housing conditions and social attitudes to adolescent motherhood. There is no link between growing up in single-parent families and the occurrence of early motherhood. Moreover, parental support plays a key role in the young woman's decision to keep her pregnancy. According to a research conducted in Moscow – Moscow region and Bryansk – 50% of pregnant girls lived with their parents (Gurko, 2003). In the Soviet era the welfare state supported young mothers who could raise a child even if they lived in relatively poor circumstances. As welfare provision has dramatically decreased in the post-communist period, teenagers can no longer rely on state support for raising their children.

In the 1990s authoritarian regulation of young people's behaviour was replaced by more flexible rules, thus leading to a rise in risk-taking attitudes among young people. Of great concern was the increase in sexually transmitted diseases (STDs). Syphilis among young girls reached a peak in 1996. In 1996, 596 per 100,000 girls aged 15-17 and 1,302 per 100,000 girls aged 18-19 years were infected; 186 per 100,000 men aged 15-17 and 500 per 100,000 men aged 18-19 were infected as well. By 2003 the disease had dramatically decreased but remained very high for both sexes compared to the 1980s and 1990s levels (*Russian Statistical Yearbook*, 2004, p 276). The number of people with HIV/AIDS increased, too. Between 1987 and 1996 the HIV virus progressed slowly but since 1997 it has entered a new phase and by 2000 had acquired a character of an epidemic. As of 30 September 2005, there were 318,794 people infected with HIV, and 1,383 persons were suffering from AIDS (www.hivrussia.org/index.php). Twenty per cent of infected people were women, and 30% of infected women were teenagers aged 15-17. Contamination through infected needles accounted mostly for the dramatic spread of the disease.

The role of political actors

In the early 1990s, the government took some steps to address rising concerns about population decline. The Supreme Soviet of the Russian Federation adopted a decree entitled 'About urgent measures for studies of population and demographic perspectives of the Russian Federation'. However, it took 10 years to implement the recommended measures. By the beginning of the new millennium, the demographic decline increased both in scope and intensity. In his speech to the Federal Assembly in May 2003, President Putin described demographic issues as the most important challenge for Russia (*Rossijskaya gezeta*, 2003, p 4). The Conception of the Demographic Development of the Russian Federation (President of the Russian Federation, 2000, p 170) identified the main objectives of demographic policies. Family-friendly policies with a special emphasis on young families, measures aimed at encouraging female participation in the labour market and child care provision were intended to create the conditions of stable population growth. However, these measures were never fully implemented. Child benefits remained extremely low. In 2005 child benefit was 8,000 roubles (approximately €233). The monthly parental leave payment, which is paid to a mother until her child reaches 15 years of age was only 700 roubles. These benefits could hardly provide an incentive for women to have children.

Governmental inertia was severely criticised, but no competing political forces came out with clear alternatives in the field of family policies. Instead, most political parties suggested the implementation of similar measures to those proposed by the government. All political parties wanted to increase the level of child benefits and improve housing conditions for young families. Most parties supported a traditional breadwinner model whereby women were confined to traditional nurturing and caring roles. This strong ideological commitment to population growth led to the formulation of reactionary proposals that could severely undermine women's and children's rights. For instance, the Liberal Democratic Party proposed to legalise early marriage as well as polygamy in order to increase birth rates. Most parties, such as 'Rodina', described fertility decline as a consequence of the erosion of traditional family values. 'Rodina' argued that the government should take a much more leading role in the field of family policies. The other party, 'Edinaya Rossiya' ('United Russia'), was equally concerned with young people's well-being and advocated for increased state and financial support for young people. 'United Russia' also advocated for longer parental leave and more generous family benefits. The leader of the 'Russian Party of Life', the Speaker of the Federal Assembly S. Mironov, believed that the Labour, Tax and Budget Codes should be changed in order to become more family-friendly. Unsurprisingly, most parties also blamed birth rate decline on abortion.

During the 1990s, Russia signed several international conventions such as the United Nations Convention on the Rights of the Child, the Convention on the Elimination of All Forms of Discrimination against Women, the World Declaration on the Survival, Protection and Development of Children. At the federal level, the most important measure was the foundation of the Russian Federation Legislation on Citizens' Health (adopted in 1993 and amended in 1998). The legislation established a right to free counselling and family planning. The government adopted specific measures for teenagers. Programmes such as 'Family Planning', 'Safe Motherhood', and 'Disabled Children' were part of a general programme entitled 'Children of Russia'.

The programme 'Family Planning' developed by the Department of Health was the most effective measure for teenagers' sexual health. Sex education courses were developed by the Department of General and Vocational Education in cooperation with the Department of Health. Family planning centres were created and by 1997 there were 296 centres. The Department of Education launched information campaigns on family planning and contributed to the distribution of 40 publications. Seven hundred and fifty videocassettes were distributed in different areas and the Department contributed to the publishing of specialised journals (Healthcare in the Russian Federation, 1999). The country experienced important legislative activity until the early 2000s. The Federal Assembly ('State Duma') drafted a Bill entitled 'About Reproductive Rights and Guarantees of Their Implementation'. In September 1997 the Government of the Russian Federation adopted the new federal Family Planning Programme for the period 1998-2000. The 'Safe Motherhood' programme also contributed to improve young people's reproductive health, especially in terms of maternal and infant care. Between 1995 and 1997, 63 scientific projects concerning at-risk pregnancies were implemented, and a new contraceptive, 'Nitrogest', was designed and tested. The main objectives in 1998-2000 were: the improvement of the legislative framework protecting mothers and children; the improvement of the quality of obstetric-gynaecological medical care for women; and the improvement of the quality of information concerning infant and mother care. In 2001, the Coordinating Council was established within the Department of Health in order to monitor the implementation of the Safe Motherhood programme at the regional level. Moreover, the government adopted a series of normative documents on teenagers' reproductive rights such as the Conception of the Protection of Reproductive Health of the Russian Population for 2000-2004, the National Plan on the Improvement of the Position of Women in the Russian Federation and the Strengthening of Women's Role in Russian Society for 2001-2005.

In 1995, the United Nations Population Fund (UNFPA) started its activity. The first Russian representative of the UNFPA was appointed in 2003. Adolescents' reproductive health was one of the main priorities of the UNFPA. The first project, entitled 'Reproductive Health and Rights of Youth in the Russian Federation' (2000-02), was conducted in six pilot regions. The second project, entitled 'Strengthening the Complex System of Protection of Reproductive Health in Smolensk Oblast' (2001-04), developed special measures for adolescents. In the 1990s, a series of public organisations specialising in teenage sexual health started to emerge. These organisations were the Russian Family Planning Association (RFPA), the international Mother and Child Care Foundation, the Russian Society for Contraception, the Russian Association for Prevention of STDs (SANAM) and Women's Future (an international women's foundation). These non-governmental organisations (NGOs) intended to improve sex education, reduce abortion rates and promote effective use of contraception, especially among the youth. For instance, the RFPA considered sex education as a part of the process of an individual's formation. In 1995 the RFPA created a new structure, Youth Centres. These centres provide information and advice in various areas of sexual and reproductive health. The Youth Centres are supported by the federal government. In 1998-2000, the RFPA and the UNFPA carried out a project entitled 'Sexuality and Reproductive Health of Teenagers' in 16 regions. Approximately 600,000 teenagers accessed information on various aspects of reproductive health. Since 1988 the RFPA has created another important project entitled 'Sex and Reproductive Health and Rights of Teenagers'. The programme was implemented in six cities, in cooperation with the Swedish Association of Sex Education. In 2001-02, the RFPA carried out an educational programme, 'About You'. The Department of Education supported the programme. Governmental initiatives were relatively modest but gained momentum in the late 1990s. The role of NGOs and international organisations remains crucial in the development of specific programmes and services for teenagers. Unfortunately, these initiatives prompted a moral backlash against progressive health policies.

As in the US and Poland, (see Chapters Two and Ten, this volume), religious organisations were at the forefront of the offensive against liberal policies. In particular, the positions of the Catholic Church in Poland and of the Orthodox Church in Russia are strikingly similar. Both oppose sex education in schools. For instance, in 1997, a regional Committee for the Protection of the Family and Life was created under the leadership of Life, a Moscow Patriarchy and Orthodox medical-educational centre. The Committee aimed to oppose liberal organisations such as the RFPA on the grounds that they attempted to destroy the family and to encourage the occurrence of a second sexual revolution. The purpose of the Committee was also to strengthen traditional family values. In 2004, the Committee took a step further and issued even more reactionary views. In particular, it suggested cutting funding for family planning programmes. Quoting German and Polish legislations, the Committee also campaigned in favour of the prohibition of abortions. Similar committees were established throughout the country (in Aleksandrov, Magadan, Saint-Petersburg, Zaporozhje, Izhevsk, Lvov, Ufa, Yaroslavl, and other regions). These committees attempted to unify parents and teachers in the fight against sex education in schools and family planning. These committees wanted to undermine the influence of 'destructive' organisations such as the RFPA.

In April 1997, a conference entitled 'The Orthodox Faith in Defence of Life and Family' spelled out its main arguments against sex education. The website of the Orthodox Church stated that 'the ideology of family planning encourages society sterilization, contraception, homosexual intercourse, and encourages children and adolescents to focus on the coarse physiological aspects of sexual relationships. 'Safe sex' threatens the moral and physical health of children and instils hedonistic notions which are alien to our traditional values' (www.orthedu.ru/books/sbornik.htm). Typically, these arguments portrayed sex education and family planning as foreign concepts that undermine the very fabric of Russian society. In this perspective, such policies supposedly lead to moral and sexual corruption by promoting guiltless and apparently safe sex. Various parties supported the position of the Orthodox Church. The Bloc 'Rodina' suggested replacing sex education programmes with preparation to parenthood and family life classes. The Liberal Democratic Party supported the prohibition of abortions for 10 years in order to boost birth rates. Russian demographists strongly opposed these proposals on the grounds that the prohibition of abortion and contraception would not increase birth rates.

Programmes for young people and children

Russian family law was consolidated in the mid-1990s. The *Family Code of the Russian Federation* (1999) provided a strong legal framework for the protection of children' rights. The Code stated that children can express their opinions, and that these opinions had to be taken into account. Protection from domestic violence was also included in the Code. The federal law 'About State Benefits to the Citizens with Children' streamlined various child and family benefits. The law consisted of the simplification of existing rules. In the 1980s, the government of the former USSR carried out a natalist policy, with a special emphasis on helping young families. For example, the programme 'Young Family', implemented between 1988 and 2000, aimed to improve the status and living conditions of young families, to broaden their social safety net, to help young parents raise their children, and to improve the social inclusion of young parents in the professional and public spheres. Various benefits were provided to young parents, such as free housing. Although teenage parents were not included in the programme, students were mentioned. For instance, a young mother could receive 200 roubles (approximately €6) when her child was born and special allowances were made for students who raised a child.

As the government and officials showed little interest in the issue, family planning policy began to develop relatively late, only in the 1990s. An archaic abortion culture was predominant until the 1980s. In 1955, abortions for pregnancies of less than 12 weeks were legalised. However, other forms of family planning were not available until the 1980s, when the Department of Health adopted the programme on the use of the IUD as well as mini-abortions. In July 1993, the Foundation of the Russian Federation Legislation on the Health of Citizens stipulated that a woman could choose to terminate a pregnancy up to 12 weeks of gestation. A termination for social reasons (homelessness, lack of income, unemployment, and so on) could be carried out up until 22 weeks of gestation. When the pregnancy had to be terminated for medical reasons, the abortion could be performed at any stage. In 1996, the government widened the criteria for legal abortions. Thirteen different life circumstances (social indications) were considered sufficient grounds for performing an abortion. Abortions for social indications among the young women in the 1990s to early 2000s were performed mainly because the woman was single, unemployed, lived in poor housing conditions or did not have a sufficient income. A tremendous U-turn occurred in 2003, when the government reduced the number of social indications from 13 to four. At present, abortions can be granted if the court has deprived the expecting mother of her parental rights, if the woman is pregnant as a result of rape, if the woman is in jail or if the father is disabled or dead. The considerable tightening of the law on abortions is likely to result in a rise in the number of illegal abortions, which are often damaging to women's health.

At present, the current legislation does not identify teenage parents as a specific group, even though adolescent parents can be included in the broader category of young or poor families. Young parents are entitled to benefits if their per capita income is less than the regional average. Certain measures are specifically targeted at students. For example, their medical expenses are partially paid for and children under two are enrolled in free medical care and food programmes. However, whether teenage mothers are entitled to welfare state support remains a controversial matter in Russian society, as some Conservative politicians support the withdrawal of benefits for very young parents. In general, state support for adolescent parents is in its infancy. For instance, there are no maternal homes for teenage mothers. The only exception to the rule is the house 'The Second Mama' in Saint Petersburg, which is sponsored by the Finnish government. It is worth noting that several consultative centres have been opened in Moscow and Barnaul.

In the late 1980s, economic and social transformations severely reduced the income of poor families. Young people's involvement in the labour market occurred earlier than was previously the case. Current legislation allows child labour from 14 years onwards and a young person can sign a work contract once they are 15 years old and once they have finished compulsory secondary education. The minimum age at which someone can get married has also been lowered. Until 1993, the Family Code stipulated that 18 years was the minimum age of consent for marriage. In 1993, the law was modified and defined 16 years as the minimum age of consent. Similarly, in 1997 the age of sexual consent was reduced from 16 years to 14 years. The Criminal Code of the Russian Federation now states that a sexual relationship with a teenager above 14 years of age is only an offence in the case of rape. There was no public debate about lowering the age of sexual consent, but 80% of school teachers were opposed to the changes made in 1997 (Gurko, 2003, p 139). Thus, sexual relationships with teenagers became legal, in sharp contrast to the much more stringent criminal law in the Soviet era. For instance, the Criminal Code of 1960 stipulated that a person who had reached full sexual maturity was committing an offence when having intercourse with a person who had not yet reached puberty. Puberty was established in court, which was a very complex procedure. The changes introduced in the 1990s are extremely ambiguous. Although they tend to formally grant some form of adulthood status to young people, both in terms of work and sex life, they also deprive adolescents of legislative protection against potential exploiters. Moreover, these modifications remain purely formal: there is no substance to the right to work since young people are proportionally more affected by unemployment than the rest of the population. Indeed, youth unemployment was 27% in 1998 although it dropped to 18% in 2001.[3]

Conclusion

The period since the early 1990s has witnessed the development of some positive policy initiatives in the field of reproductive and sexual health. Furthermore, family planning services have become increasingly targeted at adolescents. But these initiatives are still in their infancy and do not meet existing needs. Research shows that many family planning services are unavailable for adolescents. For instance, girls still resort to self-medication if they have a contraceptive problem, and seek medical help in the late stages of their pregnancy. They rarely use gynaecologists in the prevention of STDs and pregnancy (Albitskiy et al, 2001; Zhuravlyova, 2002). According to a survey conducted in Tatarstan in 2002, 61% of girls aged 15, 50% of girls aged 16 and 46% of girls aged 17 had never seen a gynaecologist (Mukharyamova et al, 2004, p 368).

But the main problem remains the development of a moral backlash against sexual health and sex education policies. Indeed, conservative political forces such as the Orthodox Church have launched various campaigns against sex education and family planning programmes. The Parliament has cut funding for the Family Planning programme. Negative reports concerning sex education have led regional authorities to ban the adoption of sex education lessons in schools. Thus, adolescent reproductive and sexual rights remain purely formal. In theory, a girl aged 15 is entitled to abortion and does not need to obtain parental consent. In practice, however, physicians often hesitate to carry out the procedure on a young girl. A girl is more likely to have an abortion performed in the private sector rather than in the public sector, which can endanger her health if the termination is not carried out properly. Social support for teenage parents is also extremely limited since responsibility for the girl's reproductive behaviour is laid on the family. The girl's parents are legally responsible for supporting their daughter (and their grandchild). The Russian Federation has not developed specific programmes for teenage parents and young parents are only entitled to state support if they fall in the category of poor or young family (which they often do). To conclude, there are some heterogeneous programmes for teenage parents but there is no set of comprehensive public policies.

Notes

[1] *Age-specific fertility rates* (ASFR) are computed as a ratio of annual numbers of births to women at a given age group to average annual numbers of women in this age group obtained from current estimates. While computing fertility rates for the age group 15–19, the numbers of women aged 15–19 are taken as a denominator, the number of births including births to mothers under 15.

Total fertility rates (TFR) are calculated as sums of ASFR for age groups within the 15 to 49-year age range. TFR shows an average number of children per woman that would be born alive to the mother if, throughout her reproductive period (15-49 years), ASFRs for the specified year remained unchanged.

2 The exact translation from Russian is 'social indications', which refer to situations such as homelessness, unemployment, lack of sufficient income, and so on.

3 See statistics at www.unece.org/stats/trend/rus.pdf, accessed 13 December 2005.

References

Albitskiy, V., Yusupova, A., Sharapova, E. and Volkov, I. (2001) *Reproductive Health and Behavior of Women in Russia*, Kazan: Meditsina.

Botcharova, A.O. (1994) 'Sexual Freedom: Words and Deeds', *Chelovek*, no 5, pp 98-107.

David, P.H. (2000) *Household Survey 2000: Women and Infant Health Project: Report of Main Findings*, USAID/Russia, John Snow Inc.

Demographic Yearbook of Russia, The (2004), Moscow: ROSSTAT.

Demographic Yearbook of Russia, The (2005), Moscow: ROSSTAT.

Family Code of the Russian Federation (1999) Moscow: Prospect.

Gavrilova, L.V. (1997) 'Reproductive Behaviour of the Population of the Russian Federation in Modern Environment', *Family Planning*, no 4, pp 8-16.

Grebesheva, I.I. (1998) 'Reproductive Health of Adolescents: Lessons Learned', *Family Planning*, no 4, pp 24-7.

Gurko, T.A. (2003) *Parenthood: Sociological aspects*, Moscow: Institute of Sociology, Russian Academy of Sciences.

Healthcare in the Russian Federation (1999) *Federal Report on the State of Health of Population of the Russian Federation in 1997*, Moscow: Meditsina Publishers.

Ivanova, E.I. (1996) 'Nuptiality among Russian Women', *Population and Society: Information Bulletin of the Demography and Human Ecology Centre*, Institute for Economic Forecasting, Russian Academy of Sciences, no 12, pp 1-4.

Ivanova, E.I. (1998) 'Fertility Rejuvenation in Russia, and its Factors', *The Russian Demographic Journal*, no 1, pp 6-11.

Ivanova, E.I. and Zakharov, S.V. (1996) 'Fertility Decline and Recent Changes in Russia: On the Threshold of the Second Demographic Transition', in D. Adamson and J. DaVanzo (eds) *Russia's Demographic 'Crisis': How Real Is It?*, Santa Monica, CA: RAND, pp 36-82.

Kon, I.S. (1997) *Sexual Culture in Russia*, Moscow: OGI.

Kon, I.S. (2001) *Adolescent Sexuality on the Threshold of the XXI Century*, Dubna: Phenix.

Lauwers, G. (2005) 'Education and Sexual Health in the Russian Federation', in N. Harris and P. Meredith (eds) *Children, Education and Health: International Perspectives on Law and Policy*, Aldershot: Ashgate, pp 149-63.

Mukharyamova, L., Albitskiy, V., Morenko, I., Petrova, R.G. and Salakhatdinova, L.N. (2004) 'Strengthening of Reproductive Behavior among Adolescent Girls in Tatarstan Republic', in E. Shatalova (ed) *Social Policy: Realities of the XXI Century*, Moscow: Independent Institute for Social Policy, pp 349-79.

President of the Russian Federation (2000) *Sobraine Zakonodatelstva Rossijskoj Federatsii* (The Conception of the Demographic Development of the Russian Federation [Presidential Order]), No 24, Moscow, 10 January.

Rossijskaya gezeta (2003) 17 May, p 4.

Rotkirch, A. (2004) 'What Kind of Sex can you Talk About? Acquiring Sexual Knowledge in Three Soviet Generations', in D. Bertaux, P. Thompson and A. Rotkirch (eds) *On Living Through Soviet Russia*, London: Routledge, pp 93-119.

Sharapova, E.I. (1998) 'Reproductive health of women in Russia: state, trends, and system of measures for its improvement', PhD thesis, Moscow: NPO for Medical and Social Research, Economics, and Information Technologies.

Sprecher, S., Hatfield, E., Potapova, E. and Levitskaya, A. (1994) 'Token Resistance to Sexual Intercourse and Consent to Unwanted Sexual Intercourse in Dating Relationships: Gender and Cross-Cultural Comparisons', *Journal of Sex Research*, vol 31, no 2, pp 125-32.

UNICEF (2001) *A League Table of Teenage Births in Rich Nations, Innocenti Report Card No 3*, Florence: Innocenti Research Centre.

Vannappagari, V. and Ryder, R. (2002) *Monitoring Sexual Behaviour in the Russian Federation*, Report submitted to the US Agency for International Development, North Carolina, NC: Carolina Population Center, University of North Carolina at Chapel Hill.

Vishnevskij, A. (ed) (2002) *Population of Russia: Annual Demographic Report*, Moscow: Centre for Demography and Human Ecology Institute for Economic Forecasting, Russian Academy of Sciences.

Zakharov, S.V., Ivanova, E.I. and Sakevich, V.I. (2000) *Adolescent Reproductive Behaviour and Health in Russia: An Analytic Review*, Moscow: Centre for Demography and Human Ecology, Institute for Economic Forecasting, Russian Academy of Sciences, Policy Project.

Zhuravlyova, I. (2002) 'Health of Adolescents: Sociological Analysis', Moscow: Institute of Sociology, Russian Academy of Sciences.

Useful websites

www.edinros.ru/news.htm?id=107955
www.edinros.ru/news.htm?id=36414
www.hivrussia.org/index.php
www.kprf.ru/about/program.shtml
www.ldpr.ru/about/program/#5
www.orthodoxy.ru
www.rodina.ru/article/show/?id=287
www.rpvita.ru/aboutus/progs/2336.html
www.rpvita.ru/aboutus/progs/2339.html

TEN

Teenage pregnancy in Poland: between laissez-faire and religious backlash

Stéphane Portet[1]

Introduction

In Poland, teenage pregnancy seems invisible. Only a few newspaper articles mention this issue and there is neither political discussion nor a real action plan concerning early motherhood. However, even if the number of teenage pregnancies tends be small, this phenomenon remains significant. Although teenage pregnancy is not publicly discussed, by contrast issues such as sexual and reproductive rights, especially abortion and sex education, are at the centre of the political debate. These highly controversial issues structure the political agenda and define political alliances and divisions, but teenage births remain taboo. The prudishness that characterised the communist period is still predominant in post-1989 Poland. While political elites regardless of their political orientation often condemn teenage sexuality or pretend it does not exist outside marriage, Polish society has experienced rapid socio-cultural changes since the 1980s. Policymakers have been unable to adjust to these changing lifestyles and aspirations. The Church and the state try to control the sex life of Polish citizens or to ban it outside the context of marriage. Moreover, welfare retrenchment and the religious backlash that accompanied the transition to democracy and market liberalism has undermined further the state's ability to implement comprehensive sexual health policies. In this context, it is not surprising that teenage pregnancy remains taboo as it points to a disturbing social reality.

This chapter provides an overview of the dynamics of this phenomenon in Poland and analyses the characteristics of the public debate. The first section presents a statistical analysis. The second section analyses the issues of contraception and abortion. The third section analyses current sex education programmes and the public debate surrounding this very controversial issue underlining the rather conservative approach that prevails in Poland. The fourth section identifies the reasons for the lack of a coherent strategy regarding teenage pregnancy. And finally the conclusion underlines the importance of cultural factors in explaining continuity and change in patterns of teenage pregnancy.

Dynamics of teenage births in Poland and social characteristics of young mothers

With 18.7 pregnancies per 1,000 women aged under 20 in 1998, Poland resulted in 9th position among 28 Organisation for Economic Co-operation and Development (OECD) countries (UNICEF, 2001). The dynamics of teenage pregnancy in Poland is rather different from other developed countries (apart from Ireland). Whereas most industrialised countries experienced a phase of significant increase in teenage pregnancy followed by a continual decrease, since World War II Poland experienced only one very short phase (1953-58) of significant increase in teenage pregnancy. This rate remained stable for over 30 years (until 1991) with around 30 live births per 1,000 women aged 15-19.[2] Since 1991, it has progressively declined from 31.5 to 15.2 per 1,000 in 2002 (GUS, 2004).

In the majority of the former communist countries, teenage birth rates strongly decreased from 1989, following a movement that started in the 1980s (Singh and Darroch, 2000, p 17). Between 1989 and 2002, the decrease was by 74.1% in the Czech Republic, 47% in Hungary, 77.9% in Slovakia, 44.8% in Slovenia, 45.2% in Bulgaria and 50.1% in Poland.

The decline in teenage birth rates mirrored a general decrease in total fertility rates in these countries. In the Polish case, the decrease in teenage birth rates and total fertility rates is concomitant but not equivalent in intensity. Between 1991 and 2002, the total fertility rate in Poland decreased by 36.5% (from 2.05 to 1.3 pregnancies per 1,000 women aged 25 to 49 years) and the teenage birth rate decreased by 52.1% (from 32.2% to 15.4% of births per 1,000 women aged under 19).

However, since 1991 the decrease in live birth rates to women under the age of 20 is lower than the decrease in the same rate to women aged 20-24. The intensity of the dynamics is higher for older teenagers. Between 1990 and 2002, the fertility rate for 18- and 19-year-old females dropped by 60% and 53% respectively, while in the group of younger adolescents the decline is lower: 46% for 17-year-old girls and 42% for 16-year-old girls. Thus, the share of births to mothers under the age of 20 decreased by only 24.7% during this period (from 8.5% in 1991 to 6.4% in 2003).

In 2003, there were 22,615 live births to women aged under 20. There were 45 births to women aged under 14 (The Chancellery of the Prime Minister of the Republic of Poland, 2004). The most recent detailed data on live births to women under the age of 20 date from 2002 (GUS, 2004). In 2002, these women gave birth to 24,331 babies in the following fashion: 289 to mothers aged under 16, 1,135 to women aged 16, 3,375 to women aged 17, 7,428 to women aged 18 and 12,104 to women aged 19. In 2002, 2,047 women under the age of 20 gave birth to an additional child.

The legal prohibition of termination and the existence of a large market for clandestine abortions render teenage abortion impossible to measure. Given the absence of statistics, one can only assume that the number of teenage conceptions is higher than the number of recorded births each year. No detailed study has been carried out since 1988 (Wrblewska, 1991). The majority of the available data for the recent period allow only a very vague outline of the social characteristics of teenage mothers.

Births to women under the age of 20 are more frequent in rural areas than in towns. The number of live births per 1,000 women under the age of 20 was 14 in towns and 17 in rural areas in 2002. However, since 1970, this rate has decreased by a larger extent in rural areas (−50%) than in towns (−46%). The spatial distribution of teenage births is rather differentiated (Figure 10.1). Births to teenage women are particularly frequent in the border regions. This was already the case in the 1970s (Wrblewska, 1999). These regions are very poor, with a higher than average rate of unemployment. This is largely due to the closing down of collective farms following the imposition of market capitalism. Although the fall of the Berlin Wall brought the re-establishment of democracy in Eastern European countries alongside civil and political rights, the imposition of capitalist rules led to the closure of non-profitable firms. Women were hit especially hard by rising unemployment and new austerity measures (Heinen and Portet, 2002).

Teenage mothers tend to have poor educational achievements. In 2002, 48.5% of teenage mothers had only completed primary school education, which a pupil normally completes before their 14th birthday; 31.1% had completed basic vocational school; 15.5% of young mothers worked before giving birth;[3] 42.3% were

Figure 10.1: Rate of live births to women under the age of 20 (per 1,000 women), by region

Source: GUS (2004), map designed by the author

financially supported by a working person; and 42.2% relied on social assistance. In 2002, 12,190 births (50.1%) to women under the age of 20 were out of wedlock (GUS, 2004). In 1990, the birth rate outside wedlock was 20.4% for teenagers. Illegitimate births have gradually become more accepted in Polish society, but the occurrence of 'shotgun marriages', that is, marriage arranged as soon as a woman discovers she is pregnant, remains high (see Chapter Nine, this volume). This is particularly true in rural areas where only 40.6% of births to teenagers occur out of wedlock.[4]

Access to contraception and the interdiction of abortion

Age at first sexual intercourse continues to decrease although it remains at a relatively high level. In 2001, it was 19.12 years for women and 18.32 years for men (Izdebski and Durka, 2002). For women aged between 40 and 41, age of sexual initiation was 19.83 years compared to 18.39 years for those aged between 20 and 24. In 1998, 31% of young people aged 15-17 (38% of boys and 23% of girls) had already had sexual intercourse. Thirteen per cent of girls and 30% of boys aged 15 had already had sexual intercourse. The rates were 46% for 17-year-old boys and 32% for 17-year-old girls (Rzdowa Rada Ludnościowa and Rzdowe Centrum Studiów Strategicznych, 2001, p 169). The proportion of 15-year-old teenagers who reported sexual intercourse is increasing considerably (Wrblewska, 1999, p 43).

Contraceptive use is becoming more common among young people. In 2001, 74.1% of 15- to 16-year-olds and 60% of 17- to 19-year-olds used a condom at the time of their last sexual encounter with an occasional partner, but only 45.9% of 25- to 29-year-olds did (Durka, 2002). However, at the time of their first sexual encounter, only 55.5% of young women asked their partner to use a condom, 22.6% used withdrawal methods, 6.6% using so-called 'natural' methods (calendar, Billings and temperature methods), 3.9% took the pill and 22% did not use any form of protection (Wrblewska, 1998).[5] Only 52.1% of young mothers use contraception but, more importantly, most of them use unreliable contraceptive methods.

The lack of detailed research on this issue renders difficult the interpretation of the low use of contraception by teenage mothers. We do not know whether these young women have planned their pregnancies, or whether the lack of contraception reflects an unconscious desire to become pregnant (see also Chapter Eleven, this volume). Regardless of their motivations, teenage pregnancies are the result of a very low use of reliable methods of contraception by some young people. It must be stressed that access to contraception remains relatively difficult. Condoms are very easily accessible,[6] but this is not true of contraceptive pills. No third-generation pill (which contains less oestrogen than the second- and first-generation pills) is subsidised by government and only four first- and second-generation pills are subsidised, at a rate of 30% to 50% respectively (Chancellery of the Prime MInister of the Republic of Poland, 2004, p 20). In 2003, the average monthly cost of the pills was of 58 PLN,[7] that is, a sum higher than 10% of a net minimum wage (Chancellery of the Prime MInister of the Republic of Poland, 2004, appendix 4). Moreover, as the private sector monopolises the contraceptive prescription market, for some young women access to oral contraception is completely impossible simply for financial reasons. At the time of the parliamentary elections in 2001, left-wing parties promised to register a certain number of third-generation pills on the list of free medicines (paid for by the State). However, the Left did not hold to its promise after having won the elections. In addition, many doctors refuse to prescribe the pill for moral and cultural reasons. If a woman can relatively easily find more understanding general practitioners (GPs) in large cities, this is not the case in small towns. Moreover, there is a strong moral stigma attached to contraception for unmarried young women. Those who do not want to be talked about and deemed as promiscuous are reluctant to buy the contraceptive pill (Nowicka, 2004). Last but not least, the 'morning-after' pill is only available on prescription.

There is no link between the prevention of unwanted pregnancies and the fear of sexually transmitted diseases, especially AIDS. Should they not fear an unplanned pregnancy, only 18% of young Poles would use a condom (Mazur, 2004). AIDS appears not to be an issue of concern. Admittedly, the Polish official infection figures are low. Since the beginning of screening for AIDS in 1985 until 28 February 2005, 9,298 cases of infection were reported. This figure includes 5,203 cases due to the use of contaminated needles. During this period, 1,581 people developed AIDS and 743 people died (Państwowa Zakład Higieny, 2005). The fear of AIDS influences the sexual behaviour of only 21.6% of 15- to 19-year-old people: 25.9% always use a condom, 59.5% are in a monogamous relationship and 25.5% avoid partners whom they consider risky. Among those whose sexual activity is not influenced by AIDS, 56% are persuaded that their sexual life does not put them at risk and 10% believe that the risk is not significant (Durka, 2002, pp 52-3). Public indifference is an obstacle to the successful promotion of condom use. Moreover, conservative organisations systematically oppose sexual health campaigns. When three Members of Parliament (MPs) of the town of Sosnowice decided to distribute booklets on sexual life and condoms, they were confronted with strong opposition from the Church and from the pupils' parents. Father Andrzej Ceślik, responsible for family questions for the Archbishop, issued an official communication stating that 'such initiatives had been stopped in the West because they led to an increase in teenage pregnancies'. The same priest declared that sexual health campaigns based on condom use were not acceptable because 'research shows that the condom use is not effective in protecting against AIDS' (*Gazeta Wyborcza Katowice*, 10 February 2005). Although the majority of Poles do not follow religious rules in relation to sex and 80% of young people think that Catholic priests should not dictate their sexual behaviour (Szlendak, 2004, pp 126-7), the Church remains the dominant moral authority. As such, it continues to formulate norms of acceptable behaviour in the political arena. In this respect, the Church assumes a clear political role. Moreover, a negative judgement issued by the Church generally suffices to annihilate any sexual health policy initiative. Such statements also obstruct the action of non-governmental organisations (NGOs) because of the difficulty in funding such initiatives. It is no coincidence that, like in Russia (see Chapter Nine, this volume), the majority of NGOs working in the field of sexual health are founded by foreign foundations.

Not only is contraception expensive and difficult to access, but abortion is illegal following a conservative backlash against women's sexual rights enacted during the Communist period. The Communist regime legalised abortion in 1956. Women could easily obtain an abortion on both medical and social grounds until the early 1990s. However, evidence of a reactionary backlash appeared in the late 1980s as 'pro-life' organisations and the Church initiated a series of vocal campaigns against abortion. Once again, the similarities with the Russian and American cases are striking. For example, in 1992 the National Assembly of Doctors adopted a Medical Code of Ethics stating that abortion for social or criminal reasons (incest, rape) was impossible. In 1993, Parliament passed the Family Planning, Protection of Human Foetus and Conditions of Termination of Pregnancy Act, often named the anti-abortion law. In 1996, when the social democrats returned to power, legal restrictions were abolished and abortion on social grounds was again permitted. However, in 1997, after the victory of right-wing parties, Parliament again restricted access to abortion. Since 1997, termination of pregnancy is allowed in only three situations:

- if the pregnancy constitutes a threat to the life of the mother;
- if the prenatal examination or other medical diagnostics point to the high probability of severe and irreversible damage to the foetus;
- if the pregnancy is the result of a criminal act.

The left-wing coalition (2001-05) never fulfilled its 2001 electoral promise to liberalise access to abortion. In fact, political parties are extremely reluctant to confront the Catholic Church on this issue, despite the fact that opinion polls conducted since 1993 show that the population supports liberalisation (CBOS, 2005). Interestingly, in 2004-05, the social democrats officially abandoned the promise of liberalising the anti-abortion law in order to obtain the support of the Church during the European accession referendum campaign. This decision illustrates the importance of the persisting gap between popular opinion and preferences and the political and religious views on abortion.

In 2003, the number of legal terminations was 174. The right to a legal abortion is almost non-existent. Even when the pregnancy poses severe risks to a woman's health, most doctors refuse to perform the termination on ethical grounds. In 1990, the number of terminations in public hospitals was 59,417, in 1994 it was 782. In 1997, after the liberalisation, only 3,047 abortions were performed in public hospitals. In 1998, once access to abortion again became severely restricted, the number of abortions dropped to 310.

This prohibition has led to the rise in backstreet abortions. The number of such procedures is estimated to be 80,000 each year (Federacja Na Rzecz Kobiet I Planowania Rodziny, 2000). Complacent gynaecologists willing to perform terminations place thinly veiled advertisements proposing 'all kinds of services', or 'the return of menstruation'. The problem is that these terminations carry a heavy health risk as the quality of the procedure depends on the cost. The price can be four to eight times a net minimum wage. Thus the majority of women have an abortion without anaesthesia because this involves an additional person (the anaesthetist) and adds an additional cost of about 1,000 PLN (approximately €250). Teenagers need to obtain parental consent at the doctor's request in order to protect themselves against being taken to court by the family. Indeed, if a woman cannot be sent to jail for having a termination, her accomplices are liable to imprisonment.

Sex education and public discourse on the sexuality of young people

The issue of sex education is very controversial. Although a large majority of Poles are in favour of the inclusion of sex education in the curriculum, the Catholic Church constantly obstructs the development of sex education on the grounds that sexual intercourse should only take place within the context of marriage.

Sex education appeared in 1973 with the introduction in secondary schools of a facultative class for the 'preparation for the life in the socialist family'. In 1975, the epithet 'socialist' was removed. In 1986, compulsory courses for pupils aged 11–14 were set up in primary and secondary schools (two hours per month). In 1987, the first sex education handbook was published. The Church strongly criticised its contents. The Ministry of Education was forced to declare that the use of the handbook was non-compulsory and was at the teacher's discretion, which became the rule between 1990 and 1992. The conservative backlash gained momentum. In 1993, the anti-abortion law included an article on sex education for teenage pupils (12 years and over). The programme aimed to teach children the principles of 'a conscious and responsible motherhood and fatherhood, the values of the family, the life at the prenatal phase and the methods and means of conscious procreation'. In many schools, sex education was not even included in the curriculum. When sex education was included in the curriculum, it conveyed traditional and conservative views such as the sanctity of family life and marriage, in accordance with the ministerial directives.

The political mood shifted in the opposite direction with the liberalisation of the anti-abortion law in 1996. A programme entitled 'Knowledge about the sexual life of the individual' was set up. It provided basic courses for teenagers. In secondary education, the possibility of providing 10 hours of instruction each year was then envisaged. The pendulum shifted again with the victory of the right-wing coalition in the 1998 parliamentary elections. A group of senators argued that the course was unconstitutional since the Constitution referred explicitly to the need to protect the family. These senators argued that sex education at school undermined the rights of the parents to raise their children according to their religious principles. In 1998, sex education was removed and replaced by classes on 'the life in the family' for pupils over 12 years of age. These courses remain optional and parents can remove their children from the classes if they wish to do so.

The role of the family is at the heart of the political debate surrounding sex education. The Church considers parental rights as completely sacrosanct. As Father Józef Augustyn (Augustyn, 2003, p 37) points out, 'the attempt of the distortion by the State of the rights of the parents to educate their children is – according to the Church – an abuse of power'. The advocates of public sex education underline the lack of open discussion about sexual matters in the family. They stress the need for enlightened teaching based on contemporary science. Even the Church recognises the need for school sex education organised by the school: 'We are delighted by the help of the School', say bishops while underlining 'but only help' (Anonymous, 1997, p 36). 'Education by the family always comes first. Education in school can only help the parents [...] For the Church, the best place for sex education will always be the family' (Augustyn, 2003, p 37). The Vatican encourages families to monitor sex education at school. Pope John Paul II recommended 'to withdraw the children if sex education goes against the principles defined by the family' (Jan Pawel II, 1994, p 13). The Church strongly supports full parental control of state education, especially in the field of sex education, in order to protect parental rights, especially families' rights to teach their children religious and moral values. Public education is thus perceived as a potential threat to the Catholic dogma. This suspicion is not entirely ungrounded in the light of the enduring conflict between public schools and religious authorities. Indeed, under the Communist regime, schools played a key role in the attempt to marginalise the Church. However, the influence of the Catholic Church remains extremely significant. Religious education is part of the curriculum. A large majority of young Poles attend the classes even when they are optional. Like the Polish Parliament, most classrooms are decorated with a cross. The Church is regularly consulted on the contents of educational programmes. In this context, the Concordat signed in 1994 is not an empty concession to marginalised clerics. Instead, Catholicism is the official religion of the state, which explains why the Church retains privileges that go far beyond preferential tax treatment for its representatives.

Religious censorship is permanent, especially in relation to the contents of the sex education handbooks. Compliance with the social doctrine of the Church is vigorously monitored. Handbooks must respect certain principles to obtain the agreement of the Church:

> Sex education must be integrated in a global perception of the human being, it cannot be only reduced to information on the physical dimension of human sexuality…. Sexual intercourse must be evoked with reference to ethics and spirituality. The fundamental principle of sex education must be the preparation for marriage and the family…. In sex education it must be stressed that the goal of the union of bodies in marriage must be reproduction. (Augustyn, 2003, pp 40-1)

The Church does not condemn sexual activity itself: 'sex education and the forming of the consciences cannot consist in repressing the needs and the sexual desires of young people'. But these desires must be controlled: 'in sex education it should be stressed that the gift of love does not only exist through sexual activity but also by renouncing sex' (Augustyn, 2003, p 45). This spiritual base sets a series of principles that must be respected by sex education. Father Władysław Skrzydlewski (Skrzydlewski, 2003, p 27) states that 'even if sexual intercourse before marriage is in fact accepted by most young people, it should be stressed that this behaviour is morally wrong. The partners in this case have sexual intercourse which does not take into consideration the possible result of this act, that is, the possibility of a child'. This priest also declares that 'the use of contraceptives is morally bad because it removes from the sexual act its first dimension: procreation' (Skrzydlewski, 2003, p 28).

Such principles are widely respected by sex education handbooks. For primary schools, the only handbook authorised by the Ministry of Education follows the doctrine of the Church to the letter (Król, 1999). For secondary schools, the Ministry of Education authorises two handbooks, which are both sympathetic to Catholic principles (Ryś, 1999; Król, 2001). In secondary schools, seven handbooks are authorised (Król, 1999; Kalinowska, 2001; Ksinska, 2001; Długołcka-Lach and Tworkiewicz Bieniaś, 2000; Szczerba, 2001; Garstka et al, 2003; Izdebski and Jaczewski, 2004). Only two handbooks present the various methods of contraception, comparing their respective reliability and underlining the risks incurred by the use of 'natural' methods. The remaining handbooks teach pupils that 'the natural methods are particularly adapted for women having rather irregular cycles' (Król, 2001, p 124), breast-feeding is presented as 'a means of contraception used since prehistory, although it is necessary to have some reserves on its effectiveness' (Król, 2001, p 126 [translation]). Textbooks often stress the risk posed by the use of the contraceptive pill, in particular, for young women (Król, 2001, pp 144-5). Contraception is even sometimes presented as an absolute evil, which 'means more than the destruction of health, destroying social ties....' (Ryś, 1999, p 277). The books also question the reliability of condoms, notably their capacity to protect people from the HIV virus. The majority of handbooks do not condone sexual intercourse outside of marriage and preach abstinence. With some exceptions (Izdebski and Jaczewski, 2004), the handbooks preparing for family life closely follow Catholic dogma. The choice of the handbook is at the teacher's discretion but teachers choose the most conservative volumes as shown by a survey carried out in the Łodz area (Kuratorium Adzkie, 2003).

These handbooks are subject to criticism, in particular from the feminist movement (Skłodowska, 2004). In 2003, the Ministry of Education decided to remove the accreditation for a handbook for presenting unreliable and biased information. However, the reading of the accredited Ministry shed some considerable doubt on the handbooks as pedagogical support for neutral scientific teaching.

In addition, access to sex education is very unequal. In 2000, 47%

of head teachers stated that they experienced difficulties in organising classes (Federacja Na Rzecz Kobiet I Planowania Rodziny, 2003b). These courses are often not treated seriously and are rarely allocated concrete slots in the timetable. Yet pupils continue to ask for reliable information, in particular regarding contraception and protection against sexually transmitted diseases. The majority obtain information from the media (Izdebski and Ostrowska, 2004). Whether the solution lies simply in an improvement in offering sex education in schools remains, however, doubtful. Indeed, the results of a 2000 study on the effects of sex education courses are puzzling. After completing the sex education courses, the proportion of pupils who thought that condoms protect from HIV decreased from 9% to 3% whereas the majority thought that condoms protect from the disease but not all the time (Federacja Na Rzecz Kobiet I Planowania Rodziny, 2003b, p 3).

Teenage pregnancy as a political issue

The question of adolescent pregnancies is closely related to that of sex education, which is a highly divisive issue. Liberals advocate sex education as a way to promote sexual health and to reduce teenage pregnancy. The Church opposes liberals' views because priests want to maintain the status of traditional attitudes to sex. What is at stake is the political and cultural hegemony of the Church. Each group mobilises studies or examples showing that the development of sex education either stimulates or reduces the number of teenage pregnancies. Sex education is even often depicted as a true Pandora's box, in the sense that it can potentially unravel a whole range of broad social problems. For instance, in 1997, during the parliamentary discussion on the liberalisation of the anti-abortion law, Maria Władyslawa Smereczyńska, a Conservative MP, declared:

> Sex education, as organised in many countries, is often simplistic; sexuality is apprehended in a instrumental and technical way.… What are the effects of sex education in the USA? [...] In 1970, 4.5% of 15 year old American females were sexually active, in 1990 the number was 61.4%, … the number of abortions increased by 800%, child abuse increased by 500%, the number of divorces by 133%, the number of people contracting venereal diseases by 255%, the number of suicides in teenagers increased by 240% and the juvenile criminality by 295%. Do we, in Poland,

wish to have the same results? Do we want to pay for the effects of sex education, with what money?'[8]

In 2001, Maria W. Smereczyńska, the then State Secretary for Family Affairs, explained that in Western Europe 'sexual education provoked a huge increase in the number of teen pregnancies'.[9]

However, such public statements remain rare since teenage motherhood has not become a significant political issue. Instead, the political debate focuses on issues such as fertility decline and abortion. The Church is more concerned with the promotion of sexual intercourse for reproductive purposes than with the fight against teenage pregnancy. Thus, the debate about teenage pregnancy is often regarded as a sword of Damocles. Public policies concerning teenage pregnancies are virtually non-existent. Only some feminist organisations seem to be really aware of the phenomenon and recently tried to push the issue through the political agenda. During one of the very rare initiatives devoted to this topic, the conference 'So as children don't have children', on 28 May 2003, Wanda Nowicka, the president of the Polish Family Planning Federation was indignant that 'in Poland, the problems of the teenage pregnancies and teenage mothers are not the subject of any political measure'. Danuta Duch, a sociologist specialising in gender studies, underlined on this occasion that 'the youth is completely left alone with sexual problems'. Kazimiera Szczuka, who reports these remarks in her 2004 book, claims that 'the lack of access to objective information concerning sex education and the restrictions on the right to abortion cause teenage pregnancies, and pose serious threats to the physical and psychological health of young mothers' (Szczuka, 2004, p 9). For Polish feminists, teenage pregnancies are a social problem that needs to be taken into account by the government. Addressing the issue of teenage pregnancies also enables them to question not only the limits of the law on abortion but also the ways in which sex education is taught in schools. Adolescent pregnancies are indeed a phenomenon that the majority regard as an evil to fight against; the progressives in the name of women's right to have sexual intercourse without the risk of pregnancy and in the name of the rights of the teenagers to live their adolescence; the conservatives in the name of 'proper' sexual intercourse, that is, in the context of marriage.

The question of teenage pregnancies is thus rife with controversies about dominant moral values. As such, it is a highly emotional issue which politicians simply prefer to ignore. Such a situation is connected with the strong taboo concerning teenage sex. When young people escape adult control (teachers, priests and so on), they clearly challenge adult authority. Of course, adults seldom welcome the fact that teenagers want to live their own lives outside their vigilant protection. However, in Poland this conflict is especially strong due to the constant negation of young people's right to autonomy as a result of the persisting influence of religion.

Perhaps more importantly, the very challenge of parental authority encapsulated by teenage sexuality puts the family in an awkward position vis-à-vis the religious doctrine. Indeed, if only a minority of Poles complies with the Catholic dogma when it comes to their sex life, the situation is quite different in relation to young people. Parents must ensure that their children are raised in full compliance with dominant religious norms. This social pressure is especially strong in rural areas. Families' reputation lies in their capacity to ensure that their children are perceived as good members of the parish. Teenage sexuality challenges both the authority of the family and the Church, and is completely 'unacceptable' for this reason. This sustains silence and taboo. Teenage pregnancies assume a broad symbolic importance and are usually connected with a discourse of fear, drama and even pathology.

Yet this topic seldom emerges in public discourses, apart from discussions around sex education and abortion or when the press describe cases of child murder, abandonment of new-born babies or suicides of pregnant girls. The annual assessment by the Polish Parliament of the application of the anti-abortion law enables progressives and conservatives to engage in a vocal confrontation on the question of teenage pregnancies. Apart from these rare moments, the question of adolescent pregnancies simply does not appear in public discussions.

Public authorities claim to be aware of what they regard as a 'serious problem' (Komunikat po Radzie Ministrów, 2002) but they never set up any policies aimed at reducing teenage births apart from sex education courses. Successive governments, regardless of their political orientation, have not commissioned any studies on the phenomenon; they simply monitor the implementation of the anti-abortion law. Indeed, one of the rare legal provisions concerning teenage mothers intends to protect their right to study (Article 2.3 of the anti-abortion law). Schools are expected to support pregnant girls and young mothers (and fathers) in finishing their studies by offering teaching support, a special timetable, extra holidays and additional sessions in the event of absence from examinations. Quite often, this legal provision is simply ignored and pregnant girls are requested to hide their pregnancy by not attending school, thus being de facto excluded from schools. Teenage pregnancy is considered by Polish society such a deviant phenomenon that it must be hidden at all costs (see also Chapter One). Public authorities have turned a blind eye to these unlawful practices. The Ministry of Education does not collect any data regarding the number of pregnant girls or of young mothers and does not ensure any monitoring of the application of the law. In 2003, no complaints were received from pupils who may have been discriminated against because of their pregnancy or their maternity (Chancellery of the Prime Minister of the Republic of Poland, 2004, p 27).

Moreover, public support for teenage parents remains underdeveloped. Local governments run residence centres for young (but not only) homeless women. In 2003, there were only 10 centres of this type including five private centres offering a total of 395 places. Four hundred and twenty-eight women benefited from a place in these centres. Young mothers, like other parents, are eligible for state aid for maternity and the education of their children. Most allowances are means-tested. To have a right to financial support, the family income per capita must be lower than 504 zl (approximately €122, that is, a little less than the minimum net wage). But receipt of such family allowances is conditional upon meeting occupational requirements as they are based on some kind of social contributions. This provision excludes de facto teenage parents, who are not entitled to family allowances in their own right. When young mothers are maintained by their relatives, the allowance is calculated on the basis of the income of the family. Thus, allowances are particularly meagre and hardly represent any incentive to becoming pregnant. Lastly, it should be noted that in the case of the marriage of children under 21 years old, the parents lose the right to family benefits. Thus, in contrast to the ongoing controversy concerning teenage mothers as a welfare burden in New Zealand, the UK and the US, the issue regarding the cost to the welfare state is never mentioned in the rare debates concerning teenage pregnancy in Poland.

Targeted programmes for the prevention of teenage pregnancy are completely anecdotal and are most of the time carried out by NGOs.[10] However, in 2004, a trial experiment was organised in 24 Polish schools. It consisted of entrusting eight pupils in each school to, over a weekend, look after dolls containing an information-processing system enabling them to behave like new-born babies. The programme, which aimed to increase awareness of the teenagers about the constraints associated with child care, was the subject of an evaluation commissioned by the Ministry of National Education to explore the development of the programme on a larger scale. Such an action contrasts strongly with the traditional passive stance of the Polish authorities, which seem to be satisfied by the 'natural' decrease of births to young women. The Millennium programme of the United Nations, which sets Poland a goal of a 75% decline in teenage birth rates by 2015, underlines that there is 'an opportunity for the attainment of the target in reference to older teenagers. At the same time, the target will be difficult to reach for younger adolescents' (United Nations and Gdansk Institute for Market Economy, 2002, p 19). The author (Wiktoria Wrblewska) of the United Nations report, when asked to cite which policies could help, proposed to:

> extend the scope of secondary-level education and to increase the number of secondary school graduates going into university education and at the same time to allow easy and common access to reliable information and contraception contributing to a better understanding of methods of family planning, including improved knowledge of human physiology and health hazards related to premature initiation of sexual activity. (United Nations and Gdansk Institute for Market Economy, 2002, p 19)

The issue of the risks incurred by young mothers and their children is raised only by the feminist movement and certain doctors. For mothers aged under 16, one notes an hypotrophy of the foetus in 30% of cases, and approximately 10 to 30% of childbirths in teenagers require a caesarean section (Federacja Na Rzecz Kobiet I Planowania Rodziny, 2003a, p 3) There are proportionally almost 1.7 times more children who are born before 32 weeks among women aged under 20 than among women aged between 20 and 24 years (GUS, 2004, p 32).

Beyond the difficulty of setting ambitious policies aimed at decreasing the number of teenage births, it is necessary to underline that various Polish governments regard this issue as a private, family affair. Such a wait-and-see policy is rather dangerous. Of course, since 1991, successive governments can be satisfied with the decline in the number of teenage births. However, the decrease concerns, above all, older teenagers whose behaviour in terms of fertility is surely closer to older young women than in the case of mothers aged under 17 years.

Conclusion: a Pyrrhic victory?

The number of teenage births has dramatically decreased since 1991. Owing to the lack of precise data, it is difficult to explain this steep decline. The number of teenage pregnancies is influenced by the age of sexual initiation, the frequency of sexual acts, the use of methods of contraception, the number of teenage mothers being determined by the proportion of live births and miscarriage, and the rate of abortion.[11] A certain number of 'cultural' factors intervene simultaneously with these behavioural and biological factors. They relate, above all, to a culture of maternity. Indeed, unless we consider that all teenage births are unwanted, it is necessary to understand the process that leads to a teenager keeping a child. As the French sociologist Boltanski demonstrates (2004), the willingness to raise a child fits in a broader culture of maternity, which is an integral part of the gender contract of a specific society. The mode of resolution of the equation between the status of woman and that of mother is connected with the wish to reproduce as a route to individual self-realisation or as a way to meet the social expectations (see also Chapter Eleven). Lastly, the culture of maternity is increasingly subjected to constraints that challenge its realisation. Women are torn between their professional aspirations and their wish to have children. This dilemma is particularly acute in Poland where child care facilities and family policies are notably underdeveloped, thus making it especially difficult for women to combine a career and motherhood.

Far from being the effect of a strong political and governmental commitment to reduce teenage births, the fall in the number of adolescent births is explained, above all, by the development of the methods of contraception and the ongoing challenges to a traditionally predominant culture of maternity. However, if the decrease in the number of births to women aged over 18 years is very significant, the same does not apply for pregnancies among younger people.

Since the early 1990s, Poland has witnessed a steady decrease in fertility rates. This decline was caused by various factors such as rising unemployment, a higher requirement from employers in terms of commitment from their employees (Portet, 2004a), higher educational levels, the dissemination of materialist and hedonist values, a new conception of the education of children, and cuts in social spending (Portet, 2004b). All these factors led to the erosion of the culture of maternity that prevailed up until 1989. According to the results of the Polish General Social Survey, in 1994, 39% of women said they would agree or strongly agree with the opinion that a life without a child has no sense, whereas this figure declined to 29% in 2002.

At present, many young Polish women no longer regard motherhood as the unique route to self-fulfilment. A professional career is also viewed as a way to self-realisation, and young women look up to alternative role models, especially in the media. These changing aspirations contribute to the erosion of the culture of maternity and explain at least partially the fall in fertility rates among women above the age of 18. However, an increasing number of people are concerned about the fall of the birth rate in Poland. The pro-natalist discourse is becoming predominant, especially in the context of the increasing influence of the Catholic Conservative party called Law and Justice in the parliamentary elections held in September 2005. As the decrease in the number of adolescent births is connected to the general trend of the fertility rate, Poland is not protected from a possible backlash. Lastly, mass unemployment among young people (37.3% for 15- to 24-year-olds for the fourth quarter of 2004) makes it difficult to imagine any rapid labour market integration. This could enhance the attraction of parenthood as a way to acquire a new social status, especially for poor, under-educated young people. The only way to definitively challenge this situation would be to overcome the traditional gender contract, which is still powerful in Poland, according to which a woman is, above all, a mother.

This calls for the implementation of a coherent sex education policy that would include unbiased views on contraception and sexual health. Liberalisation of abortion also seems necessary. Various surveys show that a large majority of Poles are in favour of such initiatives. The Church itself would surely gain some legitimacy by accepting that Poles cherish their intimacy and do comply with religious dogma. But this is extremely unlikely as rightist and populist parties have won strong popular support in the last parliamentary elections. At least in the short term, the status quo will take precedence over changes.

Notes
[1] I would like to thank Mathilde Darley for her comments and remarks on earlier versions of this chapter.

[2] Between 1955 and 1970 in France, Austria and Holland, between 1965 and 1975-80 in Italy, Greece, Portugal and Spain, between 1960 and 1985 in Sweden and Norway.

[3] This figure is calculated on the population for which sources of maintenance were known (56.7% of the whole population).

[4] In towns the rate is 58.2%.

[5] Because of possible multiple choices the sum is higher than 100%.

[6] The rate of availability calculated with the WHO's methodology was of 0.97 in 2001.

[7] 1 euro = 4 PLN.

[8] Debate at the Polish Parliament, 30 December 1997, point 2.

[9] Debate in the Polish Parliament, 18 January 2001, point 15.

[10] The first NGO devoted to young parents was created in 2004. For the moment the activity of this organisation mainly consists of gathering members and publishing a web site www.nieletnirodzice.org.prv.pl. A conference on teenage parents was planned for March 2005 but because of a lack of financial support it was cancelled.

[11] There are obviously other parameters that will not be taken into account here, such as biological fertility and sterility.

References
Augustyn, J. (2003) 'Wszystko, co w nas naprawdę ludzkie – Stanowisko Kościota Katolickiego w zakresie wychowania dzieci i młodzieży', in J. Rzepka (ed) *Zagadnienia pro rodzinnej edukacji seksuologicznej*, Mysłowice: WSP, pp 33–44.

Boltanski, L. (2004) *La condition fœtale: Une sociologie de l'engendrement et de l'avortement*, Paris: Gallimard.

CBOS (Centrum Badania Opinii Społecznej) (2005) *Komunikat z Badań – Aborcja, edukacja seksualna, zapłodnienie pozaustrojowe*, Warszawa: CBOS.

Chancellery of the Prime Minister of the Republic of Poland (2004) *Sprawozdanie RM z wykonywania w roku 2003 Ustawy z dnia 7 stycznia 1993 roku o planowaniu rodziny, ochronie płodu ludzkiego i warunkach dopuszczalności przerywania ciąży oraz o skutkach jej stosowania*, Warsaw Chancellery of the Prime Minister of the Republic of Poland.

Długołęcka-Lach, A. and Tworkiewicz Bieniaś, G. (2000) *Ja i Ty: Wychowanie do życia w rodzinie*, Warszawa: Oficyna Edukacyjna Krzysztof Pazdro.

Durka, B. (2002) *Postawy i opinie młodzieży opracowano dla Krajowego Centrum ds: AIDS*, Warszawa: TNS OBOP.

Federacja Na Rzecz Kobiet I Planowania Rodziny (2000) *The Anti-abortion Law in Poland*, Warsaw: Federacja Na Rzecz Kobiet I Planowania Rodziny.

Federacja Na Rzecz Kobiet I Planowania Rodziny (2003a) *Ciąże nastolatek*, available at: www.federa.org.pl/publikacje/mat_info/ciazenast.htm

Federacja Na Rzecz Kobiet I Planowania Rodziny (2003b) *Wychowanie seksualne po polsku*, Warszawa: Federacja Na Rzecz Kobiet I Planowania Rodziny.

Garstka, T., Kostrzewski, M. and Królikowski, J. (2003) *Kim Jestem? Wychowanie do życia w rodzinie*, Warszawa: Wyd. Juka.

GUS (Główny Urzd Statystyczny) (2004) *Rocznik demograficzny*, Warszawa: GUS.

Heinen, J. and Portet, S. (2002) 'Political and Social Citizenship: An Examination of the Case of Poland', in M. Molyneux and S. Razavi (eds) *Gender, Justice, Development and Rights*, Oxford: Oxford University Press, pp 141-70.

Izdebski, Z. and Durka, B. (2002) *Raport z badania 'Wiedza, postawy społeczne wobec HIV/AIDS i zachowanie seksualne'*, Warszawa: TNS OBOP.

Izdebski, Z. and Jaczewski, A. (2004) *Kocha, lubi, szanuje: Wychowanie do życia w rodzinie – Podręcznik dla gimnazjum*, Warszawa: PWN.

Izdebski, Z. and Ostrowska, A. (2004) *Seks po Polsku*, Warszawa: MUZA.

Jan Pawel II (1994) *Gratissinam sane: List do Rodzin*, Rzym

Kalinowska, F. (2001) *Wychowanie do życia w rodzinie*, Piła: Efka Wydawnictwa szkolne.

Komunikat po Radzie Ministrów (2002), 30 July, available at: www.kprm.gov.pl/1937_4094.htm

Ksinska, E. (2001) *Wokół nas: Wiedza o społeczeństwie: Moduł: Wychowanie do życia w rodzinie: 3 klasa gimnazjum*, Kraków: Rubikon.

Król, T. (ed) (1999) *Wędrując ku dorosłości: Wychowanie do życia w rodzinie dla uczniów klas IV-IV szkoły podstawowej*, Kraków: Rubikon.

Król, T. (ed) (2001) *Wędrując ku dorosłości: Wychowanie do życia w rodzinie dla uczniów szkół ponadgimnazjalnych*, Kraków: Rubikon.

Kuratorium Adzkie (2003) *Sprawozdanie z badania dotyczącego realizacji zaj edukacyjnych 'Wychowanie do życia w rodzinie' w szkołach województwa łódzkiego*, available at: www.kuratorium.lodz.pl/aktualnosci.php?id=211

Mazur, N. (2004) 'Czego się boimy?', *Gazeta Wyborcza Poznań*, 30 November.

Nowicka, W. (2004) 'L'avortement en Pologne', in J. Heinen and S. Portet (eds) *Egalité des sexes en Europe centrale et orientale: Entre espoir et déconvenues, Transitions*, vol XLVI, no 1.

Państwowa Zakład Higieny (2005) *Zakażenia HIV i zachorowania na AIDS w Polsce w 2005 roku – Informacja z 28 lutego*, available at: www.pzh.gov.pl/epimeld/hiv_aids/

Portet, S. (2004a) 'La Pologne comme laboratoire du nouveau modèle de protection sociale ?', *La Nouvelle Alternative*, no 62, pp 25-39.

Portet, S. (2004b) 'Poland: Circumventing the Law or Fully Deregulating?', in D. Vaughan-Whitehead (ed) *Working and Employment Conditions in New EU Member States: Convergence or Diversity*, Geneva: European Commission and International Labour Office, pp 273-338.

Ryś, M. (1999) *Wychowanie do życia w rodzinie: Książka dla młodzieży*, Warszawa: CMPP-MEN.

Rzdowa Rada Ludnościowa and Rządowe Centrum Studiów Strategicznych (2001) *Sytuacja demograficzna Polski, raport 2000-2001*, Warszawa.

Singh, S. and Darroch, J. (2000) 'Adolescent Pregnancy and Childbearing: Levels and Trends in Developed Countries', *Family Planning Perspectives*, vol 32, no 1, pp 14-23.

Skłodowska, M. (2004) 'Représentation des femmes dans les manuels scolaires polonais de "Formation à la vie en famille" 1999-2004', in J. Heinen and S. Portet (eds) *Egalité des sexes en Europe centrale et orientale: entre espoir et déconvenues, Transitions*, vol XLVI, no 1, pp 87-109.

Skrzydlewski, W. (2003) 'Konkretne wskazania etyki seksualnej', in J. Rzepka (ed) *Zagadnienia pro rodzinnej edukacji seksuologicznej*, Mysłowice: WSP.

Szczerba, K. (2001) *Wiedza o społeczeństwie: Wychowanie do życia w rodzinie: Podrcznik dla gimnazjum*, Warszawa: Wyd. Graf-Punkt.

Szczuka, K. (2004) *Milczenie Owieczek – rzecz o aborcji*, Warszawa: WAB.

Szlendak, T. (2004) *Supermaketyzacja – Religia i obyczaje seksualne młodzieży w kulturze konsumpcyknej*, Wrocław: FNP.

UNICEF (United Nations Children's Fund) (2001) *A League Table of Teenage Births in Rich Nations*, Innocenti Report Card No. 3, Florence: Innocenti Research Centre.

United Nations and Gdansk Institute for Market Economy (2002) *Report on the Millennium Development Goals: Poland*, Warsaw: UN.

Wróblewska, W. (1991) *Nastoletnie matki w Polsce: Studium demograficzne na podstawie badania 'Ankieta młodych matek' z 1988r*, Warszawa: Szola Glowna Handlowa (SGH) [Warsaw School of Economics].

Wróblewska, W. (1998) *Nastoletni Polacy wobec seksualności*, Warszawa: SGH.

Wróblewska, W. (1999) 'Przemiany płodności nastolatek', in I.E. Kotowska (ed) *Przemiany demograficzne w Polsce w latach 90. W świetle koncepcji drugiego przejścia demograficznego*, Warszawa: SGH, pp 48-63.

ELEVEN

Conclusion: welfare states and the politics of teenage pregnancy: lessons from cross-national comparisons

Corinne Nativel with Anne Daguerre

Introduction

In this book we have developed new insights into the politics of teenage pregnancy by drawing together examples from across different types of welfare regimes in the industrialised world. The main message has been that welfare state institutions, policies and narratives are critical to our understanding of early motherhood in 'varieties of capitalist states'.

There are, of course, strong and ongoing theoretical debates in the social sciences about whether essentialist or social constructionist theories should be retained to explain teenage motherhood (Musick, 1993; Hacking, 2003). Notwithstanding the personal and socio-psychological factors that help explain the onset of teenage pregnancy, we have departed from analyses and solutions directed at adolescent 'risk-taking' behaviour per se. Instead, we have focused on the *variations* between countries and tried to shed light on some of the social policy factors that might explain these differences.

As stated in Chapter One, the principal objectives of this volume were to contribute to an emerging body of literature on comparative welfare states, especially in relation to youth and gender issues, to examine and contrast public policy responses in a range of countries representing various welfare regimes, and to critically reflect upon the construction of teenage pregnancy as a social problem.

To meet these objectives, three hypotheses were formulated regarding the linkages between the welfare state and teenage pregnancy. The first of these hypotheses concerned the role of social protection towards individual households and the family. It was assumed that those nations with minimal social safety nets would incur higher rates of births to teenagers. Second, diverging social attitudes, beliefs and policies towards youth sexuality were expected to exert a significant influence on teenage well-being and reproductive behaviour. Third, we put forward that state intervention towards teenage pregnancy may be driven by differing regulatory regimes as to the appropriate timing of fertility, the pace of entry into adulthood, and breadwinner/caregiver models.

This concluding chapter returns to each of the three hypotheses and uses the key findings of the case study chapters not only to confirm their validity and relevance to the study of teenage pregnancy, but also to draw wider scholarly and policy-relevant lessons.

Why social protection matters

Teenage pregnancy has been in consistent decline in all the countries reviewed in this volume, including the transition countries of post-communist Europe (see Table A1 in Statistical Appendix, p 245). Despite this general trend, countries of the liberal welfare regime examined in Part One of the book, as well as one transition country (Russia), continue to display a relatively higher incidence of youthful pregnancies than their counterparts. Thus, our first endeavour has been to question whether minimal state protection leads to higher teenage pregnancy and conversely, whether more generous welfare provision helps to mitigate it.

There is ample evidence to support both views. One obvious fact is that social democratic and conservative-corporatist welfare states, which belong to the 'medium' to 'low' risk categories with regard to teenage pregnancy (see Table 11.1), spend a higher proportion of their Gross Domestic Product (GDP) on family-related items than countries falling under the liberal and Mediterranean models. Among the 30 countries of the Organisation for Economic Co-operation and Development (OECD), Denmark and Norway had the highest social expenditure on the family in 2001 (respectively 3.8% and 3.2%) compared to 2.8% in France, 1.9% in Canada and Poland, 1% in Italy, 0.5% in Spain and 0.4% in the US (OECD, 2005a). If the UK and New Zealand (both 2.2% of GDP) were more generous than their US cousin with regard to family expenditure, the share of GDP devoted to unemployment benefits and active labour market policy was equally low, reflecting the trend towards labour commodification, social stratification and welfare residualisation that typifies these three countries. Of course, if minimal levels of social expenditure resulted in high levels of teenage pregnancy, then nations of the Mediterranean welfare regime would be among the 'high-risk' category. As shown in the case of Italy (Chapter Seven), the countries of Southern Europe continue to rely on a familialistic model of solidarity and kinship and the great majority of young girls continue to reside with their parents until they can become financially self-reliant. Among the transition countries, Russia – whose economic 'shock therapy' has resulted in high levels of poverty and social polarisation – is close to the liberal model provided by the US. Although Poland has also seen a drastic reduction of female employment rights and an emergence of strong discriminatory employer policies, women have responded by deferring motherhood. Moreover, Poland has a higher GDP share of social expenditure than Russia, and indeed lower teenage birth rates. The level and nature of social protection thus clearly affect teenage reproductive outcomes without constituting the sole or principal explanation.

A further theme developed in the book concerned the relationship between universal access to higher education and the aspirations of young girls. The chapters on France, Italy, Denmark and Norway all underlined that public subsidies encouraging participation in tertiary education (including student housing benefits) are strong incentives for adolescent females to delay childbearing. Public spending on tertiary education is lower in countries of the liberal welfare state than in those of the social-democratic type. In 2004, excluding private and Research & Development expenditure, the UK devoted 1.1% of its GDP to tertiary education, the US 1.4% and New Zealand 1.7% compared to 2.7% in Denmark, 2.2% in Sweden and 2.1% in Norway. The trends are similar when all levels of education (primary, secondary and tertiary) are taken into account. Moreover, the percentage of young females participating in education is a revealing statistic. In the UK, it is well below the OECD average for both 15- to 19-year-olds and 20- to 24-year-olds; the US is within the mean range only for young people aged under 19. Denmark, France and Poland are among the countries with youth participation in education well above the OECD average (data from OECD, 2005b; see Statistical Appendix, Table A2, this volume). Democratising access to higher education represents a powerful means of keeping youth pregnancy at bay. At the same time, we have seen that this goal contradicts the workfarist agenda of liberal welfare states.

Additionally, one salient dimension for those 'high-risk countries' relates to the spatial concentration of poverty. The US and UK case studies (Chapters Two and Four) showed that neighbourhoods with the higher rates of teenage conceptions are also those that experience the lowest educational outcomes. Teenage pregnancy is more likely to occur in run-down neighbourhoods that suffer from a combination of social ills such as poor-quality housing, inadequate transport, lack of affordable child care, absence of permanent well-paid work, and subsequent social dislocation (see also Arai, 2003; Kidger, 2004). In the case of New Zealand and Québec, the regions mostly occupied by Aboriginal communities have not seen any decline in teenage fertility. A plain fact is that the lack of private and public sector investment in disadvantaged neighbourhoods and regions has generated cycles of no pay/low pay. The lack of decent educational and employment opportunities in the vicinity means that an early mothering career is more easily perceived as a valuable option than in affluent middle-class areas. Of course, such trends also exist to a lesser degree in the other countries surveyed in this book, for example in the Italian Mezzogiorno or the French Nord Pas-de-Calais regions, which have been plagued by industrial decline. But in Italy and France, these regions tend to be the exception to the rule, so that their teenage birth statistics are diluted in national figures and often overlooked by policymakers.[1]

Another key finding is that the nature of social benefits and services available to teenage mothers varies significantly between welfare states. In the 'low-risk' countries, social protection mechanisms are devised in ways that preclude the stigmatisation of teenage mothers. In Norway, Denmark and France, teenage mothers receive the same cash entitlements as other single mothers. Thus, social policies for teenage parents (as opposed to measures that seek to prevent teenage pregnancy) follow similar lines to those that apply to lone-parent families. The comparative welfare treatment of lone motherhood is an issue that has already received ample scrutiny in the social policy literature. As argued in another edited volume published by The Policy Press, there have been significant cross-national differences with regard to the additional direct state support provided to working lone-parents (Millar and Rowlingson, 2001). Likewise, the social policy treatment of teenage mothers is characterised by considerable discrepancies. The case study of France (Chapter Six) shows that in this country (but equally so in other countries of the conservative-corporatist regime such as Germany and Switzerland), teenage mothers are viewed with empathy, and not as a cost to the taxpayer as they are in the US. Social policy is based upon a philanthropic tradition towards infants and teenage single mothers, who are viewed above all as children in need of protection. They are offered a shelter in maternal homes and semi-independent housing schemes. Such schemes are administered at the local level, often as partnerships between local authorities, voluntary sector and church-based organisations. The schemes call upon the intervention of adult social workers and health professionals whose role it is to promote the well-being of the mother and her child. Child care, schooling of the mother, intermediation with the father and the family, help with daily matters and the like are dealt with in a comprehensive fashion. The UK has recently introduced similar housing schemes although these are found to be predominantly motivated by a desire to control paths into adulthood, and not by a truly supportive ethos (Giullari and Shaw, 2005).

In fact, in the UK, an emerging trend has been to resort to the community-based social network approach, which recognises the importance of relational resources. This focus is obvious in programmes that rely on local teenage pregnancy coordinators, peer educators and other youth professionals who remain in close proximity to their clients through information and communication technologies. Overall, increased emphasis is on the availability of teenage-friendly environments for the provision of sexual and health advice. These policies can undoubtedly be classed as best practices, although a longer-term supportive approach should be based on 'early parenthood' as opposed the more restricted notion of 'motherhood'. Policy efforts that extend professional support and service provision to the fathers undoubtedly contribute to family bonding. Evidence suggests that support from fathers or a new partner is linked with improved financial and psychological outcomes and has a positive influence on parenting behaviour (Bunting and McCauley, 2004). Although countries such as the US and the UK have recently taken steps towards including the father in the design of social policies, progress remains slow.

Why the regulation of youth sexuality matters

It has been argued throughout this book that teenage pregnancy cannot be disconnected from the normative framework that underpins youth sexuality. Michel Foucault (1978, 1985) has argued that sexuality discourse is a primary site through which power operates; it is one of the means through which both individuals and populations are controlled, 'normalised' and 'disciplined'. Foucault has labelled this particular manifestation of power 'bio-power'. How then, does a relatively open and permissive 'bio-political' approach towards teenage sexuality contribute to lowering the risk of teenage pregnancy, and conversely is there evidence that excessive moralising favours risk behaviour? The regulation of teenage reproductive health and sex education provides some useful answers to this question.

Access to contraceptive means

There is a broad consensus among policymakers that young people face concrete barriers when trying to access contraception and that governments must intervene to reduce risky attitudes to sex. Several countries have launched innovative schemes to ease access to emergency contraceptives via doctors, chemists, and sometimes schools. For example, some UK municipalities have recently piloted C-Card condom distribution schemes, which provide young people under the age of 25 with a card entitling them to free condoms and sexual health advice. C-Card outlets include several youth and community venues as well as the more traditional sexual health services. Likewise, the shift from the pill to long-acting injectable or implanted contraceptives, which are now used by one in ten sexually active American teenagers, as shown in Chapter Two, reflects changing attitudes to contraceptive access. More generally speaking, emergency contraceptives are becoming more readily available in a number of countries. These measures have undoubtedly helped reduce unwanted pregnancies by taking a pragmatic view of young people's place-based lifestyles. The recent UK policy developments in this field are to be welcomed. In view of the continued difficulties experienced in transition countries with regard to the affordability and availability of contraceptives, this policy area must continue to receive attention if progress is to be made to reduce teenage pregnancy in medium- and high-risk countries.

State legislation on abortion

State regulation inevitably affects sexuality and reproductive behaviour through a myriad of laws. Anti-abortion laws are crucial in this matter. In the European Union (EU), for example, Ireland, Portugal, Poland and Malta are the only countries where abortion remains practically illegal and abstinence before marriage is explicitly encouraged. Denying young people access to their sexuality promotes a culture of shame, transgression and social stigma in relation to sex and pregnancy. In other countries, important variations exist in terms of the legal period for carrying out an abortion: in most countries, the deadline is 12 weeks, while it is 24 weeks in the UK and the Netherlands, 14 in Sweden and 10 in Slovenia. However, these legal periods do not appear to have a systematic impact on reducing births to teenagers. The highest rates of induced abortions can be found in the Nordic and transition countries such as Russia and Poland where there the abortions are often backstreet practices (Chapters Nine and Ten). One of the most surprising findings is that legislation on abortion is not the major explanation for lower teenage conceptions, but that these outcomes result from a broad societal acceptance towards abortion.

Transmission of sexual knowledge

Sex education is undeniably one of the key instruments in the regulation of adolescent sexual and reproductive behaviour. There is an increasing recognition that democratic states must empower young people to make informed decisions about their health and well-being (Blair, 2005). We have identified four main 'normalisation' channels that are used in varying degrees and combinations across our case studies. Sex education can be diffused through (1) schools, (2) the intervention of health professionals and social workers, (3) intergenerational parent–child dialogue, and (4) intra-generational peer dialogue. It is striking that low-risk countries are those that have mostly relied on the last two (that is, on interpersonal relationships), whereas high-risk countries have preferred to resort to state intervention in the public sphere in an attempt to monitor and alter individual behaviour. The increased public funding for abstinence-only sex education in US schools since 1997, despite overwhelming parental preference for comprehensive sex education, is a patent illustration of how far direct state intervention can intrude in the 'bio-sphere' at the expense of individual well-being (see Chapter Two). So far, such abstinence-based movements have remained extremely isolated, and their attempts to attract European youth have proved unsuccessful. In transition countries such as Poland and Russia, the far-right and the Church have gained political ground diffusing reactionary slogans against the 'moral decline' and Western sexual decadence. However, the theme of Western decay is not new in Russia and has been used for anti-liberal purposes both by the Church and the Communists during the Stalinist period.

If the Nordic countries and some other EU countries such as France and the Netherlands appear to be more successful when it comes to the transmission of sexual knowledge, this is because they have adopted a liberal humanist view of sex education. However, as shown in the case of Denmark and Norway (Chapter Eight), such norms have emerged in the absence of elaborate sex education programmes in the classroom. In contrast, the chapters on Russia and Poland convincingly show that these countries are lagging behind the social frameworks as the search for a cultural consensus on sex education is still in progress. In fact, Russian, US and Polish governments seem to reject the relatively tolerant attitude towards teenage sex that prevails in most Western European countries. A further caveat worth bearing in mind is that the overemphasis on 'technical/ educational' explanations for youthful childbearing represents a distorted reading of teenage reproductive behaviour and could lead to curtailed policy responses (Arai, 2003). Indeed, France, Italy, Denmark and Norway have achieved relatively low adolescent conception and birth rates, in spite of haphazard approaches to sex education.

What clearly emerges from the contributions to this book is that various countries, regardless of their regime category, have developed strikingly different views of youth sexuality. In those countries that have embraced neoliberal market principles and religious neo-conservatism, dramatic accounts concerning sexual permissiveness have gained prominence. This is illustrated by the growing influence of the religious Right (especially in the US) and the exploitation by some post-communist governments (especially in Russia) of nostalgic feelings towards a golden past characterised by high morality and order.

Why the cultural dimension of the gendered welfare regime matters

Chapter One argued that the analysis of the relationship between teenage pregnancy and the welfare state needs to incorporate a gendered dimension. Our case studies clearly suggest that espousing a culturally sensitive perspective to the welfare state is equally crucial (Baldock, 1999; Pfau-Effinger, 2005). Culture is indeed an important factor in explaining the sociological behaviour of individuals, institutions, and indeed civilisations (Elias, 1973). The 'business' of moral regulation (Hunt, 1999) is an intrinsic component of welfare state cultures; it is embodied in welfare legislation, institutions and policies and therefore deserves more attention. While they involve a range of different actors, all the industrialised societies scrutinised in this volume display strong implicit or explicit normative schemes concerning the definition of gender roles and ritualised patterns of youth transitions. Returning to our third and final hypothesis, are we to conclude that a collective preference for fast transitions into adulthood and a weak breadwinner model increase the risk of teenage pregnancy and that conversely, slow transition models into adulthood and a strong breadwinner model contribute to minimising it?

There is no doubt that the welfare state exerts considerable influence on the aspirations of welfare subjects, those aspirations being intrinsically bound up with transitional paths into adulthood. Bynner et al (2002) note that there is a widening gap between those in the 'fast lane' and those in the 'slow lane' to adulthood according to their parents' socioeconomic status (those in the fast lane being disproportionately born to parents in lower socioeconomic groups and those in the slow lane born to parents in higher socioeconomic groups), the latter being in the position to stay in education longer and postpone parenthood until they have completed their training and started a career. The distinction (fast versus slow lane) is also applicable to the wider relationship between welfare states and young people. One of the recurrent themes is that the liberal welfare state generates abrupt transitions into adulthood whereas the period of adolescence tends to be prolonged in other countries, as time spent in higher education is normalised through parental and/or state support via legislation and public spending. Because youthful pregnancies are not fully unplanned, as stressed by various contributors to this volume, the option of early family formation is likely to become less attractive if young people can realistically opt for other lifestyles than early family formation. Here also, a moral principle, that of responsibility towards young people – that is, the intergenerational contract – is materialised in the collective and familial welfare choices of social democratic, Conservative-corporatist and Mediterranean welfare regimes.

Controlling fertility

Women's movements have profoundly recast established gender regimes. A common theme is that women have been at the forefront of the 'second contraceptive revolution' which, contrary to the 'first contraceptive revolution', gave them full control over their fertility (see note 2, p 133) and at least in most Western countries (with the clear exception of Russia and Poland), births to teenagers unsurprisingly started to decline in the 1970s. Hence the absence of strong and inclusive feminist movements is certainly a factor that has generally hampered women (including teenage women) gaining control over their own bodies, a right that is increasingly under attack in the US, Poland and Russia. In the US and the UK, the feminist movement has been historically strong but has failed to attract the support of young women from the lower middle classes, even at the peak of the historic campaign for the liberalisation of women's reproductive rights. In the US, the feminist movement has lost momentum and has failed to connect to grassroots organisations. Moreover, feminists tend to view teenage pregnancy as a symbol of male oppression and domination rather than a positive choice for young women (see Chapter Five). Among the countries surveyed, there is little if any mention of the issue of teenage pregnancy in feminist platforms except perhaps in Québec and Poland.

Meanwhile, another cultural revolution has taken place. Although historically, working-class women have often had to work outside the home to supplement the family income, the female career path only became normalised once their middle-class counterparts started to join the labour market and delay childbearing. Alternative trajectories are invariably judged against yardsticks established by the ruling class, and therefore 'it is no coincidence that [the stigmatisation of teenage mothers] has occurred at a time when middle-class women are gaining higher education and professional careers' (Wilson and Huntingdon, 2006, p 67).

The moral panic over teenage pregnancy in the US and the UK represents the Janus face of another less explicit panic, namely declining fertility rates and 'late motherhood' in consumer-worker capitalist societies. These trends are widely held to pose a 'crisis' in the context of an ageing society (Castles, 2004). Pro-natalists have argued that teenage pregnancy could in fact solve the dilemma faced by ageing societies where delayed childbearing is becoming increasingly common. As this book suggests, focusing the debate on the issue of fertility misses the point. Instead of giving credit to such debates, policymakers should in our view be essentially concerned with the well-being and promotion of autonomous paths for young people through investment in adequate educational and professional opportunities.

Future research directions

In sum, the construction of teenage pregnancy as a social problem rests upon a variety of interwoven institutional and cultural factors:

the level and nature of social protection, the vigour of feminist movements, community organisations, Church–state patterns, the transmission of sexual knowledge and education, access to contraceptives, breadwinner/caregiver models, and last but not least, the attachment to values such as individualism and universalism. Importantly, it is the complex interaction between this set of variables that contributes to shaping policy outcomes.

This book will hopefully set a trend for further comparative research in the politics of teenage sexuality and reproductive health. The availability of comparative datasets from micro surveys allowing for multivariate analyses would undoubtedly extend our knowledge in this field.

However, detailed case study research remains equally crucial. As rightly noted, social scientists have played a major (and not so innocent) part in the contemporary construction of teenage childbearing as problematic (Cherrington and Breheny, 2005; Wilson and Huntingdon, 2006). As producers of knowledge, they have perhaps too easily given in to the demand for 'evidence-based' research, adding scientific gloss to political discourse, especially through a heavy bias on traditional quantitative analysis (Graham and McDermott, 2006).

This 'academic panic' has consequently given rise to a 'veritable industry' (Furstenberg, 1991, quoted in Wilson and Huntingdon, 2006, p 64). Thus, one of our endeavours has been to recall the *responsibility* borne by social scientists to critically engage with the politics of teenage pregnancy and resist the temptation to become the purveyors of a fundamentally normative academic *prêt-à-penser*.

As far as approaching the topic of teenage pregnancy through a welfare state approach, this book has shown that trying to fit political approaches to teenage pregnancy into broad welfare state categories is not fully unproblematic. For example, even though the UK and the US are both classed as 'liberal' in Esping-Andersen's (1990) typology, there are important differences in the construction of teenage pregnancy as a social problem, with the UK emphasising health and the intergenerational transmission of poverty and the US highlighting outcomes in terms of associated welfare expenditure (Bonnell, 2004). Likewise, despite being heralded as the exemplary model, the 'Nordic' welfare state also incorporates important idiosyncracies as shown through the comparison of Denmark and Norway.

Moreover, some of the lowest teenage birth rates can be found in Asian countries such as China, Korea and Japan (see Statistical Appendix, Figure A1). In these countries also, culture has been argued to provide the foundations for a model of the family-based, so-called 'Oikonomic'

Table 11.1: The welfare regulation of teenage pregnancy and motherhood: a typology

Cultural and geographical area	Welfare state regime	Gender regime	Familial regime	Socio-cultural norms towards teenage sexuality and early parenthood	Births to teenagers: high, medium and low risk[a]
Anglophone countries (US, UK, Canada, New Zealand, Australia)	**Liberal** Equal opportunities and individual equity	**Mixed** High rates of female participation in the labour market; part-time work; lack of affordable child care	**Unstable-individualist** High rates of divorce and lone parenthood; pre-eminence of individualist values; 'fast lane' transitions into adulthood	**Conservative** Extreme ambivalence of teenage sexuality and recent promotion of abstinence-based policy (in the US, appeal to the religious Right under G.W. Bush)	+++ (US) to ++ (others)
Eastern European countries and Russian Federation	**Transitional** Abandonment of distributive policies that characterised the communist era and imposition of welfare retrenchment	**Patriarchal** High female employment levels in the communist era; welfare retrenchment has been detrimental to women	**Unstable-familial** Second demographic transition, erosion of traditional family values despite the resilience of marriage as a social institution	**Residual** Promotion of abstinence before marriage; strong influence of the Church; minimal policy intervention	+++(Russia, Romania) to ++(others)
Scandinavian countries (Sweden, Denmark, Iceland, Norway, Finland)	**Social democratic** Universalistic regime; social rights as an individual entitlement	**Egalitarian** High female labour market participation; family-friendly policies and state-funded child care	**Stable-individualist** Encouragement of youth autonomy; high rates of out-of-wedlock births	**Liberal-humanist** High tolerance, pragmatism and relative permissiveness towards teenage sexuality	+

Note: [a] High risk (annual birth rates of >35 per 1,000 women aged 15 to 19) = +++; Low risk (annual birth rates of <15 per 1,000 women aged 15 to 19) = +.

Cultural and geographical area	Welfare state regime	Gender regime	Familial regime	Socio-cultural norms towards teenage sexuality and early parenthood	Births to teenagers: high, medium and low risk[a]
Continental Europe (Austria, Belgium, France, Germany, the Netherlands, Switzerland)	**Conservative-corporatist** Social rights are attached to individual employment status; traditionally no individual entitlements	**Patriarchal** Model of the 'male breadwinner' but in decline. France is closer to the Scandinavian model in terms of female participation in the labour market and level of child care provision	**Unstable-familial** Reduced social rights for the youth in the welfare state; slow transition to employment, which perpetuates family dependency and intergenerational inequalities	**Universalist and hygienist** Encouragement of mother–infant bonding; non-judgemental attitudes towards teenage sexuality; comprehensive assistance schemes for teenage mothers	+
Southern Europe (Greece, Italy, Portugal, Spain)	**Mediterranean** Similarities with the corporatist model; welfare provision through family and kinship	**Matriarchal** Domestic decision-making power for women; breadwinner model in decline, declining fertility rates	**Stable-familial** Resilience of marriage; tradition of intergenerational solidarity and cohabitation; surveillance and inclusion of young people within the wider family circle: 'slow lane' transitions into adulthood	**Residual** Significance of the Church; minimal role for the state.	++ (Portugal) to +(others)

Note: [a] High risk (annual birth rates of >35 per 1,000 women aged 15 to 19) = +++; Low risk (annual birth rates of <15 per 1,000 women aged 15 to 19) = +.

or 'Confucian Welfare State' (Jones, 1993). To date, the Asia-pacific region is still under-represented in comparative social policy and future research on the politics of teenage sexuality and pregnancy would gain from a closer scrutiny of this region's welfare regimes.

Conclusions

Cross-national comparisons are not fully unproblematic, not least because contextual meaning often gets 'lost in translation' (Barbier, 2005). By attempting to depart from traditional welfare state analyses and incorporating a cultural lens, notably calling upon the Foucauldian concept of 'bio-power', the contribution of this volume to academic and political debates on youthful pregnancies has been two-fold: first, it has allowed us to separate the analysis of teenage pregnancy and motherhood from the private realm, which often nourishes pathological readings by focusing on individual causes and 'cures'. It has reminded us that it is a 'total social fact' (*fait social total*) in the Durkheimian-Maussian sense. In other words, teenage childbirth – like suicide – helps us understand the societies in which the phenomenon *actually* occurs. Following the example of French sociologists Baudelot and Establet (2006), who revisit the meaning of suicide in contemporary societies, the authors of this book show that a rather marginal, highly symbolic and emotional issue such as teenage motherhood is critical to our understanding of the status of youth and sexuality in the industrialised world.

Sexual activity among young people is common worldwide and policymakers must acknowledge this fact. In the developed world, three quarters of young women have had sexual intercourse by the age of 20. Providing teenagers with accurate information and normalising access to contraception and abortion can reduce the risk of unwanted pregnancy. At the same time, those who do become mothers must be provided with comprehensive health and social assistance. We have identified several examples of good practices in those areas.

However, given the main argument developed in this volume, which has consisted of stressing the significance of political commitments to the universal principles of social justice, protection and solidarity, the conclusion can only be that seeking to alter individual behaviour remains a partial if not an inappropriate approach. Rather, the socio-spatial environments in which children grow up to become adults and the regulatory frames that support these transitions deserve more attention. It is in this sense that welfare states matter in explaining teenage pregnancy.

Note

[1] The example of the Franco-British INTERREG project, 'Let's talk about love', running from 2005 to 2007 between the Somme and Kent shows that policymakers are starting to acknowledge the spatial dimension of teenage pregnancy and seeking to develop local and regional solutions. These types of transnational pilot projects could set examples of good practice to be followed by other countries.

References

Arai, L. (2003) 'British Policy on Teenage Pregnancy and Childbearing: The Limitations of Comparisons with other European Countries', *Critical Social Policy*, vol 23, no 1, pp 89-102.

Baldock, J. (1999) 'Culture: The Missing Variable in Understanding Social Policy?', *Social Policy & Administration*, vol 33, no 4, pp 458-73.

Barbier, J.-C. (2005) 'When Words Matter: Dealing anew with Cross-national Comparison', in J.-C. Barbier and M.T. Letablier (eds) *Politiques sociales: Enjeux méthodologiques et épistémologiques des comparaisons internationales* (Social policy: The methodological and epistemological challenges of international comparisons), Brussels: Peter Lang, pp 45-68.

Baudelot, C. and Establet, R. (2006) *Suicide: L'envers de notre monde*, Paris: Le Seuil.

Blair, A. (2005) 'Calculating the Risk of Teenage Pregnancy: Sex Education, Public Health, the Individual and the Law', in N. Harris and P. Meredith (eds) *Children, Education and Health: International Perspectives on Law and Policy*, Aldershot: Ashgate, pp 129-48.

Bonnell, C. (2004) 'Why is Teenage Pregnancy Conceptualised as a Social Problem? A Review of Quantitative Research from the USA and the UK', *Culture, Health and Sexuality*, vol 6, no 3, pp 255-72.

Bunting, L. and McCauley, C. (2004) 'Teenage Pregnancy and Parenthood: The Role of Fathers', *Child and Family Social Work*, vol 9, no 3, pp 295-303.

Bynner, J., Elias, P., McKnight, A., Pan, H. and Pierre, G. (2002) *Young People's Changing Routes to Independence*, York: Joseph Rowntree Foundation.

Castles, F. (2004) *The Future of the Welfare State: Crisis Myths and Crisis Realities*, Oxford: Oxford University Press.

Cherrington, J. and Breheny, M. (2005) 'Politicising Dominant Discursive Constructions about Teenage Pregnancy', *Health*, vol 9, no 1, pp 89-111.

Elias, N. (1973) *La civilisation des mœurs*, Paris: Calmann-Lévy.

Foucault, M. (1978) *The History of Sexuality: An Introduction*, New York, NY: Vintage Books.

Foucault, M. (1985) *The Use of Pleasure: The History of Sexuality* (volume 2) New York, NY: Vintage Books.

Giullari, S. and Shaw, M. (2005) 'Supporting or Controlling? New Labour's Housing Strategy for Teenage Parents', *Critical Social Policy*, vol 25, no 3, pp 402-17.

Graham, H. and McDermott, E. (2006) 'Qualitative Research and the Evidence-base of Policy: Insights from Studies of Teenage Mothers in the UK', *Journal of Social Policy*, vol 35, no 1, pp 21-37.

Hacking, I. (2003) 'What is Social Construction? The Teenage Pregnancy Example', in G. Delanty and P. Strydom (eds) *Philosophies of Social Science: The Classic and Contemporary Readings*, Philadelphia, PA: Open University Press, pp 421-7.

Hunt, A. (1999) *Governing Morals: A Social History of Moral Regulation*, Cambridge: Cambridge University Press.

Kidger, J. (2004) 'Including Young Mothers: Limitations to New Labour's Strategy for Supporting Teenage Parents', *Critical Social Policy*, vol 24, no 3, pp 291-311.

Jones, C. (1993) 'Pacific Challenges: Confucian Welfare State', in C. Jones (ed) *New Perspectives on the Welfare State in Europe*, London: Routledge, pp 198-217.

Millar, J. and Rowlingson, K. (eds) (2001) *Lone Parents, Employment and Social Policy: Cross-national Comparisons*, Bristol: The Policy Press.

Musick, J.S. (1993) *Young, Poor and Pregnant: The Psychology of Teenage Motherhood*, New Haven, CT: Yale University Press.

OECD (Organisation for Economic Co-operation and Development) (2005a) *Society at a Glance: OECD Social Indicators 2005*, Paris: OECD.

OECD (2005b) *Education at a Glance: OECD Indicators 2005*, Paris: OECD.

Pfau-Effinger, B. (2005) 'Culture and Welfare State Policies: Reflections on a Complex Interrelation', *Journal of European Social Policy*, vol 34, no 1, pp 3-20.

Wilson, H. and Huntingdon, A. (2006) 'Deviant (M)others: The Construction of Teenage Motherhood in Contemporary Discourse', *Journal of Social Policy*, vol 35, no 1, pp 59-76.

Statistical appendix: Teenage fertility in OECD countries

Figure AI: Annual births per 1,000 women aged 15-19 in selected industrialised countries (2000-05)

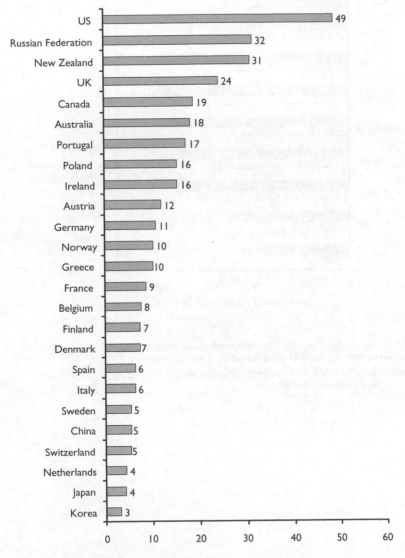

Source: UNICEF statistics (2006) *Global Database on Fertility and Contraceptive Use*, www.childinfo.org/eddb/fertility/index.htm

Figure A2: Age at first sexual intercourse in selected countries[a]

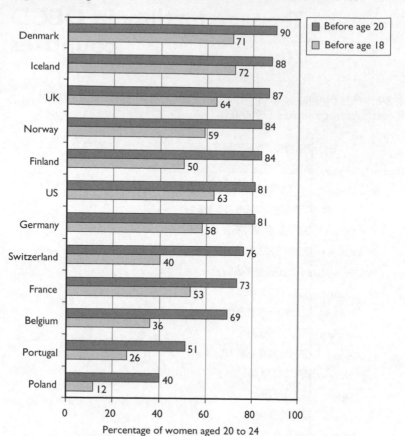

Note: [a] Percentage of women who report having had sex before age 18 and 20. All women surveyed were age 20 to 24 (data for different years in the early 1990s).

Source: UNICEF (2001) *A League Table of Teenage Births in Rich Nations*, Innocenti Report Card No. 3, Florence: UNICEF, p 13.

Figure A3: Evolution of teenage birth rates per 1,000 women aged 15-19 in five countries (1970-2000)

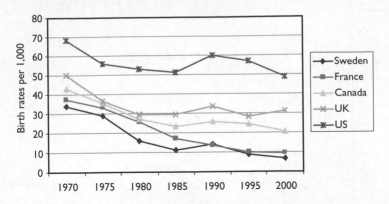

Source: Darroch, J., Frost, J. and Singh, S. (2001) *Teenage Sexual and Reproductive Behavior in Developed Countries*, Occasional Report No 3, New York, NY: Alan Guttmacher Institute, p 103.

Table A1: Teenage birth rates, by year, and percentage change in birth rates, by period, 1970 to mid-1990s, in selected countries

Country	Rate						% change		
	1970	1975	1980	1985	1990	1995[a]	1970-85	1985-95	1970-95
Australia	50.9	40.9	28.1	22.7[b]	22.0	19.8[c]	-55	-13	-61
Austria	58.2	47.1	34.5	24.4	21.2	15.6	-58	-36	-73
Belgium	31.0	27.8	20.3	12.6	11.3	9.1	-59	-28	-71
Canada	42.8	35.3	27.2	23.2	25.6	24.2	-46	4	-43
Czech Republic	49.0	61.2	53.1	53.3	44.7	20.1	9	-62	-59
Denmark	32.4	26.8	16.8	9.1	9.1	8.3	-72	-9	-74
England and Wales	49.7	36.5	29.6	29.5	33.2	28.4	-41	-4	-43
Federal Republic of Germany	43.3	26.2	19.5	12.1	16.8	13.2	-72	9	-70
Finland	32.2	27.5	18.9	13.8	12.4	9.8	-57	-29	-70
France	37.4	33.1	25.4	16.9	13.3	10.0	-55	-41	-73
Greece	36.9	46.5	53.1	36.4	21.6	13.0	-1	-64	-65
Iceland	73.7	64.1	57.7	33.7	30.6	22.1	-54	-34	-70
Ireland	16.3	22.8	23.0	16.6	16.8	15.0	2	-10	-8
Italy	27.0	32.5	20.9	12.7	9.0	6.9	-53	-46	-74
Japan	4.4	4.1	3.6	4.0	3.6	3.9	-9	-4	-12
Netherlands	22.6	12.6	9.2	6.8	8.3	5.8	-70	-15	-74
New Zealand	64.3	53.7	30.6	30.6	35.0	34.0	-52	11	-47

continued

Table A1: contd.../

Country	1970	1975	Rate 1980	1985	1990	1995[a]	% change 1970-85	1985-95	1970-95
Norway	44.6	40.3	25.2	17.8	17.1	13.5	-60	-24	-70
Poland	30.0	31.4	32.9	35.1	31.5	21.1	17	-40	-30
Portugal	29.8	37.0	41.0	33.0	24.1	20.9	11	-37	-30
Russian Federation	29.7	34.5	43.6	46.9	55.6	45.6	58	-3	54
Scotland	47.3	40.0	32.6	30.9	31.8	27.1	-35	-12	-43
Spain	14.3	21.9	25.8	18.5	11.9	7.8	29	-58	-45
Sweden	33.9	28.8	15.8	11.0	14.1	7.7	-68	-30	-77
Switzerland	22.2	15.3	10.2	6.7	7.1	5.7	-70	-15	-74
US	68.3	55.6	53.0	51.0	59.9	54.4	-25	7	-20

[a] Data are for 1996, not 1995, in Austria, the Czech Republic, Finland, Iceland, Norway, Poland, Portugal, Sweden, Switzerland and the US. [b] The 1985 birth rate is the average of 1984 and 1986. [c] The birth rate for 1995 is actually for 1994.

Notes: All data presented reflect 'age in completed years'. Where age was defined as 'age attained during year', as in the Federal Republic of Germany and France, birth data were adjusted.

Source: Singh, S. and Darroch, J.E. (2000) 'Adolescent Pregnancy and Childbearing: Levels and Trends in Developed Countries', *Family Planning Perspectives*, vol 32, no 1, p 17.

Table A2: Teenage births, income inequality and women not in education[a]

Country	Annual births per 1,000 women aged 15-19 (2000-05)	Gini coefficients (2000)	% of women aged 15-19 not in education (2003)
Australia	18	30,5	20,2
Austria	12	25,2	16,3
Canada	19	30,1	15,1
Denmark	7	22,5	11,2
Finland	7	26,1	13,7
France	9	27,3	14,7
Germany	11	27,7	8,4
Greece	10	34,5	14,4
Ireland	16	30,4	14,3
Italy	6	34,7	16,7
Netherlands	4	25,1	18,4
Norway	10	26,1	10,7
Poland	16	36,7	3,4
Portugal	17	35,6	21,9
Spain	6	32,9	13,4
Sweden	5	24,3	11,3
Switzerland	5	26,7	19,7
UK	24	32,6	22,8
US	49	35,7	16,3

[a] The table shows: teenage birth rates (as in Figure A1); an index of income inequality where higher values indicate greater inequality (the Gini coefficient based on per capita household income); and the percentage of 15- to 19-year-old women not enrolled in education in 2003.

Sources: UNICEF statistics (2006) *Global Database on Fertility and Contraceptive Use*, www.childinfo.org/eddb/fertility/index.htm; OECD Factbook (2006), available at www.sourceoecd.org/factbook

Index

Page references for figures and tables are in *italics*; those for notes are followed by n